HIPPIE TALES

of the

NORTHWEST WOODS

HIPPIE TALES
OF THE
NORTHWEST
WOODS

'BUCKWHEAT' BOB HARRISON

MILL CITY PRESS

MINNEAPOLIS, MN

Mill City Press, Inc.
322 First Avenue N, 5th floor
Minneapolis, MN 55401
612.455.2293
www.millcitypublishing.com

ISBN-13: 978-1-62652-892-5
LCCN: 2014910628

Cover Design by James Arneson
Typeset by Biz Cook

Printed in the United States of America

Contents

Prologue:

Gulf, 1976

The island is small, only about a square mile, but you couldn't tell that this morning. It was beginning to snow and visibility was down to a couple hundred feet. Looking inland from the small cove—where a small skiff is beached at the medium tide line and a nineteen-foot clinker is moored to a plastic milk container buoy outside the low tide line—you can see a path rising through alders and salmonberries to a plateau shrouded by conifer trees. If you look carefully up the trail you can barely make out the shake wall of a cabin. The trail ascends at maybe a 15 percent grade, up about thirty feet, but since you always seem to be in a hurry when walking up you are always puffing a bit when you reach the sheltered plateau where the cabin sits.

Looking just above the high tide line on the beach, there are the skeletons of old boats in various stages of disintegration. You also see a number of containers, plastic jugs, and plastic and metal jerry cans, again, in various stages of decay. You find old paint cans half full of solidified paint, with the brush forever encased in the gunk. There is a funky shed with just a roof, containing all kinds of wondrous stuff such as rectangular pieces of plywood, pieces of frayed plastic rope, a mess of rusting nails, screws, nuts, and bits of hardware of unknown origin.

There are one or two outboard motors with covers off and corrosion all through them, proof that they have not been tinkered with for several years. In the vicinity of the motors are scattered parts, which probably went with one of those engines sometime in the past. Perhaps not. There is a sense that nothing is completed.

The scene on the beach is fairly representative of most semi-inhabited beaches in this part of the world, not, I hasten to add, the beaches inhabited by summer people or the otherwise idle rich, but rather those inhabited by common folks scufflin' to survive. I know this seems like a mighty slovenly way to live, but there is a method to this style of life. First off you have to understand that the person or persons inhabiting this location probably have very little money, which means they cannot afford to purchase new things. Any hardware is a precious commodity here. As a matter of fact, many of the things they own have been given to them or bartered for in one way or another.

The Indians of the Northwest Coast were "Cedar Culture" people. Cedar is an amazing resource, mainly owing to its straight grain and its relative weather resistance. The Indians made clothes, housing, boats, tools, and almost everything from cedar. You will notice that cedar is also the material of choice of the white man. All you need to roof or side a house is a saw, froe and mallet, and some nails. Shakes. Presto. It must be admitted, however, that it can be hard to find straight cedar near the coast because of the lack of soil and prevailing winds, which affect growing conditions. But, as if in compensation, the ocean brings in many wondrous things. You always have your eye out for driftwood and flotsam that might contain a few cedar shake bolts. You can make a house, chairs, tables, smoke house, boat, fence, containers, furniture . . . almost anything out of cedar.

Another thing you may notice on the beach is that much of the junk has been collected from the beach. Now you may wonder what the Christ someone would want to do with some of this stuff but, then again, how are you going to dispose if it? I mean, the beaches of the Pacific Northwest, and probably all the beaches on earth, are the ultimate garbage dump for all the surrounding civilization.

The ideal solution to the pollution problem would be to take all that crap—old bacon packages, plastic this, plastic that—fill bags full of it, go to the nearest town, and strew it all back where it came from. Believe me, the poor folks who live around these parts don't generate very much non-biodegradable garbage of their own. They are, in fact, pretty good scavengers. For some demented people there is real satisfaction in re-using things in imaginative ways.

Take those rectangular pieces of plywood: they are a commodity that will probably become extinct with the proliferation of plastic (read "fiberglass") boats. What they are is hatch covers. Any boater with any sense would attach a line to an eyebolt on a hatch cover to keep from losing it over the side in heavy seas. From a count of old hatch covers on the beaches of the world, you would find that an awful lot of people don't have much sense. But, what the hey, a boater's loss is a beachcomber's gain. You can build houses, tables, damn near anything with hatch covers. I once made a bush wheelbarrow out of a couple of two by twos, a long steel bolt, a hatch cover, and a bicycle wheel.

So really, what you see on the beach is a bunch of stuff that mostly came from the sea, and might someday have some earthly use to the lunatic who lives in this particular cove. Of course, most of the scenery we have been commenting on is not visible, because the whole gulf is covered with about three inches of snow.

Looking up the path smoke can be seen streaming out of the chimney. It (the chimney) is about six feet of rusty pipe off at an angle, guyed with some rusted baling wire and a hat perched precariously to the top. Just your normal bush stove pipe. The chimney is protruding from an ancient shake roof. There are charred shakes around the roof jack, evidence of near disasters in the past. The roof is atop a pole-frame shake cabin, which began life as a storage shed and worked its way up to primitive shack, after several tenants had domestic aspirations that transcended living in a storage shed but fell a bit short of what most people would consider to be civilized habitation. The floor was an uneven surface, made up of various sizes of two by something plank of random dimensions, which had fallen off a lumber barge and eventually found their way into that particular cove.

Most of the planks you find on the beach have been around for a while. And around and around. Over the years they come in on the high tide then out with another high tide to end up God knows where. They have a tendency to be split and rounded on the ends because of continuously banging against things during their endless migration. If a person had enough of these planks to build a floor and if he fit the planks by cutting the ends off with a chainsaw then he would have a pretty classy-looking floor. Except that the planks seem to vary in thickness up to a quarter of an inch, so it's best to lift your feet while you walk around. Again, a typical bush cabin.

But this day there was snow on the ground and everything looked white and formless. Smoke was coming out the chimney. The door opened and the man came out on the porch. He walked to a tree, which had something hidden inside a burlap sack hanging from a limb, pulled his Old Timer knife from his belt and proceeded to cut loose a quarter of venison. He trudged back to the cabin and disappeared inside. He was about five foot, ten inches tall; medium build; light brown somewhat scraggly beard; and slightly bulbous nose. That was all you could tell, because he was dressed to the chin in various un-matched woolen garments, garnered from the Sally Ann (Salvation Army in Canadian vernacular) in Vancouver, and God knows where else, with a brown woolen toque on his head. This left very little of his features visible.

The wind was blowing southeast at twenty-five to thirty knots, which would be inconvenient if you lived unprotected from the sou'easter; that's why lee shore coves, like this one, are at a premium. In 1976 there were still some lee shore bays available for squatting. The smoke from the pipe became much darker as the man damped down the stove. Several minutes later he emerged from the cabin. His outer layer now consisted of a yellow slicker without the yellow hat, and black gum boots up to his knees. A backpack with a sleeping bag attached was hanging by one strap over his shoulder. He held the hunk of deer meat in a plastic bag in one hand and gripped an Enfield .303 in the other.

The Enfield .303 was a Godsend to the bush hippies of the '60s and '70s. They were mass-produced in England to arm the home guard back in the dark early days of WWII. The rifle was bolt-action with a small clip. It was light in weight, reasonably accurate up to a hundred yards or so, and, the most important thing, could be had for between thirty and fifty dollars. You could get ammunition almost anywhere, but many folks used re-loaders to refill their cartridges.

The man trudged down the steep trail to the shore. The tide was in and the dinghy was bobbing in the foot-high lee waves. He grabbed the mooring line and pulled the dingy to shore; loaded the pack, rifle, and venison inside; untied the bow line, jumped into the skiff, kicking off shore as he did so. He pulled out the oars before he could be swept back onto the beach and started rowing out into the bay.

The thought of going out on this day was a bit scary; the outline of the clinker anchored about fifty feet off shore could barely be seen. The snow was blowing furiously and visibility was down to about fifty feet. This is the time when anyone with the slightest amount of sense would have said, "To hell with it, it's too dangerous to go out in a boat in this weather." People who live with the elements, and who are not artificially protected from them, develop a different attitude about nature. They are aware of the power of nature; in this case that powerful entity is the sea, probably the most powerful of all, unless that honor should go to the desert or areas of extreme cold. I don't think there is anything that can match the sea in making a person feel small and insignificant.

Those who live with the elements learn how to live with them or they don't survive. One thing they cannot do is become fearful. If they could not laugh at the danger they would become phobic and have to leave the water. Sometimes this makes them do some weird, if not stupid, things. I suppose it is something like the soldier who is confronted with seemingly random events that could end his life and yet shrugs his shoulders and says, "If my number's up then there's nothing I can do about it."

Well, face it. You'd have to be pretty crazy living like this in North America toward the close of the twentieth century, wouldn't you? The point is, if you live on the sea you will learn the sea, understand the sea, and trust your karma to be good, if there is such a thing as good karma. And you must challenge it once in a while, just to prove that you are not afraid. You challenge it, albeit very prudently. Ordinarily. There are, however, special occasions when one must sail just one point closer to the wind, dangerwise. This was one of those occasions.

The man rowed out to the clinker and tied the dinghy to it. He transferred his possessions into the boat. The clinker had a beautiful nineteen-foot cedar plank, ship-lapped hull painted white with black trim. Sails were wrapped around a detachable mast, tucked inside and running the length of the boat. He climbed aboard the clinker, made his way to the stern, hoisted the anchor, lowered the propeller of his six-horse Johnson into the water, and pulled on the starter cord. It fired on the third pull. He let it idle for a minute or so, went to the bow and cast the line, crawled back to the stern, pulled up the stern anchor, and then took the handle and started for the mouth of the cove.

He was headed for a somewhat larger island about a mile west of his cove. You might think it was stupid of him to go out into the ocean without a compass. Actually, it probably was. This is what I've been talking about. It would be very difficult for anyone to miss the island that was his destination, even if he only had ten feet of visibility. All he has to do is follow the line of the chop in the water. He knows the winds, and the winds blow the water, so he knows the water. If he follows the waves, with the boat at a ninety-degree angle to them, he will hit the island, no doubt about it. There might be a question of where and when he will hit the island, but hit it he will.

This is of some importance, because the West Coast is very recent geology. Things are sharp and jagged. There hasn't been enough time since the land emerged from the sea for erosion to have smoothed things. There are many rocks and shoals in these waters. The man will spend some time in the open strait after he leaves the haven of his island, so it really pays to be very observant.

Probably the most dangerous things out in the water are deadheads, logs floating vertically in the water with one end either just above or just below the surface. Some deadheads are famous. They float through eternity along the waters of the Northwest Coast. Those that have been spotted by the government have flags attached to them so boaters can see them. I remember very well seeing one come slowly, inexorably, into my bay, maybe ten feet per day, and recalling seeing it halfway around the island several months before. But in a sou'easter, with fifty-foot visibility, the only defense was to run the boat dead slow. The man knew the tide was still rising, which meant there would be a tidal current of about five knots flowing from the south, so he made a slight correction in the angle the boat made to the wave lines.

After a few minutes he heard the faint sound of waves splashing on rock. Since he knew that snow deadens sound he slowed down the motor still more, till he was barely moving, and peered intently ahead. He certainly didn't want to run aground, as he had done once several years ago. He smiled wryly remembering waking up after a party in town, finding himself in his boat, stuck on a beach somewhere at low tide, and having no recollection of how he got there.

Since the sou'easter was blowing the boat toward shore, he killed the motor and ran to the bow with his pike pole to fend off any rocks they might encounter. Suddenly a small island emerged from the snowstorm and he jabbed quickly at the rocky shore, stopping the boat. He pushed off the shore, wallowed in the crest of the waves for a moment, almost swamping, gave the pole a sharp push sideways to turn the boat around, then dove toward the stern to try to get the motor going before they beached. He tripped during his dive and almost ate the motor cowling. He swiveled the motor up until the prop was just below the surface of the water, so it wouldn't shear from hitting a rock, pulled the starter, and, thank God, she fired on the first pull so he headed out into deeper water.

Everything was OK now. He knew precisely where he was, around a small point from his destination, and he could have motored in blindfolded. Thankfully he slowly motored around the point and into a small bay. Out in the deep water there was a buoy made out of a one-gallon bleach bottle, holding up a rope attached to an anchor. He steered the clinker to the buoy, which had another boat tied to it; he tied up, let down his stern anchor, and attached his bumpers. He transferred his pack, gun, and venison to the dinghy, jumped aboard, untied the line, and started rowing toward shore.

He beached the dinghy and threw out the stern anchor. Then he tied the boat to a landline attached to a tree on the shore. Although he didn't notice, having seen this beach many times, it was a smaller version of his own. It had less stuff, but different kinds. This beach had shakes lying around everywhere and some toys, either reasonably functional or broken, so it was obvious that children lived here.

He hoisted his pack and sleeping bag, grabbed the meat and rifle, and started toward the trail running off to the left of the beach. He could already hear the sound of guitars, flutes, bongos, and Indian drums. The trail was littered with all of the accoutrements of primitive life on the beach. He trudged up the snowy trail.

The cabin was a small shake house, with shakes sticking out in all directions, as if the builder had to get a roof over his head as quick as possible, and to hell with aesthetics. Now he could feel the energy and hear the animated voices inside. There was an evergreen wreath hanging around the doorknob. He stopped at the edge of the clearing and let out a hoot to let everyone around know that a friend had arrived. After a short while he walked up to the shack. He put his gun in a corner of the porch, took off his pack and laid it alongside the rifle, then took off his gumboots. He grabbed the venison, opened the door, and stuck his head in.

He glimpsed a tableau that included a beautiful tree, with popcorn and paper decorations hanging from it, three small children playing, three young women feverishly bustling around the kitchen area preparing some pretty good-smelling food, and three young long-haired guys sitting on homemade chairs, playing guitars and drumming. A half-finished bottle of homemade wine was visible on the table, and the air smelled like there had been a fire in the rope factory. Everyone looked up simultaneously and started grinning.

One of the musicians said, "All right, it's Allen." One of the women came over and hugged him first, and then everyone came around. Allen sniffed the air and said, "I see you still got some of that home-grown from last fall. Merry Christmas everyone."

Preface

After a six-year Odyssey that began as a programmer/analyst for the California General Services System Analysis Office in Sacramento, through five years in the woods in southern Oregon, I washed up on the shores of Lasqueti Island in the majestic British Columbia coast.

Sitting in my squatter's shack I pensively gazed out upon the sea specked with small islands studded with sharp rock and stunted Douglas fir trees. Several tug boats were visible, slowly towing freight barges destined for small communities along the B.C. coast and on up to the Gulf of Alaska. My friends, Dick and Judy, were with me. It was 1978. We were partaking of various refreshments and discussing and dissecting the collapse of the hippie tribal movement, which we had thought in the recent past might save the planet and usher in a new age of cosmic consciousness. (Snicker, snicker).

A copy of Karl Jung's *Memories, Dreams, Reflections* had made it to the island and we had all read it, as we read pretty much everything that made it to the island, including three-month-old newspapers. Some of us had battery-powered radios, but even the excellent CBC broadcasting was no match for a good book.

Jung was fascinated with the puzzle of primitive tribal structures and what made them viable. Extinction was always on the horizon, a fact not always understood by city dwellers, who at least believe they are safe from the natural environment if not from their fellow homo sapiens.

Jung found that the cornerstone of the tribes he studied in Africa and the American Southwest was a strong central tribal myth that all members bought into. Among the advantages of this structure was that the community was saved the expense of lawyers. Violating the myth was grounds for death or banishment. For example, Jung found the Hopi had a central tenet that their rituals were responsible for the sun (god) rising. Not performing their rituals properly would have dire consequences.

The lack of a strong central binding myth was the problem with the alternative lifestyle movement. In some instances, strong cults caused disastrous consequences, such as what happened with the Manson family. In retrospect, the emerging technological control of Western civilization was at least partially responsible for the hippie rebellion, and the idea that these freedom-loving individuals would or could submit to authoritarian control of the group was not possible. We could see this in retrospect.

I have pondered this conundrum for many years. Some forty years later, I have come to the realization that we will never understand how viable tribal structures evolved. It had to be some sort of survival of the fittest, certainly, and much trial and error. Evolution is slow. All we get to see is the successful tribes and cultures. Some cultures may have developed the necessary ingredients for survival quickly (doubtful) but most probably evolved over centuries and even thousands of years. But we will never know. How many did not have the luck or good fortune of the survivors and became extinct? We will never know. The only information we have is from stories handed down from many generations. Using this information to understand tribal historical development would certainly not be good science. The aboriginals in Australia have been living on the continent for at least 35,000 years; large numbers of tribes survived and inhabited the entire continent until the arrival of the white man.

Even if the hippies had understood and bought into tribal dynamics, which of course we did not, at best we were attempting to rewrite our destiny over a period of several years instead of hundreds of years. If one can get over the stigma of us living on a dying planet, we did have a lot of fun much of the time. I'm going to take you on my version of the trip. I hope you enjoy the ride.

Introduction

I grew up in the Sierra foothills in Northern California. I fished and hiked in the rugged granite canyons of the Feather River country. My family on both sides emigrated from midwest in the middle 1800s. As a kid I got pocket money mowing lawns with a push mower in 100-degree-plus temperature, then later worked knocking almonds, bucking hay bales, picking peaches, and swamping boxes. I also worked as a tail-off man in a door and window factory (sawmill) and in a fire suppression crew on the middle fork of the Feather River. I was interested in all things electronic and had a ham radio license when I was fourteen years old.

I was too immature and insecure to be successful in engineering school and failed to graduate. I got married, and went to work for IBM soon after I left school. IBM and I didn't get along too well. I was quite passionate about my distaste for things like corporate greed and institutionalism. It took me some time to realize that I was capable of pissing people off.

Post-IBM my marriage broke up and I went through some bad patches. I eventually went to work for the State of California Franchise Tax Board. At the same time, I discovered the Beat Generation and jazz. Whoa.

I was always intimidated by those sophisticated city beatniks, so I didn't mingle with them but I admired them from afar. I got heavily into the Tao. On the job I became a programmer and systems analyst, and at the same time I was writing poetry and growing a beard.

Then came the Trips Festival at the Longshoreman's Hall in San Francisco in January 1966; I discovered hippies and totally dug the scene. Over the next several years my second wife and I spent some weekends in the Haight-Asbury visiting hippie friends. In 1970 my second wife Polly (we'd be together for a few more months) and I dropped out and took off in our VW van to the Promised Land, wherever that might be. I was thirty-three years old. We lived with fishermen friends in Newport Beach for several months. I had heard of some communes in rural Oregon and I yearned to return to the woods and just dig life. I had put in a lot of time in the civilized world and I wanted to go back to the country and live a spiritual life. At this point either fate or karma took over and has continued to rule me to this day.

On my way to the Vortex I Festival outside Portland, Oregon, fate escorted me to Takilma in the southwestern part of the state, and that set my life for the next five years, and the start of fifteen years without money, property, electricity, a vehicle, or potable running water. I had just enough money left over from my state job to last until I learned how to be poor. Remember, I was in early middle-age at this time. After several years I realized the tribal movement had ended in the U.S. and my only desire was to get totally away from civilization and learn to live off the land, or as close as I could come to this ideal. Canada was the place.

I ended up with my partner, Mara, and her two children, Bret and Maia, on Lasqueti Island in the British Columbia Gulf of Georgia. We were Americans, didn't bother to get permission to stay in Canada, had several hundred dollars to our name, and didn't know a thing about the country.

This short bio is not intended to impress you about our exploits, but to explain my vantage point for producing these stories. Us hippies is gettin' older, and I feel that history of the bush hippie way of life will soon be lost forever.

When I read back over these stories I wonder if anyone will believe them. I wonder if I believe them. The perspectives are totally from what (I thought) I saw or stories told to me. Obviously, other people involved with these incidents saw things from their own vantage point, so I make no claims that these stories are the cosmic reality of the events.

I also noted upon reading that the stories only deal with events rather than the sociological dynamics of living in this alternative environment. I hope I put down the feel of living on the edge.

1

The Beginning

After living life as a beach bum in Orange County I decided the city, even on the beach, was not going to make it for me. There were too many drugs and too much negativity regarding the legal establishment. As I was about to leave Newport Beach forever (hopefully) I heard about a happening in the Pacific Northwest: the first Sky River Festival. I provisioned my self-customized VW van and set out in quest of the festival. I got the idea after seeing a poster in Mr. Natural's Health Food Shop a couple of blocks from the Newport pier. The information was sparse. It didn't even tell which state it would be in. I headed up the coast to the Pacific Northwest, which would become for the next several years my physical and spiritual home, with enough food to feed an army and a half-pound of Oaxaca buds.

I picked up a lot of hitchhikers on the way up Highway 101. This was the summer of big migration from the East Coast, and all the highways across the country were filled with long-hair freaks thumbing from somewhere to somewhere else.

While visiting with friends in Fort Bragg I began to hear rumors of the Vortex Festival to be held somewhere near Portland, Oregon. It sounded promising.

My plan was to follow the coast highway 101 to Astoria, then head inland along the Columbia River to Portland. I drove up beautiful Highway 1, which joins Highway 101 at Leggett, California. The first part went according to plan. Then I picked up two hitchhikers, a boy and pretty girl. They asked me where I was going and I told them I was going to Portland via 101. The girl asked me if I had ever heard of Takilma. I said I had not and she began telling me how beautiful it was and that it was becoming a drop-out hippie haven. I found out later that she was trying to find her boyfriend, who was supposed to be staying there.

At first I wasn't inclined to change my travel plans, but then I began to wonder how I was going to have adventures if I stuck to a script. Against my original desires, I decided to check out Takilma. We drove up 101 to Crescent City then up 199 toward Grants Pass. Just across the Oregon border, we arrived at O'Brien, then turned east across the east fork of the Illinois River to Four Corners, then south toward California, about ten miles away. We entered a narrow valley. The first landmark was an old house with a sign over the door that said "Love." There were several junk cars scattered around and old, deteriorating wooden outbuildings. We passed several half-decent houses along the road, though most were shacks with junk in the front yard. Far out. Dogpatch. I was starting to like the place already.

Young people were walking the road in various degrees of dress. My impressions of Takilma were getting more positive all the time. About a half-mile down the road we came to what I was to learn was the "Mirage Garage," the original unfinished plywood crash pad in the community, which had a drawing of an octopus crawling over the wall. Outside the door a squat, swarthy guy with long black hair, straggly black beard, Indian headband, and loincloth was vigorously chopping firewood. All around and down to the river, about a hundred yards away, about a hundred naked hippies were swimming and hanging out. Ah ha. I had never in my wildest imagination envisioned anything so cool. I stripped off my clothes and joined the gang.

I was somewhat conspicuous because so much of my body was white but it didn't bother me in the least. I didn't wear clothes while at a swimming facility for the next fifteen years.

After a couple of blissful days I took off for the fabled Vortex Festival, bringing along several of my new friends from Takilma. We found the site at McIver State Park, southeast of Portland. I parked my van then we grabbed our stuff and walked down the dirt road into a beautiful, narrow valley that would be my home for the next three days, donated by the state of Oregon and facilitated by that wonderful Republican governor Tom McCall. The governor and the Rainbow Family, later sponsors of Gathering of the Tribes, reached an agreement to provide McIver Park, food, electricity, stage materials, and medical facilities for the Vortex Festival.

The move to McIver Park was not entirely altruistic, rather it was an attempt to defuse a potential confrontation in downtown Portland. There had been information from the FBI that the American Legion Convention in downtown Portland had catalyzed a movement to hold a counter convention in the park across the street. The young political radicals and the authorities thought there might be a bloodbath. This was shortly after Kent State, and there was a lot of anger.

I would be remiss if I didn't mention that McIver Park was circled by National Guard troops, though they stayed out of sight during the entire weekend. I intermingled with the probably twenty thousand beautiful young people and for the first time felt totally accepted, even though I was as much as twenty years older than most of them.

I looked around and said, "Toto, we're not in California anymore." I probably didn't say that, but I should have. The first thing I did was sit down in a circle of folks who were sharing a joint. On at least one level the passing of the marijuana was a ritual quite similar to Indians passing the peace pipe, to pass our energy in accord. The ritual got a bit of a boost because the illegality of the act affirmed our belonging.

This particular passing of the joint was super special because there were two narcs sitting in the circle. We knew they were narcs because they had DA haircuts, shades, and were talking hipster lingo. We'd pass them the joint and they would do a very poor job of fake inhaling. It was fun because there was nothing they could do, and God forbid they accidentally got a drink of the Kool-Aid. That was a good start to the weekend.

I ran into a young singer from Portland; she saw my guitar case and latched on to me. Pot, LSD, and mescaline were for sale cheap or were given away. Johanna and I tried some mescaline and had a grand time. I had found my tribe. The music was local and pretty bad. That was good because the people who were into enjoying a music festival went home and the gathering of the tribes continued. I'm sure I'm not the only one who felt that we didn't need all those high-living uptown bands. Personal interaction is where it's really at. One of the offshoots of the festival, at least from the straight community point of view, was that it had attracted a lot of hippies from out of state who decided that Oregon would be a wonderful place to live. Many tribes were formed in Oregon after Vortex 1.

Tom McCall was actually decisively re-elected in the next election. No wonder we all fell in love with Oregon.

After the festival, Johanna and I split to eastern Washington to pick apples. She lost interest in me when she realized that I was no kind of musician and in all probability never would be. We picked for several days, then Johanna ran into a drummer friend from Portland. They split back to town and I was alone, just like that. I started working on music. I had always wanted to be a singer and could just barely get around on the guitar a bit, so I decided to go for it. I had brought along several song books, *Hill and Range Country Hits, Hank Williams' Greatest Hits, and Gordon Lightfoot's Greatest Hits.*

One day I started having acute anxiety attacks. I was weak and was even afraid to climb the picking ladder. This had never happened to me before. That was the end of my apple picking this time around. I considered that some acid might help to sort out the situation, but before making any decision I threw the

I Ching—I know, I know. I didn't save the pentagram but it said something like, "You are very weak and defenseless. Don't try to do anything [except] flee to a very small town." That cleared everything up. I packed, got my pay, and took off for Takilma. I offered to drive some of the other pickers to Seattle. I dropped them at a friend's house and it was there that I found out that Janis Joplin and Jimi Hendrix had died. I was infuriated that these musicians could so selfishly injure the spirit of the movement, bring the whole movement down and not care. That was the day the music died for me. It just confirmed what I had learned at Vortex. Who needs the fucking music industry?

I arrived in Takilma and the whole scene had changed. All the school kids had gone back to wherever they came from, and the city folks had gone back home. The few who were left took stock of their new world. I arrived at the Mirage Garage. Harold recognized me right away and gave me a wonderful greeting. I'm flattering myself that my personality was more enticing than the remains of the half-pound of Oaxaca.

Aries Jerry and Allen were a bit older than many of the other hippies in town. They both obviously had been living on the street for a long time. Jerry looked like he might have been a biker. Allen was the self-styled guru. He was magnificent; he died a couple of years later, and I grieve for him to this day. Harold told me that Allen had scored a big bag of peyote buttons from his affiliation with the Native American church, and had held a peyote meeting in "the Meadows" the day before I arrived. The Meadows was a large tract of land on the west side of the river that was originally a squatter's area and later was purchased by the Meadows family. The significance of this event was that it brought the whole new town together for the first time. It seemed that the ones who were still around would constitute the new community.

The communication was incredible. These were weird, tough people; and there was no fear in self-plumbing the depths of their souls. These were the old-time crazies. Not everyone was into this space, of course. Everyone had his own reason for being there at that time. It wasn't always fun. When we contemplated the misery and suffering in this life, we decided that this must be the penal planet. We must have done something really bad to have ended up here. Exploring inner space was not always fun.

Most of the hippies were living either on government land or unoccupied private land, living on food stamps and very little else. Allen lived across the river in the Meadows, where he was in the process of building a house . . . shack?

The fall pastel colors had begun to take over and the day was quiet and beautiful. I stood for ten minutes watching (and listening) to a woodpecker working on a dead Douglas fir with the sound echoing through the valley; a mesmerizing experience. Harold came out of the house and said, "I've got a tab of blotter acid. Would you like to share it with me?" I had to think. Several years before I had had a really crazy acid trip and I hadn't done any since, though I had done mescaline a couple of times. Then I looked back at the woodpecker and thought, *If not here and now, then when?* I told him, "Sure." So we washed it down and waited for what would happen next.

We were getting high and Harold started talking about Allen and the wonderful thing he had done with the peyote meeting. He said, "You know, he's working on his house and he's tired from last night, why don't we go over and give him a hand?" So we did. We gathered our gear and walked about fifty yards down to the river. We took off our footwear and waded the river, which was quite low at that time of year. We walked on the dirt track and into a beautiful meadow with dry grass, oaks, and fir trees.

As we approached the house I could see a roof, a floor, and nothing else. No walls. I then noticed that the cook stove was burning away and Reba, Allen's wife, was happily cooking. No walls, just a cook stove. Allen was naked, lying on a palette on the floor; long, sinewy, black hair and beard, long Jewish face reminding me of so many paintings of Jesus. He was lying on his back with his head propped up, gesticulating and preaching to several disciples who were sitting around his pallet, the sun low in the sky, not obstructed by walls, and he had a golden halo around his head. Swear to God.

Every few minutes a new small group, maybe with a couple of kids and a dog, walking stick, and packs, arrived saying, "Well, we thought we would come over and help Allen with his house."

Everyone in town, at least on this side of the river, just gravitated to the energy spot. Pretty soon, after they had all re-introduced themselves to each other, they began to discuss the future. Winter was coming and stable dwellings were in short supply. Someone suggested that they could start a free store. This caused a bit of a squabble since a number of people were allergic to the word "store", no matter the context, so they decided to set up a "free goods exchange." Patrick suggested that we needed to buy food in bulk for better prices: a food co-op.

My God. I was looking back and forth between the glowing Allen and the discussion about the new community, head buzzing on blotter acid, and thinking, "Wow. I'm seeing a primitive society being formed and I'm probably the only one here who realizes it."

Needless to say, the house didn't get built that day. However, the next day a bunch of us showed up and started working on his mansion-to-be. I don't think any of us had any experience in carpentry. Allen didn't really have a plan so we each sort of took over and expressed ourselves. "Want a window here, Allen? Ok, I'll make one: cut some boards, nail them together, and attach to the wall beams some way and voila! A window. Now we'll just build the wall around it. The whole process was hilarious. You carpenters shield your eyes. I can guarantee there was not one right angle in the place. But it got done and was used for many years. It still may be standing, for all I know.

The next day I was very excited about what I had experienced and I tried to explain it to Allen. He cut me short, questioned my validity, and really challenged me. I was quite devastated by his reaction and came crashing down from my beautiful high. Both Jerry and Harold came over to me a bit later and said, "Boy, Allen really tore into you. Don't take it too seriously. He's a really cool guy." I agreed with them that he was really a cool guy. I left town with the situation buzzing in my head. My male ego was bruised.

I realized, however, that this was a new situation for me. Who was I to the rest of the world? I had been a fringe beatnik and was into Tao and Zen in the early '60s. I first dropped acid in maybe 1966, but had not dropped out until six months ago. I had now entered the world of, "You are what you manifest." Talk doesn't cut it. Do it. I hadn't manifested anything yet. In the past I had felt comfortable hanging with longhairs, because I had been interacting with hippies for several years. But I had been steadily employed, so I didn't have my own hippie street cred, and was not totally one of them. I got many points, however, for being thirty years old, wow, and quite hip for an old guy. I probably exploited that for all it was worth.

Now it was a new game. I had to find out *who* I was and what I was going to *be* in this new environment. Allen had nailed me, and I hated it because I wanted to be Allen; I wanted to be an old-time crazy, goddamnit.

Later, after I had manifested myself and became Buckwheat Bob of the fabulous buckwheat pancakes, I gained his respect and became considered as one of the old-time crazies. From several perspectives this wouldn't seem to be a particularly desirable goal in life but we were into living, whatever that meant. Allen and I would look at each other and start laughing. What a wonderful feeling to have the respect of someone you really look up to. I left Takilma and spent the winter in Sacramento.

2

New Year's

After I left Takilma in the fall I spent a couple months in Orange County and then back up North to Sacramento. I spent Christmas with my family then left for Takilma on December 26, 1970. I had scored an ounce of what was purported to be "organic mescaline" but was actually some very good acid mixed with Nestlé's Quick to give it the right color. I didn't care; it was good stuff.

It was frigid when I arrived at Takilma. There was about six inches of snow and it got down to about ten degrees at night. Harold and Delores and the kids, along with a young lady, Rebecca, were living in the Mirage Garage. There were maybe thirty people living in the area. Some, like Charley and Joyce, had been there the winter before, which had been mild, but most of the folks were new at this, penniless, on food stamps, and freezing their asses off. Gemini Bill was walking around barefoot in the ice and snow. Some of the residents, and probably most of the people still living in Takilma that winter, had left the Bay Area several years before, when they felt the collapse of the city scene and some migrated north through Lou Gotleib's Morningstar Ranch on to the Mendocino coast, camping out on the Navarro River. They were somewhat used to living in a primitive style but not adjusted to the rain, snow, isolation, and cold of southern Oregon. It was a hard life. There was only one single female (Rebecca), no money, no tobacco, no pot, no liquor, no electricity, no running water, and no car to get them into town for their monthly food stamps, and no books to read.

When I pulled in to the Mirage Garage Harold came out and said, "We expected you two days ago" (Christmas). I hadn't communicated with anyone since the end of September and was totally shocked that they still remembered me from all the people who passed through there that fall. I realized that this would soon be home.

I arrived with some food, some books, and the ounce of acid. Hosting this distinguished guest, who actually had a vehicle, was a social triumph for Harold and Delores. I had never been an honored guest before.

I guess I don't have to tell you that everyone living there in those days was crazy. Some saint or demon had driven them (us) to this extremity of life and different people's crazy manifested itself in different ways. But it was all held together by a spiritual commitment made by all members of the tribe. Do your own thing, just keep it real.

We were not immune to the infrequent infestation of fellow members of our species whose only personal asset was the ability to detect any kind of positive energy that is not directed at them or created by them and try to usurp it or destroy it. There are a lot of these people. Energy rip-offs. When a person came into town he would see a bunch of stupid vegetarians just right for exploitation by his or her street theater. And they were right, up to a point. We always did like being entertained. In very few instances would the person be physically or socially ostracized from the group. They just didn't share the energy; and in most cases, after some major attempt to nuke the community, sometimes violently, they left as failures. We had all done psychedelics together and really related on that level. I remember Robert saying, "I love everyone here but I don't like some of them." I think that summed things up pretty well.

My arrival caused a bit of a spark in the spirit of the community. Anything new would have sufficed. New Year's was coming up soon. We heard that there was going to be a community New Year's Eve party at the log cabin, a structure about 900 square feet right next to the Takilma store.

I drove Harold, Delores, and Rebecca, plus everyone else who could fit in the van, the half-mile to the log cabin. The fact that there was a vehicle at the cabin that night could have had disastrous consequences later that evening.

As my host, Harold had possession of the NQ acid, which he began to dole out soon after we arrived. Harold and Delores had recently returned to the U.S. from Canada after living on one of the islands in the Gulf of Georgia in British Columbia for several years as undocumented Americans. I know in retrospect what it feels like to have to leave that area and return to the real world. It is not easy.

At this party there was no smoke and no beer or wine. All we had for, er . . . *refreshment* was the acid. Lets see, there was Gemini Bill, Charlie and Joyce, Brian and Pam, Lance and his wife, Medicine Man, Rebecca, and a number of people I don't remember now. And there was music, of course, though I can't remember if I played that night or not. Gemini Bill was playing, and so was Lance. I guess there were about twenty-five people in all.

Harold was giving out the acid and licking up the leftovers. Charlie Two-shoes and Brian Bones were going around hitting up people for change to buy a lid. Panhandling was not unusual for this duo. They were usually bumming in front of the store to buy wine, but this time it was for pot; a more noble endeavor, I suppose.

It was going to be a long night. It seemed like a hopeless task to get enough spare change from this destitute group to buy any pot, but lo and behold they came up with the twenty dollars that an ounce would cost.

Who was the only one here with a vehicle? Me. Where was this mythical marijuana? Wonder, Oregon, about twenty-four miles down Highway 199 toward Grants Pass. Medicine Man, Charlie, and Brian came up to me and said, "Would you drive us down to Wonder?" I said, "No way." Then Medicine Man asked me if I would lend them my van. It seemed that the life of the party was up to me. I finally decided to let them use it. This was probably a sort of a test of my commitment. I don't know.

There was little road traffic in the winter of 1970, so the possibility of an accident didn't bother me too much. I said, "Sure, go ahead." I wasn't really worried about the car but I was concerned that if it broke down or something, they might freeze to death. So I had that to think about.

Sometime later the trio made it back and walked in with this skinny bag of pot and set it down on the table. Hippies came charging to the table. They dumped out the pot and started rolling it up, stashing joints, rolling as fast as they could. One minute and twenty-four or so seconds later that lid was gone. We lit up and the party resumed.

Charlie and Brian started the spare-change routine again. I don't know how long any of this took but it doesn't matter. We weren't going anywhere and time has very little meaning on acid. This was an all-nighter. So Charlie and Brian manage to get another twenty dollars or so and asked if they could use the car again. I said sure and they were off again.

At this point Harold, who Charlie Two-shoes had dubbed Harold the Barbarian, started having a minor freak-out from taking a bit too much LSD. He would have been one of those bartenders who would sip leftover drinks all night.

A good freak-out in these environs, with nowhere for anyone to retreat, was not pleasant to contemplate. I started trying to communicate with him. I found out that one of the things he was having trouble with was his general communication skill; he was a really weird guy even in this environment. His specific problem was his inability to relate his experiences in Canada. Most of the folks here were recently out of the city and could not relate at all to that severe work-intensive lifestyle away from civilization.

I got him talking about their life up north. Differently from most of the kids in the room, I was fascinated by his stories of making it in the real bush. I started thinking about doing that someday. For now I was having too much fun here.

After I listened to him for a while he calmed down. Several years later, the way he had been living in Canada was just what I wanted to do.

The boys returned with another bag of dope. Our reflexes must have sharpened because it only took forty seconds for it to disappear. I don't remember too much more about that night.

Rebecca and I moved into the Taj Mahal, an A-frame down behind the Mirage Garage. The Taj was tiny, maybe no more that ten by ten feet. It had a miniature cook stove and a miniature heat stove, but you couldn't heat the place. There were holes in the walls. There was a loft just wide enough for two people to sleep side by side. During the several days we were there the drinking water on the table stayed frozen solid. I got pretty anxious to get out of there. I left in a snowstorm for Sacramento two days later, taking the only single female in town with me.

After reading this I realize the force must have been with us back then.

3

Here to Stay

In the early spring of 1971, I pulled into Takilma for the first time as a self-proclaimed "resident." When I stopped at the side of the road I was greeted by a number of my friends from the previous winter. There may have been several reasons for the happiness at my arrival: (1) They were hoping I had brought an intoxicant, (2) they grooved on my possession of a functional van, and/or (3) they just loved me. I think it was a combination of the three.

I had just dropped into another galaxy, but I had to figure out how I fit in. I had to learn how to be a part of the community. I just had to live and see what happened. The day might start slowly as I crawled out of my van, started a fire in the pit, brewed up some coffee, sat on a log, picked my guitar a bit, and fixed breakfast. Then I'd usually go visiting.

The community basically consisted of the Mayor and his family at the "Love House." he owned the Love House. He was older than most of the hippies, had a successful firewood business, and was looked up to as the local authority by many.

There was a Jewish commune of mostly New Yorkers at the "Magic Forest Farm;" several people who rented small shack/houses along the road; the family at the Mirage Garage; and the river rats who were squatting in various shacks they had put together along the river bed. On the other side of the river was the Meadows and then "Talsalsen," a rent-a-shack community, run by Johnny, who had once worked as an engineer for NASA.

Since there were few motor vehicles, people spent a lot of time walking or hitchhiking. Of course, if you had a vehicle, as I did for a while after I arrived in town, you had to be neighborly enough to pick up everyone who wanted a ride.

Speaking of that, I became the bus driver for the dreaded trip to Grants Pass on food stamp day. The van would hold ten or twelve people. I'd drive forty-five miles to G.P., pull in to the food stamp office, and unleash twelve or so scruffy hippies, in their patched clothes, onto the unsuspecting natives. Before I opened the doors I would admonish them that, goddamnit, they needed to be back here at a certain time. Faint hope. "Rules? You're setting rules? You're on a power trip." OK, whatever. Then like cats—pshooo! They're gone.

The usual schedule was to pick up food stamps, of course, then on to the supermarket and Rogue Gold discount cheese, and the VD clinic, if needed. I think we put a lot of stress on the straight community. Sorry about that.

By the time I got everybody and all their shit back in the van and started home I was a bit short-tempered. I got a few demerits for this attitude from some of my neighbors. I didn't know how to tell them that I didn't fully enjoy being a traveling secretary and drill sergeant. I didn't become "just another guy" until my van blew up and I was walking like everyone else.

A political note on the attitude of Cave Junction toward Takilma hippies. We were unable to go into about half of the businesses in town, those with "We Do Not Solicit Hippie Patronage" signs in the window. These establishments included bars, of course. They didn't really need signs. We also were not allowed in the only dry goods and hardware store in town, several grocery stores, and both movie theaters, including the drive-in. All local police, the State Patrol, and the county sheriffs kept close watch on us while we were off the reservation.

When we reached Four Corners after a trip to town and looked up into the mountains ahead, we wanted to shout, "Free at last! Free at last!"

At least in the beginning, 1970 or so, our focus was on creating a tribal community through the release of our inner spirit, slowly expanding outward and encompassing the entire planet; maybe the Universe. Well, we were dreamers.

Habitations were varied. There were a few tents, a teepee, a wooden teepee in the Meadows, Long Larry's wall tent, and a lot of scrap wood shacks and camps. In most of the homes along the road, on a typical day, there would be a number of people hanging out. No one ever knocked at a door. We would whistle to let the people know we were there and then enter. Anyone knocking had to be police. If there were intoxicants they would be consumed, of course. The women were often cooking stuff in the kitchen and there would be music if any musicians were present. The wandering minstrel life was alive and well. No electricity, no radio or recorded music. Musicians would go from house to house, hook up with other musicians, and then move on to the next promising location. It was a movable party.

I mention this because . . . When I got to Takilma I had the best guitar in town, a very fine Epiphone Frontier. Everyone wanted to play it. In the beginning I wasn't confident in my ability. Several things bugged me. I was envious of the musicianship of some of these kids, a lot of rock-and-roll and blues stuff that I didn't know. I was an old fart, late to start playing music, and I played mostly country and folk, which I thought the kids would find corny.

I was in a quandary because if I didn't play my guitar everyone else would use it. Things changed for me one day when during a kitchen music session at the "Funky Egg," Charlie Two-Shoes looked at me and said, "Buckwheat, seems I remember that you played a few tunes last winter. Why don't you play a song or two?"

The rest as they say is history. I played for a while, the kids liked my music (or any music truthfully) so . . . my tribal function became providing music and traveling around to outlying communities trying to bring the tribes together. And party of course. Allen approved.

Since our physical needs were small, everybody shared. It wasn't the law, it was the love. On naming conventions, most people in the valley had nicknames. Some of our neighbors had warrants out, so they obviously didn't want to use their real names. No one used a last name. Even the relatively law-abiding citizens like myself didn't want our names on any official documents. Another reason was that it's easier to remember nicknames than real ones.

Some of the monikers were Gemini Bill, Bowie Bill, Billy Gulch, Crazy Jim, Mining Claim John, Mad John, Rainbow Bob (one blue eye and one brown eye), Buckwheat Bob, Cleveland Bob, and Jesus Bob (not particularly religious, it just seemed that every time he did something someone would say, "Jeezus, Bob"). The names allowed the holder to set his or her persona. They could be self-initiated or could come from some differentiating characteristic. Women tended to use more earthy names such as Rainbow, Willow, Sunshine.

Since we had more or less eradicated the valley of police, from time to time it became a haven for some bad groups of people. It was much like the badlands of Oklahoma, Texas, and New Mexico toward the end of the nineteenth century. Along with the hippies, mostly middle-class city kids, there was a group of armed country kids who kept life interesting.

The first tribe I remember was the small Ishanabe group. There were about six of them and they were pretty self-sufficient. They traveled on horseback and were armed. They camped in the Meadows and were quite amiable. There were also the Gunslingers, more on that later.

The next infestation came from an armed Moslem tribe (no Arabs in the group) that resulted in an actual Old West type of duel and shotgun death of the Moslem tribe's leader. This event is dealt with later in the book.

Lastly, a group of armed paranoid people led by a Vietnam vet, brother of Bowie Bill, arrived and camped on Hope Mountain. They were belligerent with the locals and most people were very worried by their presence. Eventually Rainbow Bob and Moses were killed and beheaded after a drunken confrontation.

From time to time seriously disturbed individuals arrived. Some stayed for a while but at least early on, besides one non-fatal shooting and a few anxious moments there was no super violence from those "passing through."

4

Takilma Rifles

It's hard to impose rationality upon the events that took place in southern Oregon in the late 1960s and early 1970s. The Takilma valley was a particular anomaly. The "town" was situated where the east fork of the Illinois River flowed down the Siskiyou Mountains. Takilma consisted of a country store with a gas pump and the road was literally on the way to nowhere. The unpaved road ran due south, ascending into the mountains; it passed several mining claims, climbed into California, and then ended. Anyone coming through town would have specific, if occasionally nefarious, reasons for being there, or else they were lost.

There was some private property in the area, mostly owned by people of limited means and aspirations, small ranchers like Lou Duval, and wackos like the Reverend Rowe, who excavated a UFO landing pad on the other side of Hope Mountain. Much of the private land was unoccupied by owners, and much of the rest was owned by the government as National Forest, which has always been a magnet for the less responsible members of society. The store/gas pump was owned by Andy; to his and everyone else's discomfort, Andy hated and detested hippies.

I guess there is something to this karma stuff, because the valley soon saw a migration of weirdoes who saw its isolation and the disinterest of the local constabulary a large plus for their way of life. The first group was the Fanatic Family. Many of the first immigrants were folks who had worn out their welcome almost everywhere else in North America. They were wild and crazy, the first dope-crazed, gun-totin' bad asses seen in this part of the country since the mining days. This fact contributed to the relative disinterest of the police. Andy ended up being the purveyor of goods and services to some of the dirtiest, meanest scum in the country.

It must be stressed that although the police had no particular interest in what was happening in the valley, many of the local rednecks, particularly the loggers, were intensely interested. For them it meant many things, including the fact that pit-lamping for deer, and poaching generally, was at least marginally more dangerous with these people hanging out in the woods. There were many other reasons for the rednecks antipathy, some valid and others less so.

Although in the pre-hippie days the general décor in the valley had not been particularly fit for inclusion in *Better Homes and Gardens,* with the new residents it could qualify for *National Geographic* articles on poverty in Africa or Asia. I mean, tourists could drive down Takilma road past the Mirage Garage and see naked men, women, and children sitting on logs next to the road smoking marijuana and I don't know what all, with rifles and shotguns leaning up against trees and within easy reach.

From my understanding, the first incursion by the political establishment into this disgrace began with several deputy sheriffs and the local health department arriving and demanding to inspect the Mirage Garage for health violations, particularly relating to outhouse arrangements. Possible pollution of the river was a recurring theme in the efforts to get rid of these vermin.

I don't know what they expected to happen, but one sheriff came on the property and threatened the Fanatic Family, who were residing there at the time, with physical punishment if they didn't allow access. Black Willie asked if they had a warrant to enter the property. When none was produced, the deputy walked onto the property. Black Willie knocked him down then pulled his pistol and stuck it to the deputy's head and threatened to blow his head off if he didn't "get the fuck out of there." These scum cursed a lot, too.

The upshot to this confrontation was a deputized posse on horseback rounding up the members of the family. It took several days and they were all rounded up, except Takilma Nick, who escaped the area.

The law in Josephine and Jackson Counties was rather parochial at that time. All sides of the law were on the same team, more or less. If an attorney were to have any chance of being successful here, he or she would have to play a lot of ball with the police and the judges. An illustration of the clubby atmosphere happened when Allen was arrested for cultivation of marijuana, even though it was not growing on his land (he owned no land) and there was no physical connection between him and the plot. He had trouble getting a local lawyer so he hired one from Eugene. The first thing the judge said was, "What's the matter, the local lawyers not good enough for you?" Strike one.

All the prisoners were found guilty. The defendants hired the Jackson County ACLU lawyer; he appealed and the convictions were overturned. However, that lawyer was probably a marked man after that.

The raid and its aftermath definitely proved that there were in fact "crazy gun-totin' hippies" in the area, probably loaded on LSD. The general paranoia increased in the straight community. Any embellishment of the gun mythology tended to make the valley safer. The rumor began, propagated mostly by Takilma Nick, the self-appointed sheriff, that there were armed revolutionaries in the woods.

Shortly after the raid some of the more hardcore rednecks formed the Illinois Valley Betterment Association, a militia group committed to the idea that the valley would be considerably bettered by getting rid of "them goddam hippies down in Takilma." The method decided upon was to raid the town and burn them all out.

It seems that there was a spy in their midst who tipped the Fanatics that a raid was coming. At the appointed time, the convoy got about halfway to their destination when a hippie emerged from behind a tree with a rifle pointed at the lead vehicle. He walked up to the driver and said, "If you'll look down the river bank, on your right you will see a number of people with rifles pointed at your convoy. We don't want any trouble, so why don't you go back home and leave us alone." The loggers went back home and endured the taunts of other tough guys saying, "How come you got run out by a bunch of long-haired sissies? Haw, haw, haw." End of round two.

One of the rights of spring for some of the local redneck kids was to "Hoo Ray" Takilma, like the trail riders from Texas used to do at Abilene and other trailhead towns during the cattle driving days. The teenagers would drive down Takilma Road, shoot into a big tree, and then make their escape out of town. There was at least one incident of a deputy sheriff shooting a shotgun at a young hippie couple skinny dipping in the river.

The Meadows was inhabited by a group of serious pacifistic vegetarian hippies, nicknamed Veggie Chumps by some of the rougher citizens around town. They were something of a counter balance to the Fanatic Family and their followers. As the community began to grow there were a number of different philosophies on life and reality represented. Since there was a large, fairly inaccessible area in the Meadows, a rumor began circulating that this was the headquarters of the Takilma Rifles, a paramilitary revolutionary offshoot of the Fanatics, who had several thousand rifles buried, awaiting the revolution.

This was all bullshit of course, though the rumor enhanced the idea that it wasn't healthy to mess with Takilma. It also had unforeseen consequences for the future. The parents of one of the girls living in the Meadows went to the local sheriff's office and asked how they might find their very spiritual darling daughter, who lived in the Meadows. They were told that it would be dangerous to go to the Meadows since everyone who resided there were revolutionary guerillas hiding out with guns. The Takilma Rifles must have been happy that their disinformation program had been so successful, though I'm not sure the Meadows people appreciated it.

Did the Takilma Rifles really exist? Well, yes and no. The whole hippie consciousness at that time was balanced on a fine line between fantasy and reality. Everyone was allowed to create his own reality. The only caveat was that he actually manifest his reality, not just talk about it. The Gunslingers were an example of this. We all knew that their shtick was 90 percent bullshit, but no one was willing to pass judgment on the other 10 percent.

By the time I was involved, the myth of the Rifles was generated mostly by Takilma Nick. He looked a bit like Buffalo Bill and always had a gun belt with his latest weapon holstered. Only two other Fanatics were still in the area by the time I had arrived.

Certain dudes drifted into the role of greeters, people who met the new folks arriving in town, especially females. Nick was one of the most accomplished. He had a very courtly manner he used with much success. He had a line of BS a mile long, and I must admit that much of this story uses him as a source. I do not claim absolute accuracy. Nick and I partnered for a while, at a camp on Cedar Creek on an agricultural enterprise that ultimately failed, and he appointed me an officer in the Takilma Rifles. I can't remember what rank, and my responsibility was "communications." The duties were quite nebulous, but the general idea was to try to devise some sort of early alert system we could use if we were attacked by one group or another that didn't like us. I can't remember if I actually worked anything out, but I was, by God (or by Nick), a member of the Takilma Rifles.

A number of city couples, sometimes with kids, arrived in southern Oregon searching for . . . something. They fell in love with the beauty of the country and the easy lifestyle. For a lot of guys the courting and mating games were pretty intense. City people mainly create their world through words and abstractions. In the country words don't have a lot of weight if not followed up with actions.

The pretty city ladies had a tendency to be attracted to the self-assured bush hippies and many had a field day with the local studs. Some of their guys went back to the city and tried to devise ways to get even with the bitch; most of the ways involved the children. There were several cases of abduction, legal and otherwise, and there was quite a panic.

Some of the most vulnerable were the families who lived in the Meadows. There was an unimproved road along the ridge, with the river between the Meadows residents and the main road. Residents could be easily caught with no way to escape. My camp was a couple of ridges south of the Meadows and I decided to blaze and maintain a well-disguised trail using a series of discarded mining flumes (ditches that had been used to transport water to the "diggins") as the backbone of the trail.

I liked playing in the woods. I always had, even as a child. I didn't have any desire to carve out an empire in the wilderness, just to hang out, take care of myself, and learn to be a woodsman. This put me in bad repute with some of the newer city hippies who were into property and improvement.

Fortunately, the camp and trail were not needed by mothers and children, but occasionally it was a hiding place for low-level fugitives like Big Steve, who was somewhat wanted in a marijuana cultivation case. It was mistaken identity of course, but best not to turn yourself in. Sooner or later they will probably forget about it. The real hippies didn't like the gun consciousness, but the Takilma Rifles became a part of the folklore.

As a part of the self-appointed elder and Takilma Rifles communications officer, I tried to teach the hippies how to be outlaws, since we were all sitting targets in the valley. So, did the Takilma Rifles really exist? It certainly did on the fantasy plane. And it was good enough to get the Gunslingers raided by the police.

5

Ashland

I had been gone for several days visiting somewhere in the Pacific Northwest. I can't remember what subversive mission I had been on this time. The last ride dropped me off in Cave Junction, Oregon, in the early afternoon. Pretty town. Nice town if you didn't happen to have long hair. Population of about seven hundred; a backwater, but located at the junction of Highway 199, which is the interchange between U.S. Highway I-5 at Grants Pass and Highway 101 at Crescent City, California, and the Caves Highway, which leads to that great tourist attraction, the Oregon Caves.

The first thing I noticed in CJ was that there were a hell of a lot sheriff's cars around this small country town. I didn't think too much about it at first. Preparatory to hitching the last ten miles home I went into the market (the one that did solicit hippie patronage) and bought some groceries and a couple of bottles of beer and wine. I hiked out of Cave Junction south on Highway 199, then turned east onto Caves Highway. I had begun to notice that this Josephine County police car had been following me ever since I left the market. They were driving at walking speed, which was a bit disconcerting.

With my pack and guitar I trudged to the first wide pullout, which had a nice oak tree you can lean up against while waiting for a ride. I had been planning to lie back against that tree and enjoy a bottle of beer. When I reached my hitching spot I dropped my guitar and pack and sank down with my back against the trunk. When I looked up I saw that police car had made a U-turn and had pulled up right across the street from where I was sitting. The deputies just sat and watched me. I began to have the feeling that my presence was not totally appreciated at this moment. In full disclosure, I had been kicked out (or asked to leave) a couple of towns by this time in my moderately young life.

All I really wanted to do was to pop a beer and relax, but I had the nagging feeling that if I so much as intimated that I was going to have an open container in my vicinity I would end up in that police car within seconds. Since I had never been in jail, I certainly didn't want the first time to be in Josephine County. My other worry was about how I was going to get back to Takilma. Hitchhiking was legal in Oregon, but rural police were not always bound by the law.

My political dilemma in those days was that I was older than many of the people in the community. I was strongly committed to the sort of Utopia we were trying to build, and I believed it could be created if you worked hard enough. Since many of the kids were pretty young and naive about interaction with the local community, especially the police, I tried to teach them as much as possible, but it was important that the straight community did not see me as a leader. I hated politics, and I didn't want to get my name on any "person of interest" list. I knew my cover might be blown if they detained me here, even if they let me go. If I couldn't put my thumb out how was I going to get a ride?

I sat stewing for about a half hour, with the police across the street watching me the whole time. Finally, a very nice lady in a pickup stopped and told me to hop in. Whew. When we arrived at the Takilma store I felt as if I had passed through Checkpoint Charlie, from the slave world into the free world. What a relief. I told the lady of my recent travails in town, and she reached under the seat, pulled out a quart of home brew and handed it to me as I stepped out of the pickup. Home. Safe.

Most of the time, the police who patrolled the southern county area were very fearful of the local hippies. Guns, LSD, free love. Well, maybe that free love wasn't such a bad idea. If only they could figure out a way to get some of it. Most of the time I lived in Takilma the police wouldn't have gotten out of their car to investigate anything short of a murder; certainly they wouldn't roll down the window if they saw someone sitting beside the road smoking pot. They saw this often. It actually got so bad that if the police wanted to question a potential witness in a case, they went to the Mayor and asked him to go tell this person that they weren't going to hassle him, they just wanted to ask him a few questions. Must have been like that when Butch Cassidy and the gang arrived home in *Robber's Roost* after a hard week robbing trains. I have a photograph of myself when I got out of that car, sporting a tree-limb walking stick with a door handle for a knob. Pack, guitar, and a bottle of home brew. This picture is on the cover of this book.

As soon as I got out of the truck, everyone hit me with it—*it* being the massive busts that had happened in the past two days. They had busted about fifteen people for various things. Charley Two-Shoes had been rousted at 4:00 a.m. one morning and taken to jail for "overdue library books."

They busted the Mayor because a snitch had managed to buy an ounce of pot from someone while they were both in the Mayor's house. Of course, everyone in town was in the Love House several times a day, since his was the first house on the corner coming into Takilma. Shabby though it was, it was about the best house in town. It was the general meeting place.

Out-of-towners were often hanging around his house. There were a lot of transients, as well as narks, around in those days.

They got Allen because his squatter's cabin was the closest habitation to a small pot garden that was found. All this was stupid. Allen and the Mayor went to court and beat the frivolous charges, but still they had to go to court and, in several cases, hire a lawyer. It was a hassle and, of course, that was the whole idea.

Several people were nailed pretty good, though; Charley Tuna and Billy Gulch among them. They would have gotten Scorpio Don too, but it so happened that . . .Well, I guess I'd better tell the story.

Some time before the event I am relating, Black Michael and the Godzilla Wrecking Company returned to Takilma from Eugene. In the entourage was a raving English beauty named Nancy, fresh from London. She had somehow ended up in Eugene. She probably had severe culture shock while experiencing the Wild West frontier town of Eugene, Oregon. Well, she was from London, after all. As if that weren't enough she ran into Black Michael, and ended up in the woods in southern Oregon with a bunch of totally crazy mountain hippies.

She loved it. She loved several of the guys around town also, and I remember one night when she preferred me to Allen, which was an unusual and notable event. But I digress.

In the course of time she met up with Scorpio Don, who was an ex-con who was probably wanted by the law. She dropped out of the Godzilla Wrecking Company to hang with a real Wild West outlaw.

We didn't pry too much into people's pasts. The present, that is another story. In a small community personal privacy doesn't exist. I guess when the big bust was happening, Don and Nancy were down the lower Illinois River preparing to go horse camping. They were getting their rigs together when they heard the cops were after Don. The two evidently saddled up, crossed the Illinois River just ahead of the police, rode up over Chetco Pass, down the rugged, rocky Chetco River canyon, through the Kalmiopsis Wilderness, and disappeared after finally reaching the town of Gold River on the coast. I guess this lady must have had some interesting tales to tell to her chums back in London.

So I had arrived home to discover that since the rednecks hadn't been able to burn us out, a task that would be a lot more satisfactory than getting help from the authorities, they had decided to rely on the police to "Get rid of them goddamn hippies." The police also let it be known that there were sixty-five warrants still to be served. I was relieved when I heard that, because sixty-five was about three fourths of the total population, and it was ridiculous to think that most of the people had done anything so serious that it would require a warrant. I decided that was probably just a bluff. They also said that they would be watching the roads, and if anyone was caught harboring known or suspected low-lifes, shame, shame. We all holed up for a few days wondering what to do.

Our local self-styled promoter, David, secured a hall in Ashland to hold a benefit for the incarcerated, and he asked the musical groups the Miracles of Wonder and the East Fork of the Illinois River Boys (of which I was one) to perform at the event.

The problem was figuring out how to get there. The regular roads were being watched, so they said. Robert, the squire of the Little Funky Egg Company, decided that we could take back roads, mostly glorified logging roads, across the mountains. Ashland is only about thirty-five miles as the crow flies, but we, fortunately or unfortunately, were not crows. Most of the time we took 199 to Grants Pass, then drove south on I-5 to Ashland. Although this route was at least sixty miles longer than the "shortcut" we proposed to take, most people were not interested in using these old and neglected logging roads.

We snuck out of town in the evening, successfully evaded the hypothetical blockading forces, and finally arrived to semi-pandemonium in Ashland. There was a large turnout at the hall, near Lithia Park, and terrific vibes with the music, politics, and the anticipation of a great time.

However, the local constabulary were not too sure they wanted us bush hippies in town at all, much less inflaming the locals. Actually, they were very sure they didn't want us there at all.

I don't have any idea what they thought was going to happen. When we arrived there were a number of straight looking people with walkie-talkies and guns trying to look inconspicuous while squatting behind hedges and in doorways. It made us a bit apprehensive. The East Fork of the Illinois River Boys were about halfway through our musical set when the police came in and shut us down. They didn't have any specific reason, they just . . . did it!

Ashland being a college town, a big political debate erupted about rights, police harassment, whatever, and there was some feeling that we might resist the order. Through all the commotion, David was tearing his hair out. Figuratively speaking. At the hottest point in the debate someone said, "Hell, I have a farm outside of town. Why don't we all go over there and party?"

I guess we weren't dedicated revolutionaries, even though we had that reputation among the police and straight community. There was nothing we liked better than a party, so we loaded our stuff in vehicles, careened to our new friend's farm, and had a wonderful time. End of riot in Ashland. Things soon cooled down and life went back to normal, though I suppose life was not too close to what most people would think is normal at that.

6

Lucy

I don't know how many folks have actually been able to communicate with an animal such as a dog or a cat. I mean, really communicate reasonably abstract concepts. I know that a lot of people teach things to animals by rote, much the way they teach children. One thing that you have to realize is that you are considerably more intelligent than the animal, so the job isn't for the animal to get into your consciousness, but for you to get into the animal's consciousness. I think this is the essence of good teaching.

Now let's say right here, it's my feeling that there are smart pets and there are dumb pets, just like there are smart people and dumb people. And if you have a dumb animal there just isn't much you can do with it. But if you have one of the smart ones and can establish a mutual understanding it is a pretty awesome experience. Like the relationship I had with my cat, Lucy.

Lucy was born in Sacramento of Mrs. White, a hippie cat that was supposed to have gotten into someone's LSD stash and really got stoned and was kind of strange after that. I don't know all the details, but she must have discovered the joys of sex while she was under the influence, because she was the horniest cat I ever saw. I mean she had six litters in three years, and most of the kittens that weren't given away died in some way or other, as cats are wont to do.

I got Lucy, a gray striped tiger when she was six weeks old. I lived in an upstairs apartment and she just seemed to be a normal adorable kitten, though she didn't seem to like too much affection. One time she got out into the hallway and went down the stairs and got lost. She thought that the apartment on the floor below was ours and really got freaked out. So that was the last bit of adventurousness she showed for a long, long time. I think she began to mistrust life just a bit after that experience.

I moved to an older upstairs flat where she had a lot of rooms to play. She found a way to get into the attic, where she probably raised havoc with the local pigeon population, so life was complete.

One of the things she would not do was go outside. After we had lived in the house for several months, she finally stepped onto the porch and would sit and glare at all the cars, dogs, and other menacing things passing by on the street. After several months of scouting the outside world, she got brave enough to go to the bottom step. She was to show caution about her immediate environment her whole life. That's why she lived to die with her boots off at around age fifteen. But I digress. She finally worked up the courage to venture onto the sidewalk. Just as she had accomplished this memorable feat, a dog came flying around the corner, saw her, and chased her up one of the enormous Dutch elm trees that Sacramento, the Tree City, was famous for. For the rest of the day she wouldn't (or couldn't) climb down from her tenuous perch in the tree. In desperation, I finally called the fire department. They used to make house calls for cats back in those days. The fire engine parked and ran up the hydraulic ladder. This was before the cherry picker bucket.

If Lucy didn't like the dog, she downright hated these guys in this red, noisy diesel truck with this thing that was rising toward her; and who was this guy with a big hat climbing up the ladder? She didn't appreciate that at all. Trying to back away from him she fell out of the tree, right onto our balcony, where my wife and I were watching the show. Lucy was catatonic for a long time after that. That was not to be the last time she was to spend large periods of time in trees. I think this experience pretty much confirmed her initial impressions of the world, and she never ventured outside that house again.

My wife and I moved again, to a house with a yard in an older residential neighborhood. Lucy was old enough to be aware that something very bad was going on when she observed us packing. This was confirmed when she was put into the car and driven across town and carried into a totally strange house. She hid in a closet and wouldn't leave for a day and a half. When she finally left the closet, she was still so freaked out that she darted through an open window. I figured she was gone for good. As it turned out she was gone about three days and came back just as cocky as could be, and proceeded to become the scourge of the neighborhood.

She was not your cuddly type of cat; most of the time she didn't want to be held at all. If she did ever feel lonesome or deprived she would allow herself to be cuddled and petted for about a minute max, then she'd extricate herself from your grasp.

Still, she would get lonesome. When we would go away for the weekend and leave her in the house we soon learned that we had a three-day limit. Everything was just fine as long as we were gone no more than three days. If we stayed away longer she would wreck the joint. Even back then I think she was trying to reach a social agreement with me. "Hey, Bud! I'm part of this family, too. Show a little respect."

Lucy escaped from the house one time while she was in heat. This was not too difficult to understand, because she always seemed to be in heat; or at least thought she was. This happened about every three weeks, if I recall correctly. She sounds suspiciously like her mother now that I think of it.

So here she was, about to deliver her brood, though she seemed to be the last one to know what was going on. My wife was back east visiting her family. Lucy had finally chosen a nesting place, in my middle dresser drawer. This location had been something of a compromise on her part, because I think she really wanted my bed, and I kept moving her someplace else. However, as the great moment arrived she became very agitated, obviously terrified because she didn't know what was going on. When she started delivering, she climbed out of her drawer, dragged herself into the living room, lay down on the carpet, and looked at me. I didn't want her having kittens on my living room carpet much more than I wanted them on my bed, so I carried her back in to her nest in the drawer. She jumped down again and came back onto the living room carpet. The only way I could get her to stay in her nest in the dresser drawer was to stand by the dresser and pet her while she delivered the first kitten.

She was really freaked when it came out, but then she started purring and licking the newborn and suddenly figured it out. Then she turned toward me and gave me a scornful look that seemed to say, "What the hell are you doing here? Can't you see I'm busy?" Typical woman. From then on everything seemed to be OK. She was a surprisingly good mother to her kittens, which were a weird group. I didn't really notice their strangeness right away, because I was too busy playing midwife.

We had no furniture in the family (trip) room. We sat on cushions on the floor, one of which was a red satin-looking pillow that had gold tassels on it (a Christmas gift from my seven-year-old daughter, from my first marriage). Lucy commandeered the pillow for her nest and nursing ground, and defied me to remove her. Pretty soon it had so much hair and crud caked on it that I would never have been able to get it clean. She had also pulled all the tassels off, of course, so I finally conceded defeat.

The house rules were that she was not allowed up on the kitchen table or the counter, and certainly was not allowed to steal food. She followed the rules unless provoked. Either she obeyed the Law or she was very good at not getting caught. Still, after her kittens were old enough to follow her around, whenever we left the house and then returned home we could look through the kitchen window and see six cats, momma and the five kids, sitting on the kitchen table and staring at us. Of course, by the time we got in the house they were all gone so there was nothing we could do. "I don' know . . . wha-choo talkin' 'bout. No spika da English." I suspect Lucy could hear the car coming and would get up on the table just for spite. Maybe not. She always was good at keeping vigils.

She was a very competent but not particularly enthusiastic parent. My wife and I decided that we were going to pull an escape from this work world and get on the road, so we reluctantly moved into an apartment downtown preparatory to leaving society as we knew it. We got rid of all the kittens except Little Lucy, a miniature version of Big Lucy. Lucy was getting really sick of this kitten hanging around, and she really began tormenting her offspring. I was to notice her sadism toward other cats at least once more during her life.

We finally managed to give the little one to a couple of hippie friends who lived just up the street. They had a baby. Several days after they took the cat, they decided it would be fun to take Little Lucy back home for a visit, so they came visiting with the kitten and their little boy. Lucy was beside herself. I'm sure that from her perspective not only were they giving Little Lucy back, they were giving us a baby also. This was just too much. She scratched them both and fled to the bedroom to sulk.

This period in her life would probably stand out as the most idyllic. She didn't know it yet. Terrible things were about to happen. I had given my notice at work, had customized the inside of the VW delivery van, designing a bed, which took up most of the inside of the van. The bed was a plywood box with a hinged top, so that underneath there was a very large storage area. It worked fairly well. The thing we didn't know was how Lucy was going to take to a 400-mile ride to Newport Beach, in southern California, in a motor vehicle. The vet agreed to give her a shot that would put her totally under for twelve hours. Hah. She never went totally out once. She was dopey and drugged to the gills, but she was not, by God, going to nod out and let God knows what happen to her during this harrowing trip.

We finally got to Orange County, even though I had to make it from the grapevine with a broken accelerator cable. My wife had to operate the accelerator by pulling a string through the back window of the van, while I shouted out instructions. This was not to be an entirely stable existence we were all entering. We arrived at Mel and Esther's apartment in Newport, one block from the beach. We parked the car and left the window open so Lucy could see out. We went inside. Lucy got out of the van and prowled the neighborhood and discovered a rip in the kitchen window of our friends' house. She climbed up and jumped through. What she didn't know was this window was the cat door for the domestic female, who just happened to be nursing a group of newly born kittens in her box right below the window. Lucy never made it to the floor. The local cat met her in mid-flight and they both tumbled through the window. Lucy lost a bit of hide in the scuffle, and verified that she hated life both generally and specifically.

She was afraid of the ocean, and there were a lot of dogs in the neighborhood, but she began to learn how to fend for herself and live in the van with the window cracked enough for her to get in and out.

Mel and Esther were commercial fishermen. The city had reserved the area adjacent to the Newport pier for the use of fishermen, if they fished from dory boats and if the boats were launched from the beach and were stored on the beach at the end of the day. These fishermen were truly free people. When they arrived through the surf with their catch they would roll the boats up as close as they could get to the sidewalk, take out a wooden cutting board, which fit across the gunwales of the boat, erect a fish bin with several partitions for fish, hang a scale from an oar (which had been leaned against the boat with the blade rammed into the sand), and be open for business. Choose your fish and it will be dressed however you want it.

When the business went a little flat later in the summer, we decided to close everything up and take a vacation. The first stop was Yosemite Park, which was a pretty wild place in 1971 what with the hippies and the park bears, etc. There were some interesting young people near us in the campground selling organic mescaline, which was said to be very pure. Lucy, of course, was with us. The van was her home. I can't remember too much about her attitude to this trip, but let us say that she had become if not a willing at least a seasoned traveler . Mel, Esther, and I had something of a religious experience while hiking up to Bridal Veil Falls in the Yosemite valley after sampling some of the mescaline we acquired in camp. As we connected with the main trail we encountered a sign that pointed out the trail to Mt. Whitney, 238 miles down the crest of the High Sierras, This seemed to be an omen and we decided that we must make that hike. We departed Yosemite and decided to travel north on Highway 395 past Lake Tahoe up into Plumas County. During World War II my father had been foreman of several Forest Service camps in the vicinity of Lake Almanor, and I hadn't seen the area for a number of years. When we lived in Sacramento my wife and I had come up this way several times, and in searching the logging roads I had discovered a beautiful meadow and small stream, which I thought might have been the site of Camp Almanor in the 1940s. We took Mel and Esther to the beautiful spot.

This was Lucy's first encounter with raw nature. She stood on the front seat on her back feet with her front paws against the window, observing the environment without moving, until after dark. When the campfire finally burned down we could hear all the little varmints scuttling around the camp. Lucy jumped out of the car window and you could hear little feet thundering all around the camp trying to get away from this monster newly unleashed upon the landscape. We got up the next morning and Lucy was nowhere to be found. We lounged around and hiked, drank beer all day, and then set in for the night. I was really getting worried about my cat. There were coyotes, mountain lions, and other bad stuff out there, and Lucy was, as we have seen, a city cat. She finally staggered into camp the next day in the late afternoon; she walked into the little creek that ran through the camp and just stood in the cold water with a look of beatitude on her face, as the water soothed her sore feet. She must have gone exploring and gotten lost. It must have been a scary experience for her, but you wouldn't have known it by looking at the way she was strutting around.

We returned to Newport Beach. As soon as we got home we just about bought out the local outdoor shop, equipping ourselves (as we thought) for the long hike. All I can say is, the guy who ran that shop saw us coming.

My wife did not go with us. There was nothing in the world she would less like to do than to hike 250 miles through the woods and high mountains. She had her sights set on several bronzed surfers who hung around the beach. Anyway, when I finally returned from the hiking trip, which I had to do in two pieces because of a traffic violation I had to deal with, it was obvious that our marriage was over. I decided to try to find the Sky River Rock Festival, which was to be held somewhere in the Northwest, no one knew where, and I hit the trail of adventure. This trip, and the people I met, would come to change my life entirely and magnificently.

After the Festival (I found the Vortex Festival near Portland, Oregon, instead of the Sky River, which was somewhere in Washington). I returned to southern California for some reason. As I sat in my van in the middle of a gigantic traffic jam, I wondered what the hell I had come back for. I found that my wife had moved into an apartment, and she was going to kill the cat, because she didn't find Lucy and her lack of cuddliness a satisfying companion at all. I decided to take Lucy with me on the road, because I thought a lot of her, and she certainly had had a hard life for the past few months.

Some of my friends from Newport Beach had moved up to Sugarloaf, a town and mountain peak near Big Bear Lake in the San Bernardino Mountains. It was now November and very cold up there at night, but beautiful during the daytime, and very peaceful, since the summer people had long since departed. There were many closed-up summer cabins. Needless to say, Lucy was in heaven up there: very few people, lots of trees and brush, no ocean, no dogs she couldn't handle, no loud noise. One evening I went outside for a walk.

She approached me quickly, purring and meowing like mad. She would look at me, meow, turn away from me and go a few steps, turn and look at me and repeat the procedure. It reminded me of Lassie trying to make Timmy follow her to the well, where someone had fallen in and was drowning. I said, "What the hell," and followed her. She led me to an abandoned summer cabin. She was really purring now. She crawled under the porch and came back out and meowed and looked at me, then repeated the activity several times. She was telling me, "Look what I found. We could move in here and be very happy." It really blew my mind. We were beginning to communicate like companions.

I was looking for a place to hang and decided to check out the desert to find out if I could be happy living there, instead of Oregon. Lucy and I went south to the Imperial Valley, looking for work picking fruit. There was no work at that time, so I took a Westward turn at the Salton Sea, to check out the Anza-Borrego Desert.

I really loved the desert, as I love all of God's country that has not been screwed up by the white man, and I probably would have thought about staying there except that this happened to be Thanksgiving weekend and I realized how close everything in southern California was to Los Angeles: The desert along the highway was twenty miles of RVs, off-road vehicles, motorcycles, noise, and bad vibes. After one night there I took off screaming.

I ended up celebrating Thanksgiving in Brawley, in a third-rate Mexican restaurant, feeling lonely and blue. Since there was not going to be any fruit picking in the near future I decided to get back up north as fast as I could. As it turned out I was delayed by a trick Lucy learned, and was to use at times in the future. We were camping just out of town in my van, and Lucy jumped out of the window, which she was allowed to do, but she refused to come back. She was not comfortable traveling yet. I couldn't catch her, so I drove into town, did some stuff, and then came back. It took several trips but she finally allowed me to catch her, then off we went.

From southern California we traveled back to the Sacramento Valley, and hung around until the day after Christmas. Then I took off for southern Oregon.

The weather in Oregon was fierce, being below freezing for several weeks. Lucy and I finally arrived in Takilma in the late evening on December 27, 1970, bitter cold. I got out of the van and walked toward the Mirage Garage.

Lucy jumped out the window onto the ice and was immediately pursued by all the dogs in town, across the field and up a Douglas fir tree. I tried to get her down for two days. Man was she pissed. For two days I tried to coax her down from the tree, but all she would do is sit and wail her heart out. She finally came down and I babied her as much as I could, to atone for her having to live in an unheated van.

I decided to leave town before I got snowed in, and Rebecca wanted to go to Berkeley and try to find an old boyfriend who was supposedly living there. The night before we left town it snowed about a foot but I had been smart enough to put chains on the van before it started snowing. Rebecca, Lucy, and I charged out of southern Oregon in my magic van for the sunny climate of northern California. We landed in Richmond, staying with some friends, and started the process of getting the chill out of our bodies. Rebecca took off for Berkeley, and Lucy and I were a duo again. We stayed with my friends for a week or two. Lucy had become extremely adept at making a home wherever the van happened to be parked, even in the city. I would leave the window cracked enough to let her in and out and she would make her own fun during the day.

Her typical routine when we came to a new spot was to spend a period of time looking out the window, checking out the lay of the land. Once she had an idea of what was out there that might like to make a lunch of her, she would look for a safe shelter within a few feet of the van. Once she found this she would widen her territory and become quite self-sufficient. She reverted to her old habit. She seems to have decided that if she left the van early in the morning and she stayed during the day, we wouldn't leave. She also became extremely sensitive to any activity that might indicate that we were getting ready to hit the road. I don't know how she knew this, but she did. I would get up and go out to the van and she would not be there. I would wait, and finally she would show up late in the afternoon, pleased as punch.

This bothered me, because I was getting ready to leave and didn't know how to trap her. The solution came to me as a gift. One evening Kathy, the wife of my friend, who had to get up very early in the morning to go to work, told me, "Lucy is so cute. When we leave in the morning she is curled up asleep on the front seat."

I said, "Good. Tomorrow morning why don't you close the window so that she can't escape."

The next morning I packed my gear out to the van and there she was, glaring at me through the window. She was really pissed at me for the dirty trick I pulled on her.

I spent the winter between Sacramento and a commune in a little foothill town named Rackerby. Lucy really liked it at Rackerby, the more so because I parked just a few feet from a pile of firewood, which made a wonderful fort for her. I knew that I would have trouble cornering her when it came time to leave. The morning I was to go I saw that she was still in the van. I got a group of my friends together and said, "I'm going to lock Lucy in the van. Now I want you to set up a picket line between the van and the wood pile, because when she sees me coming she is going to make a dash for the wood, and if she makes it I will never get her out."

My friends laughed at me, said no cat was that smart. Ha. Ha. So they stretched out the line, I walked up toward the van, Lucy jumped out and shot between someone's legs and dove into the wood. I spent several minutes cussing out these stupid hippies. They didn't laugh at me anymore. Somehow I managed to corner her the next morning, but we played many funny games over the next few years. Fortunately, I was always just a little bit smarter than she was, but sometimes it was a close call.

We had several adventures on the road. One night I was asleep and Lucy came through the window with a mouse she had captured, dropped it on my stomach, and started playing with it. I woke up with a start, and gave Lucy a whack; she went one way, the mouse went the other, and I had a mouse in my van for a week or so until I caught it. Oh, well.

Heading back up north I began an incredible fifteen years with more magical happenings than anyone can ever hope for. I met a very lovely young lady in Portland, and stayed with her for a while. I parked across the street from her apartment in northwest Portland, next to a building that had a tiny garden for Lucy to play in. In case of emergency, I led her across the street and showed her the apartment house where I would be staying. It had several thick shrubs just outside the door, which could provide cover in a pinch. After several days I had to take my van downtown for some reason. Lucy was nowhere to be seen; out cruising the neighborhood evidently. I called her but she either didn't hear me or didn't want to come. When I returned from my mission the old parking space was not available and I had to park down the block. I called her again, but no luck. Later on that evening I was walking home with my lady friend, and I told her about my cat problem. She was positive that I'd never see the cat again, and she was sad, because she was a cat lover. As we neared her apartment house I said, "I think she's probably in those bushes there," the place I had pointed out to her earlier. I no sooner got the words out of my mouth when she stalked out of the bushes, giving me one of the worst cussing outs that I have ever had. The lady was a believer after that.

After a short trip to visit Mel and Esther, who had moved north and were working for a fruit grower in the hills around Hood River, I moved to Takilma, where I lived for the next five years. It was late spring and the weather was a lot different from the last time Lucy and I had been there. She was quite comfortable living in the van. For a while we parked in the front yard of the Mirage Garage.

Later I moved the van to Robert's Little Funky Egg Company, a sort of extended family, where I lived for about a year. Robert had raised chickens when he lived in Marin County and he brought his brood up to Takilma when he moved.

By this time Lucy was feeling pretty good about life. The dogs didn't seem to give her too much trouble, and there was plenty of trouble to get into: lots of real animals were lurking in the hills, including bears, mountain lions, and coyotes.

Somehow Nick talked me into setting up a camp in Cedar Gulch for the purpose of overseeing a clandestine operation. I was bankrolling the project, which of course never made any money, but it was a very fun time, living in a plastic tent and cooking over a campfire. It became a sort of vacation hangout for some folks down in the valley who wanted to get away from the wall-to-wall people for a while. It also became the guerilla camp for the Takilma Rifles, of whom Nick was self-appointed general and I became the commander of communications by field commission.

Lucy liked the camp just fine. Real mountains and no dogs. Sometime during the summer I started hanging around with Mara at the Funky Egg and left Lucy with Nick at the camp.

Nick liked to tell tall tales, but there was usually some truth to his stories. Nick liked guns. He was always trading and dealing. At this time his favorite weapon was the .36-caliber cap-and-ball revolver. He loved to forge balls (bullets) over our campfire.

I was talking to him one day and he started to tell a Lucy tale. Nick didn't ordinarily like cats. Like most macho guys he liked dogs. He told me that one night Lucy came tearing down the mountainside and ducked into his bed. He jumped up just as a coyote came crashing into camp, evidently in hot pursuit of Lucy. He saw Nick and did a U-turn and took off. Nick pulled out his revolver and fired a couple of rounds in the direction of the retreating coyote. Nick told me that pretty soon Lucy left the bed and sat on a tree stump in plain sight of the forest, and commenced licking her paws, as if to say, "Come on back. Me and my buddy can take care of you any day."

That same summer Long Larry, the Texan logger, came to visit Nick at the camp. One of the most plentiful rodents in that part of the country are pack rats. They live in dens created with mounds of sticks and whatever else they can find. Some of their dens were several feet high. They are regular rat size, and the reason they are called pack rats is that they steal anything they can find, anywhere. They have been known to steal jewelry and money among other things. Real pests. They are nocturnal so they are seldom seen. Larry didn't like cats any better than Nick did, though now Nick was boring everyone within earshot about Lucy's exploits.

When they got ready for bed, Larry threw his ground cloth and sleeping bag on the ground and went to sleep. When he woke up the next morning and turned over he found himself staring at three dead packrats lined up next to his head. At least two were lined up. The third had only a head and a tail. Larry later admitted that this was probably not his favorite way to wake up, but he very much appreciated the gesture. Lucy was just watching over her guys.

I returned to camp one evening after possibly ingesting some psychotropic substance(s). I got in my sleeping bag and watched Lucy, who was sitting near me looking my way. Pretty soon she padded to my sleeping bag purring up a storm. I let her come into the bag and we had a love fest. After a while she wriggled out of the bag and sat a few feet away and looked at me. She seemed to say at the time, "I love you, daddy, but you left me and now I've got another buddy." I was sad about this state of affairs but conceded that it was a just decision. Then she got up and came back and got in the sleeping bag, again purring like a machine, and stayed most of the night.

We often walked together in the woods. One day we started together and climbed over the ridge to the Meadows, going cross-country. We got separated but I wasn't concerned because she knew how to get back to camp. She didn't return, however, and I started to worry a bit. I heard tales of her having been seen in the area. Chris, who owned Cedar Gulch and was letting us camp there, told me, "I saw Lucy just walking down the trail yesterday. You know, she isn't all cat. I think she's part mountain lion."

That was a laugh, but I was happy that she was still around. I heard another story, from a girl named Suzie, who had a camp in the Meadows by the river. She said that Lucy visited her one evening. Suzie fed her and Lucy stayed around. When Suzie woke up the next morning, Lucy was gone but there were two pack rats laid out near her tent. Who was that, the Lone Ranger?

In the meantime our agricultural experiment had failed. Nick left the camp and I moved in with Mara. We were not sure if Lucy was still alive. We hadn't heard anything lately.

In November there was a hard freeze that lasted for over a week. One day someone told me he had seen Lucy up by the old camp and she was in pretty bad shape. I walked through the frozen woods and found her. She looked pregnant, which I couldn't figure out, because we had her fixed after her first (and only) litter. I think the problem was that there was no drinking water. Everything, including the creek was frozen solid and she was severely cold, hungry, and dehydrated. I carried her home and we babied her for a while. She was soon back in fighting trim and happy to be inside for a change. Although that house had holes in the walls and the fire didn't come anywhere near heating the house, it was a big improvement for her.

Her tranquility was soon shattered, however. Judy (the girl I had met in Portland) came to live with us for a short time, and she brought a white city cat named TK (for Takilma Kitty) with her. Lucy was not pleased. She took it all in fairly good grace. There were no serious altercations that I can remember. TK was a total klutz and adored Lucy. They seemed to have divided the house, giving TK several safe zones where Lucy wouldn't bother her, but in between the zones Lucy would spring out and clobber her. TK loved it. The situation seemed to satisfy them both.

When we would go outside to cut firewood or just to walk around, the cats would play mountain lion. At least Lucy would. They would take turns stalking each other. When Lucy pounced on TK she would give her a pretty good whack. The problem was that Lucy would have to pretend that she couldn't see the white city cat creeping up on her through a wide-open clearing. I wish I had a picture of the disgusted look on her face during the charade.

Mara bought a teepee and set it up in the Michels junk yard in O'Brien. Ed Michels was a freelance mechanic who kept the hippy vehicles in more or less running order. I used to play music with his wife, Flo, who had played years before with some of the better musicians in the LA area. Mara and I sort of resumed our relationship, since I had a squatter shack a few hundred yards away. One of the problems with a teepee is that it is very hard to keep out unwanted guests, like skunks and civet cats. Lucy had a food dish, and the local civet cat would come to check it out every night. Normally these are cheerful animals, since they have no (intelligent) natural enemies. Except some wasted hippies. One-time Donnie shot one that came into his bedroom. He shot it with a .22, making the house unlivable for some time; the bullet also put a hole in the water heater.

Under normal circumstances these animals are harmless. However, when a skunk enters your abode, and you are lying in bed with the cat alongside of you, everyone is in a tense state until it finally leaves. It's very unnerving to hear the critter tapping along the counter looking for scraps, and you hope that it does not fall off and shoot a cloud in frustration. We finally decided that if we hid Lucy's food bowl maybe the skunk would go away.

We made at least one mistake in the execution. We moved the bowl while Lucy was out. She came back in a while later and walked to her now missing bowl. Her tail became rigid and she looked up at us. Then we made our second mistake. We decided to make a joke about the missing bowl. "Ha, ha, it took the whole bowl this time, Lucy."

That night, when the skunk made its nightly visit, Lucy was off the bed like a shot. We yelled, "Lucy, no!" But to no avail. She chased the skunk behind the teepee liner, and then here came the stink. Mara, Maia, and I walked to the Michels' trailer to try to find a bed, but they shouted, "Get the hell out of here. You stink." We spent the next several nights in my cabin. We sealed the cat door so Lucy couldn't get in because she had been very close to the skunk when it let go.

Mara and the teepee moved on and Lucy came to live with me in my eight-by-six foot shack. I soon found evidence of mice in the cabin. It wasn't a particularly tight abode, but Lucy would just lie on the bed and watch them playing on the rafters. I said, "Lucy, you are not doing your job." She glared at me with a look that said, "You're out of your freaking mind if you think I'm gonna climb the walls to catch those things, just because you're too lazy to help me." She had a point. I left a dollop of peanut butter out on the floor for bait, so Lucy wouldn't have to climb the rafters. When I got back I found two dead mice on the floor; a week later I found the third, which had crawled under my bed before it expired.

One time I was living temporarily in one of the trailers in the junkyard. The front door was always open because it wouldn't latch. I went away for a few days. Ed Michels commented when I got back, "That ol' cat didn't leave the doorway while you was away." The old watch cat.

When Mara and I decided to leave for Canada we gave Lucy to some friends. I visited her once when I came through town. She didn't seem to know me. She certainly didn't owe me anything at that point. She was later adopted by some people who lived in Lincoln, California. They had a little farm in the woods and she was treated like royalty until she finally died at about age sixteen, approximately forty miles from Sacramento where she was born.

7

Gunslingers

In the 1970s, the demographics of rural southern Oregon would break down into a lot of rednecks, a bunch of hippies, and a few undefined splinters, such as the gunslingers. They were mostly young uneducated kids from the southern U.S., though one had been a White Panther in Portland and another was from southern Oregon; kind of young redneck rebels and ex-felons who had fallen in, to some degree, with their middle-class counterparts, the hippies. They all did LSD, and had fun. They chose their own ways of expressing themselves, ways that included wearing .357 magnum revolvers and carrying shotguns with them, and acting out tough mountain-man fantasies. This troubled the local vegetarians more than somewhat. It also troubled the local police.

At the time of this incident, the Gunslingers were living in the middle of town, probably not the best place for a bunch of borderline sociopaths who wanted to be left alone. One day a bunch of sheriff and state trooper cars roared into town and disgorged a number of officers, with M-16 rifles along with the chief of police and the fat little district attorney. They also brought along the press. The cops hid behind trees and surrounded the house, which had a number of women and children inside. We all walked down to see what was going on. Not too much interesting happening out there so far this week, so people gathered from all over town to watch the show. It was like a football game and we were the fans in the bleachers. The reason the cops didn't continue the raid right away was that they were waiting for a couple of cops to arrive with the Browning automatic rifles.

When the BARs finally arrived the cops moved in. It seems they had information that the long lost rifle cashe, supposedly buried in the Meadows, were actually buried at the house the Gunslingers were living in. We had a lot of fun with that. The cops' ears were really burning from the helpful comments they were getting from the bleachers. There was a ratty-looking young couple in the back of the police car. We figured they were probably the snitches who gave the phony information.

Of course the police didn't find any guns or anything else incriminating. They finally climbed back in their cars and burned rubber out of town, snarling, with our catcalls ringing in their ears and various appendage salutes. I wouldn't want to be in the snitches' shoes when they got back to the station. I guess that's what you get when you use meth freaks as information sources.

Shortly after this incident the Gunslingers decided to move out of town and away from civilization, as we then knew it. A big mining company wanted to sew up all the claims on a creek up near Tennessee Pass. They hired a professional claim-jumper to try to get title to the claims held by the current owners. In the old days claim jumpers used to be pretty bad. They would occasionally kill someone to get title to a claim, but they don't operate that way anymore. Mostly. The standard drill is to try to find some illegality in the registered paperwork, or try to prove that the person was not working the claim properly. Things like that.

An old gold miner named Bob Cutler had some claims up Tennessee Pass. The claim jumper had tried to buy the claims, and then when that didn't work he made some threats. The old miner was about seventy-five years old, and he was a little bit worried that he might wake up murdered some morning, so he signed his claims over to the Gunslingers. They moved up to the pass.

The next time the claim jumper came to talk to the miner he said, "No, I don't own them anymore. I sold them to the Gunslingers, so you can fight it out with them." For some reason, the claim jumper never went up to talk to them.

Thinking back on it, I guess the Gunslingers were pretty much green horns at living in the bush. They did some rather humorous things until they started to get their trip together. One time they decided to go dynamite fishing. They found a deep pool and tied a rock to the stick of dynamite and threw it into the pool. Boom. No fish. Not one.

One of the Gunslingers, Shawn, dug a bear trap and tried to lure a bear by heating honey in a pan. Unfortunately the honey pan was directly on a Coleman stove, with the flame high. They polluted the air for miles around when that honey burned up. I bet they scared the shit out of every bear within a half-mile of there. Then the pit caved in.

Shawn did another rather humorous thing. Their claim was about five miles from what you could call a town. They had a vehicle but they would have to walk the last mile, packing enough food on their backs for about ten people, including women and kids. The trip back home, fully loaded, was over the pass, which meant going up probably seven hundred feet, then down the grade; and then you had to ford two creeks. Not a real tough trip but not too much fun either, especially after about the tenth time you did it.

Shawn really liked refried beans. One time he unloaded his pack at the claim, and he proudly showed the folks that he had lugged a case of Rosarita beans all the way from town, on his back. His triumph was short lived, however, when one of the ladies mentioned that he could have had just as many beans if he had brought up five pounds of dried pinto beans and cooked them.

The Gunslingers did, however, have some success at living off the land, even with the small amount of game available in their area. On one occasion I went hunting with Shotgun Paul. We came back with a quail, two porcupines, and a rainbow trout. Game being scarce, this was considered to be a pretty good hunt. Here's how it happened.

Shotgun said to me, "Say, let's go hunting. See if we can get us a deer." I thought that would be an adventure, so I got my single-shot .22 rifle and he got his 16-gauge pump shotgun. The beauty of the pump is that you can put several types of shell in it. If you see a deer or bear you can pump the chamber until you get to a shell with a slug or 00 buck. If you see a bird or small animal you can use birdshot. Paul loaded his own shells so hunting was reasonably inexpensive. One reason a lot of people have re-loaders is the constant paranoia that the government is going to start registering ammunition, or worse, restricting its sale.

We started walking up the road, and after about half a mile a deer jumped. Shotgun pumped a slug into the chamber and shot at it, but the deer was too far away and those slugs aren't accurate over about thirty feet. A little while later I got lucky and shot a sitting quail with the .22. As we were crossing a bridge we looked in the creek and spotted a trout that looked about twelve inches long near the surface of the water. Shotgun pumps to birdshot into the chamber and lets it fly. The impact stunned the fish and I went in the water and pulled it out. On the way back Paul bagged two porcupines.

We got to the claim at about dusk and I skinned my first (and so far only) porcupine, with so little light that I could hardly see the knife. I avoided most of the quills somehow but I would recommend that if you are going to skin a porcupine, do it when you can see what you're doing.

We fried the porcupines. Although it had a very good taste, it probably was not the best way to prepare it, for two reasons. First, in the summer and fall they are very fat and greasy; and second, they are about as tough as shoe leather. My recommendation would be to parboil them most of the day or pressure-cook them for a while, pour off the water and fat, then either use them for stew or fry them.

After a lot of work for several years the gunslingers ended up with a very fine garden. When the corn got real good, Shotgun would sit all day in his chair next to the garden, maybe smoking a little weed, and reading fuck books. With his shotgun beside him, he'd watch the crows in the trees as they tried to decide whether or not they wanted to play chicken with the delicious corn.

Occasionally one would fly down and test him out. Sometimes the bird would win; sometimes Shotgun would win.

I must tell you that Paul was not a great shot. He would blow away more ears of corn than the crows could have eaten, but it was the principle of the thing.

If the Gunslingers heard of gun trouble, or if people were being hassled by the police, a couple of them would go to Takilma with guns and keep an eye on things. I almost always enjoyed the company of the Gunslingers.

8

Hitchhiking

I was riding in the back seat of a disheveled '67 Pontiac. The driver was wearing a T-shirt and cap. He had wild hair and a long, lean face. The woman with him was slovenly. The driver kept speeding up and slowing down, and swerving, seemingly unable to drive in a straight line. Every few seconds he would duck his head down to be closer to the radio and would ask the woman, "Heard anything yet?" At one point we almost hit a bridge abutment. I was getting nervous.

Hitchhiking was my exclusive mode of transportation for almost fifteen years. This particular ride was one of the few truly unhinging experiences I had during this time, though I regularly hitched from British Columbia to California and points in between.

On this particular trip I had been picked up just south of Duncan, B.C., on Vancouver Island. I was on my way from Victoria, the provincial capital, on the south end of the island, to my home, an island just off Qualicum beach about eighty kilometers north of Duncan. I had been in the car for about five minutes when I decided that I wanted out. This ride didn't feel right. However, it is not easy to jettison a ride once you are aboard. I certainly didn't want to insult the driver, especially this guy. I didn't know what his problem was, and

I didn't want to know. Now how do I get out? We were in downtown Duncan, and there was a traffic light ahead. I said, "I'll get out at the next street. I have a friend who lives up there."

He stopped and let me out. I thanked him for the (short) ride and settled my gear so that I could stick my thumb out again. To my disgust the car pulled into a restaurant about a hundred yards down the road. I was not going to start hitching again when he might go back to his car, see me trying to get a ride, and take exception to the obvious surmise that I had not been happy with his company. I ducked behind a building and waited until they had gone on down the road.

You may judge that I was being overly paranoid about this whole situation and maybe you're right, but I managed to hitch many thousands of miles over those fifteen years, and can still count my fingers and toes, so I must have done something right.

Hitchhiking is a way of life, or at least a facet of life, rather than just a means of transportation. You must trust your karma, because you have very little control over what will happen to you once you stick out your thumb. As such it is always an adventure. To the establishment you become a nomad, someone who is suspicious and unwanted, at all times in all societies. The police don't like you and don't want you around. I have had more trouble with the police than I have had with bad or weird drivers. In most states it is forbidden to hitch on freeways. Highway ramp designers make sure there is no safe way for anyone to pull over to pick you up.

A hitcher must adopt a special mental attitude in order to be successful. First, he must not be constrained by time. He has no control over how long it will take to get to where he is going (if in fact he knows where he is going). He can't be too paranoid about accepting a ride. I can't remember ever turning down a ride, though I may have done so. There are just too many variables to try to control. Fate is your commander. In all probability fate is always the commander, however most often we don't realize it. When you are hitching you always know it.

Hitching has cured me of many hang-ups. When I was young I was fearful of riding with people who didn't appear to be as good of drivers as I imagined myself to be. You can't have fears when hitching. Even if you are with a noticeably bad driver, if he (or she) has lived to maturity, the odds of this being the one fatal trip would seem to be small. If the driver is young it might be a little more cause for worry, but not much. Fate again. The other potential fear of course is homicidal maniacs. Of the two, if I had to choose which to worry about the most, it would be the bad driver. I have had some rides with really weird people. I had to be on my guard, but I have hung out with a number of really weird people, so generally I know how they think. I'll give you an example.

I was hitching north on I-5 from a rest stop just north of Grants Pass, Oregon. I can't remember my specific destination. The guy who stopped was a redneck in a Ford pickup with a gun rack, cowboy hat, and a bottle of Galliano wine, one of those three-foot-high bottles. He didn't fit the profile of someone who ordinarily picked up hippie hitchhikers, and he was fairly drunk, so I knew I wouldn't be bored. He took a long drink of Galliano then offered me the bottle. Of course I drank. Rule one, never refuse whatever this kind of person offers you, within reason of course. He was looking at me with suspicious squinty eyes. His driving was not good. He was weaving quite a bit. He pulled into the fast lane and passed a truck, then pulled back into the slow lane. He glanced at me and said, "Well, we made it that time. The way I figure it if your number comes up, that's it. Your number's up." He squinted at me again. I agreed with him—that was my philosophy, too. Actually, if he had any brain he would have realized that if I didn't feel like that it would be pretty foolish to hitch at all. Do not show fear or paranoia. That is what he is looking for. If I had shown fear he would have tried to see how daring he could get before I peed my pants or gave him reason to drive off the road and do something physical.

Thinking back I realize that much of my watchful attitude was developed in my early twenties when I used to hang out in cowboy bars. I didn't like to fight but some of my acquaintances did. You can usually avoid trouble with these aggressive types by not pushing the wrong buttons, and by paying attention. Problem is, who hangs out in these kinds of bars for the purpose of paying attention? A few patrons are fights going to happen, and with these our old friend fate takes a hand, for good or ill.

I judged the guy I was riding with might be a fight waiting to happen, but by being careful the threat of confrontation did not seem to be too great. The threat of getting into a car wreck did. But again, I was not going to tell him he made me nervous nor ask if he would please drop me off on the side of the road. In Oregon you can hitch on the freeway, and civilization as we know it does not seem to have collapsed because of this. The cowboy and I had both pissed on the fencepost and found out that we had some philosophy in common, so we sipped wine and talked about this and that. I told him I was a sometimes country singer, and generally we had a pretty nice ride; except, I was constantly reminded of his driving problems, and tried to think of how I could get out of the truck without offending him. It wouldn't be real cool for me if he got pulled over either.

The conversation eventually turned to his desire to see the Oregon coast. I experienced a glimmer of hope. Several roads to the coast intersect I-5. The next one was about twenty miles down the road, and I spent the next few minutes extolling the beauty of the coast, especially on a clear spring day. As we approached the next turnoff, I suggested that he let me off and go on to the coast. He was hesitant. "Gee man, you need a ride. I'd hate to leave you off out here." I said that it was a nice day and I was in no hurry. It would really be a shame if he missed the coast. He regretfully bade me adieu and headed west. To be successful you must at least feel that you are in control of the situation, but never forget to pay homage to fate.

Everything about hitchhiking is unexpected except that there will be some anxiety, hard physical labor, and inconvenience. There is no free lunch. Some of the unexpected things are truly wonderful. These experiences make all the hardship and uncertainty of life worthwhile. In retrospect.

One time I was hitching north on I-5 and had been let out at Mount Vernon, Washington. Washington does not allow hitching on freeways and exhibits a very negative view of hitchers in general. I was stuck in a particularly unpleasant spot, because the freeway was raised at this point, and the on-ramp was at the bottom of a rather steep hill. There was little room for someone to pull over, which was seemingly academic, because there were about four other hitchers at the on-ramp and very few cars entering the freeway there. Oh well, another minor inconvenience.

A short time after I was dropped off I heard someone shouting from up on the freeway. I looked up and saw that a motorist had pulled over and he was waving for us to come on up. He could have gotten in trouble for stopping. We all scrambled up the hill and got in his car. It turned out that I knew the driver. He had been a neighbor on Lasqueti Island for a short time. We had not been friends, but we had conversed several times. Coincidence?

Another time I was in southern Oregon hitching to Portland, and got picked up by a guy who was towing a vehicle. He worked for a company that bought cars at auction and towed them to Portland. He dropped me off in Portland. Nice ride. A week later I dropped onto the freeway heading south, across the road from where I had arrived. A pickup stopped. You guessed it. The same guy who gave me the ride up was on his way back down south for another auction. How can you beat that?

An anecdote, which will maybe illustrate the vicissitudes encountered in hitching, happened while I was driving. This was before my van broke down, and I radically changed my mode of transportation. I was staying with friends in Sacramento, waiting out the winter and preparing myself to settle in the Northwest for the rest of my life. Maybe. Some of my young friends in Sacramento were going to get married.

This was to be a classical Catholic Church wedding, and was more than I could handle. I loaded the van and hit the road, leaving a note behind apologizing for my precipitous flight, and egregious lack of manners. It was pouring down rain and for some reason I decided to go north on Highway 101, a difficult drive up the coast, rather than I-5, which is a straight shot north. I would drive west on I-80 toward the San Francisco Bay area, then turn off on Highway 37 to 101 at Novato, then north on 101.

There was a short stretch of I-80 at Davis that was not freeway, so hitching was allowed. As I drove by I looked to the side of the road, and saw a guy with his thumb out with inadequate foul-weather gear. Next to him were a huge steamer trunk and a regular-sized suitcase. I had to stop for this bizarre character. We loaded up his stuff and I asked him, "What the hell are you doing out here with all that stuff? Seems like it would be hard to find anyone with enough room for you and all your gear."

He told me that he was a traveling historian. His ambition, upon which he was well advanced, was to hitchhike to every county in the United States. His trunk was filled with his typewriter and manuscript. Evidently he would camp out at a Denny's restaurant at night, drinking endlessly free coffee refills, and write the day's happenings. He'd sit at a table or booth. The working folks probably found him more interesting than the drunks and cab drivers they usually saw in the middle of the night, and the U.S. was operating under a slightly different economic model in 1971 than it is today.

Anyway, this guy said that I would be in the book. I took him a few miles out of my way, because I was really fascinated by his trip. Also, it's always encouraging to encounter someone who is crazier than me. This trip was starting out with a satisfyingly bizarre twist.

I motored on uneventfully until I hooked up with Highway 101, and started north. It was dark by now and still very rainy. At the north end of Cloverdale I saw two drenched and forlorn-looking hippies at the side of the road, and I stopped. The guy and girl were quite relieved. I doubt if they expected to get a ride after dark, and there was no place to spend the rainy night if they didn't. They were doubly happy that I was going as far as Eureka, where they lived. The distance was about 180 miles, and I'm not sure that I would have gone all the way that night. More likely I would have found a place to pull over and camp, but I certainly didn't want to put them back out in the rain. The night was dismal. This portion of 101 is narrow and twisty and there were some small rocks on the road that had fallen from the hillside. A few miles down the road I put my foot on the brake pedal and . . . nothing. Pedal to the floor and no brakes. I wasn't carrying extra brake fluid, because I had not had any brake problems. I did, however, carry John Muir's VW repair manual. This book was a Godsend to all VW addicts who had to do their own repairs.

This was a perplexing situation. Visualizing the highway ahead, I couldn't think of a place where I could purchase brake fluid at this time of night. Even if I pulled off and spent the night by the side of the road, I would still have to find someplace to get brake fluid in the morning. Although the highway is narrow and curvy in that area, there wasn't much traffic and with the four-speed box I didn't use the brakes much anyway. My main concern was the rocks on the road. This was the only situation I could foresee that would require quick braking. I had to discuss the situation with my new friends. I said simply, "Well I've got some bad news. I have no brakes and I don't know where I can get any brake fluid. I intend to continue on, I don't think I will have too much trouble. You are free to travel with me, or get off at the next exit. Whatever you choose."

From their perspective I'm sure that this was a serious dilemma. With the rain coming down outside, the chance of getting a ride that night was negligible. It didn't take them long to decide to go down with the ship if necessary, so they stayed on board.

My next problem was that it had been a long day for me and I was getting tired. It became harder and harder to concentrate. Finally, after dodging rocks for about forty miles we reached Rio Dell, and a lighted sign that read "Café." There was also a long, mostly vacant parking stretch along the side of the street, so I was able to coast to a stop. We went in and had coffee, and relaxed for a few minutes before hitting the last stretch. We made it to Eureka with no problems.

This was the most dangerous stretch, however, because there was quite a bit of traffic and many stoplights. I had to anticipate the lights so that we could coast to a stop before each intersection. We finally made it through town, turned off on their road, into their driveway, and stopped. We had made it. As you can see, hitchhiking can be very boring, but it can be exciting on occasion. I hitched to town the next day, bought some brake fluid, hitched back, bled the brakes, and continued on up the road. No problems.

Hitching from my island in Canada to California was fairly common for me. Portland, Oregon, was usually the first stop on the trip. The hitchhiking ban in Washington state meant that I had to get south of Seattle before dark the same day I left Vancouver, B.C.

Let me digress and say that if you are hitching through large metropolitan areas, you are advised to become familiar with the city bus schedules. It's hard to hitch from local interchanges. People don't want to stop, and even if they do they are usually locals who will exit the freeway on an off ramp just down the road. This kind of ride doesn't really do you much good. What you really want to do is get through this damn town as quickly as possible. You always run the very real possibility of being let off far from the freeway.

This happened to me once, but that was enough. I got a ride at the U.S. border from a Canadian who was vacationing south, and who really liked the U.S. That part was OK. The problem was that he had a whole bunch of beer stashed in the back seat and we started drinking. It was a real fun trip until he let me off in Renton, Washington, after dark. I had been having so much fun I forgot to pay attention to where we were going. Where in the hell is Renton? I walked from the off ramp to a gas station to get a map and find out how to get back to I-5. I got my bearings, but I didn't have much hope. I mean, who will pick me up? And would I want to hitch with someone stupid enough to pick me up here at this time of night?

As general insurance I looked around for culverts or bushes I could sleep in overnight, if I needed to. I walked back up to the freeway and got a quick ride from a soldier who was on his way back to Fort Lewis. This ride, though only about forty miles, was like a miracle. First, I had gotten through Seattle. Second, there was a covered waiting area outside the fort intended for soldiers who needed a lift somewhere. Many vets stop by to see if someone needs a ride. I got a ride from there all the way to Portland one night. If I didn't get a ride I could throw my sleeping bag on the bench and sack out. Wow.

I had been there for a few minutes when a car pulled up and a middle-aged guy got out. He told me that he would give me a place to stay if I wanted. I said sure. Then he said we'd go to a local bar and have a couple of drinks.

Sounded good to me, so we drove to the nearby neighborhood bar. We sat down and someone saw my guitar and asked if I wanted to play a tune. I got it out and sang for about three hours and had a wonderful time. Everyone really got off.

Finally closing time, and this guy is starting to get amorous. I thought, oh shit. I don't want to have to go through this. However, I knew I could handle the guy and as it turned out he couldn't make any moves because he was married. When we got to the house his wife was just delighted to see me. I slept in the spare room and the guy took me back to the bus stop in the morning.

The point is that you want to get through the cities as quickly as possible. If you have a bus schedule you can find a bus stop, get on the right bus, and go clear to the other end of the city on forty cents or so. The downside is trying to get on a city bus with a fifty-pound pack and guitar, walking down the aisle and banging into everyone. Very embarrassing, but it does get you to where you need to be.

You hope to get a single ride all the way to Portland. It's kinda scary in southern Washington. They have militia billboards and local radio stations with commentators who make Rush Limbaugh seem like a choir boy. You surely don't want to get caught there at night.

Once you get to Oregon you feel like you have escaped from the Iron Curtain or something. Hitching is legal in Oregon, and you never get hassled.

You seldom get hassled. I got interrogated three times in five years. Not too bad, I guess. Actually, the hassles were more for existing than for hitching. At least existing in their space. But they didn't actually do anything. I remember hitching with a lady friend from a rest stop in southern Oregon. The trooper interrogated us for a few minutes then he told us he wasn't going to give us a ticket because we weren't breaking the law. Huh?

Oregon doesn't even have the freeways fenced off in many places. They actually seem to be a part of the earth. You can make a leisurely trip through Oregon. But as you get to southern Oregon, Medford and Ashland, you begin to get your game face on for California.

You leave Ashland, the last stop in Oregon, and start up into the Siskiyou Mountains right away. California laws about hitchhiking are quite similar to Washington's, though I don't know if enforcement is as tight-assed. The problem is you don't want to get dropped off on top of the mountain. You could freeze to death in the winter and there never seems to be anyone entering the freeway at Mt. Shasta or Weed in the middle of winter. The plan is to get a ride that will get you to Redding, at least. For me Red Bluff would be best because I could get to Highway 99 on down to Chico then figure out how to get to my parents' place from there.

I'll give you an example of the winter problems crossing the Siskiyou Mountains. It's about four thousand feet high on the top of the plateau, and it's about fifty miles across. This fact can be very scary in December, since you can't hitch on the freeways.

One time I was hitching back up north. I got dropped off at Red Bluff at the I-5 on-ramp. There was another longhair with his thumb out when I got there. We got a ride with a mountain guy, who lived near Dunsmuir. He offered to take us to his cabin for the night. We could have a party and he'd take us back to I-5 in the morning. It was very tempting, but I just wanted to get through the mountains. The temperature was below freezing, there was snow on the ground, and a new storm was expected. I got dropped off on one of the few non-freeway stretches that had cross traffic. Hitching was legal at this spot. I soon got a ride from a woman who was going about fifteen miles to Weed.

I took it. It was getting late now. Everything was shut down and there would be a car entering the freeway about every ten minutes. Looks like I rolled snake eyes this time. I decided that I wasn't going to get a ride, so I picked up my pack and guitar and walked to the hotel that doubled as the bus station.

I got a ticket to Grants Pass, where Highway 199 meets I-5. I decided to splurge for a motel room for the night before hitching back home, about fifty miles south on Highway 199. When I woke up in the morning and turned the radio on I found out that a big storm had hit late last night, and the Siskiyou Pass was closed. See what I mean? You have to stay in touch.

It was the same problem going south. I was hitching at Ashland one time, and this really grotty guy driving a beat-up Studebaker, spilling smoke out of the exhaust, pulled up. I asked him where he was headed and he said south. "I'm thinking of going down to the Sierras." I thought quickly. There are two places he could turn off I-5 to get to Highway 89, which runs south through the mountains. One of them cut off at Mount Shasta. Not good for me. The next was Red Bluff. Good for me. So I said, "Let's go."

This was a really weird guy. I forgot to tell you that he had a young pit bull pup in the back seat. I put my pack back there and we took off. The story he told me was that he just got out of prison for killing a Hell's Angel at a 7-Eleven. Of course, it was all bullshit. Probably. But a mind that can conjure up this kind of stuff has to be a little scary, even if it isn't true. I had to be very careful what I said.

For some reason I told him about some friends of mine who had gone hitchhiking from southern Oregon, stoned on LSD. I said that I didn't think that was too bright. At this point he decided that I was a square john, whatever that was. While we were talking the dog was eating my sleeping bag.

When we got to Mt. Shasta and the Highway 97 turnoff, I persuaded him to take me to the next turn-off, which was Red Bluff. When we got to a gas station, where I was going to get out, he looked at a map then looked at me and said, "You done fucked me."

I said, "Wait a minute, I intend to buy you a tank of gas and tell you how to get to the mountains." We parted friends. I don't need too many like him. Hitching between Canada and California in the winter can be an adventure.

When I left Canada the first time, I decided to move back to the U.S. to play music. I was wondering what to do with my stuff. Yes, even I had stuff. Getting rid of most of my belongings took care of itself when the kitchen burned down with most of my possessions inside. I saved my guitar from the fire, and I jury-rigged my blankets around the stuff I wanted to take with me, lashed them to a partial pack frame, and started south.

I can't remember too much about this trip south. I was going to visit Clyde and Candy in Sweet Home, Oregon, and figure out how to survive by playing music. I was traveling with my pack secured (I thought) to the roof rack. At the Brownsville exit my pack flew off the rack onto the freeway. The driver stopped, and I jumped out and ran back toward the pack. Most of the cars swerved to keep from hitting it. The last car coming aimed for the pack and drove over it. The blanket exploded like a bomb. Luckily there was not much but clothes in the pack but it was a bummer. I started walking and hitching toward Brownsville with what was left of my pack, mostly pieces of my old Kelty frame, and trying to hold onto my heavy guitar case. I walked the two miles to Brownsville, and stepped into a hamburger shack at the side of Highway 228. I ordered a burger and cup of coffee. For about an hour I tried to hitch the last seven miles to Crawfordsville, and finally gave up. I called Clyde to come and get me. I was through. I swore I'd never hitchhike again. Total bummer.

Clyde was a dealer in car bodies, parts, and various other activities such as hauling, and *Gypo* logging, Anything he could do to make a buck. We were sitting in his kitchen with a beer and he asked me, "How would you like to buy a car?"

I said, "You must have read my mind. I'll never hitchhike again." He had a '64 Ford Falcon for sale for a good price and as soon as I got my Canadian money changed I bought it. It was a year and a half before I was back in Canada, standing on the roadside with my thumb out.

I only hitched cross-country once and that was an interesting experience. I have lived my whole life within one hundred and fifty miles of the Pacific Ocean.

Social interaction is a very important part of hitchhiking, as was alluded to earlier. Unless you're a total sleaze you feel indebted to the person(s) who pick you up. Reasons abound as to why people pick up hitchhikers. Some guys pick up people as possible sex partners, some because they have hitched themselves and understand what's going on. Some are curious. These are the best because we could weave them some entertaining tales.

Several times I got picked up by Christians. Mostly I enjoyed our conversations. Many of those who would pick people up back then were fairly new to the Christian thing so we could really talk. I got a ride in a van one time. The guy had a dog in the back. He spent most of the trip down the Smith River bemoaning the fact that his dog didn't have a soul, and couldn't go to heaven. I can't remember what I said to him, but he seemed to be feeling better when he dropped me off.

I remember another time when this guy picked me up. I got in the back seat and as I got in I spied a bible on the front seat. Ah hah, we're going to get into it pretty quick. The guy was maybe thirty years old, swarthy with a hairline mustache. I noticed him looking at me in the rearview mirror. Finally he asked, "What are you?"

Damn good question. I had to think for a while. Finally I said, "I'm a seeker after knowledge."

He pondered that for a minute or so and he said, "I guess that's a good thing to be." End of conversation.

Standing beside the road has its own vicissitudes. By the nature of your method of travel, and general appearance, you are perceived as being on the lowest rung of society. The untouchables. The reactions of motorists are varied. You sometimes get certain hand gestures from drivers. Some truck drivers will honk their air horns when they get next to you. I've had bottles thrown at me, had people yell insults, and on one occasion a hay truck driver threatened to hit me. Of course it was bullshit; he would have had to fill out an accident report if he actually made contact. He came as close as he could. I didn't flinch, though I was prepared to bail out at the last second if he didn't straighten out the wheels.

Occasionally women with children in the car would actually change lanes to the fast lane when they'd see me. I assume they thought that somehow I could levitate into the car and then have my will with her (them), if she stayed in the slow lane. I don't know. But the constant barrage of negative energy can be quite exhausting. Another cute trick is for a car to pull over several hundred yards from me so I would grab my pack, sling it over one shoulder, grab my guitar, and gallop toward the car. When I got close they would take off. Good for conditioning, though.

The police also were an interesting diversion for hitchhikers. The existence of people with no visible means of support seems to be quite similar to a red cape to a bull. Come to think of it they are bulls. Ah hah.

When I was living in Orange County in 1970 I decided to complete my journey along the John Muir Trail that runs from Yosemite Valley to Mt. Whitney, two hundred and thirty-eight rugged miles. Earlier, I quit the Muir trail at Bishop; I had to get back to Newport Beach to deal with a traffic ticket, and was going to return to complete the southern part of the trip later. I managed to hitch from Newport Beach to San Bernardino. San Berdoo is an interesting place, I guess. It is east of LA and on the edge of the desert; it is also the gateway to the San Bernardino Mountains, famous for Big Bear Lake, and awful forest and brush fires. Berdoo is bare land, hotter than hell, recipient of most of the LA smog, and inhabited by uptight rednecks. I got stuck at a Highway 395 entrance one evening with a number of other hippies,

The police seemed to be redneck lowriders. Big, red-faced and with a sneer for us. When they came past us they would burn rubber and look to see if we were impressed. I got sick of this whole scene after a while. I had a bit of controlled substance with me. I rolled a joint then hid my stash in a discarded drink cup, which was part of a huge pile of fast food refuse beside the entrance. I lit up and we smoked it all the while smiling at the cops as they burned rubber. When we finally got a ride I retrieved my stash, and away we went.

Back to my cross-country adventure. I am definitely a West Coast boy. I had broken up with my girlfriend, Betty, and had to get out of town for a while. I decided to visit my brother in Colorado Springs. I started my journey from a spot on 80N in Portland, with a juvenile boy named Mark. This turned out to be a good deal, because people would stop to pick us up if they saw a teenager.

The first ride was from a traveling salesman. He didn't care much for me. He was going to Montana somewhere and took us all the way to his turnoff. We spent the night in Billings. Mark and the salesman stayed in a motel and they dropped me off at Rim Rock Ridge above the town. I spent a pleasant night there and they actually picked me up in the morning.

We got another ride right away and it took us all the way to Arvada, Colorado, where Mark was going to visit some friends. I didn't know the country at all and didn't realize that Arvada was a military retirement community and just slightly uptight.

We arrived at the friend's house, and since no one was home we decided to wait in the back yard. About fifteen minutes later the cops arrived, with sirens and lights flashing. Mark explained that he was a friend of the people in the house, and I was just tagging along. Turns out that the people who owned the house knew Mark but they weren't expecting him. There was some question about whether he was a runaway or not.

While the operation was going on I was writing a letter to a young female friend of mine detailing the events. The cops talked to me a bit and couldn't find anything to detain me for. That was the good part. They also took pains to explain that if I were caught hitchhiking anywhere in Colorado it was an automatic thirty-day jail sentence. They indicated that my continued presence in Arvada was not desired, and asked me if I would like for them to give me a ride to the city limits. I said that was not necessary. Although I was new to this outlaw bit, I knew that I didn't want to ever get into a police car unless forced to.

My dilemma was that I was free from the police but I didn't know where the hell I was, didn't know how to get to Colorado Springs, and knew I couldn't hitch. I mean, did you ever hear of Arvada? I didn't think so.

I was walking down a residential sidewalk assessing my options, which consisted of slim and none, when I saw a van going the other way on the street. I was thinking of sticking my thumb out after looking for cops. Although the van was going in the opposite direction, I didn't care. I wanted out of there. Before I could stick out my thumb, the van stopped by the curb on the other side of the street and the driver beckoned for me to come over. I told my story, and the driver said, "Get in, we'll take you to Denver." That wasn't where I was headed but it seemed to be a better proposition than walking around Arvada and getting picked up for vagrancy, or worse. They dropped me off in the hippie part of Denver.

Well, at least I had some protective covering at my new location, and I was also getting a dose of an alien culture. As I was standing on the street corner, a car with several blacks in it sped by. A woman, who looked a lot like Angela Davis, stuck her head out the window, poked a finger at me and said, "We're going to burn you." Far out.

Several minutes later a police car stopped next to me and a young officer got out. He had a black mustache, and hair down to his collar. I figured that maybe this dude wouldn't be too bad. He looked at me, opened the back door of the car, and said, "Get in."

I asked him, "Am I under arrest?" I knew he couldn't detain me without reason.

He clamped his teeth and replied in a more forceful growl, "Get in."

I knew that the law was on my side. I also knew that I was looking at thirty days if I pissed this asshole off, so I slid into the back seat. Thankfully he didn't close the door. He checked out my ID and looked in my pack until he got bored. Then he softened a bit and said, "We have to check out transients. Militants are bringing weapons into the area and we have to try to stop the traffic." I almost said, "Don't you think the militants may have discovered cars and trucks are a better way to smuggle arms than in a pack sack on the side of the road?" but a sign saying thirty days flashed before my eyes and I didn't comment. I said to myself, "Bob, you're not in Oregon anymore."

Needless to say, I got off the street. I slipped into a hippie restaurant and called my brother. I asked him if he could pick me up. He said he could, but it was several hours before he could find the place. In the meantime I had a good meal and played a few tunes on the guitar and had a generally good time. My brother finally arrived and I spent a very enjoyable week with him. The family was really intrigued by this freak from the Left Coast. When it was time to leave, my brother drove me to the Wyoming border. I'd had enough of Colorado for a while.

I got a quick ride to Cheyenne and then the rides dried up. I decided to hole up for the night in a field between the road and the railroad tracks. I inadvertently camped near the exit of a railroad tunnel. It's amazing what a job a tunnel does in amplifying a train whistle. Well, live and learn.

The next day I got a quick ride to Kirkland, Wyoming, and there the trail seemed to end. There were a number of hitchhikers on the freeway. I guess hitchhikers is a misnomer, because though it was permissible to be adjacent to the highway, it was verboten to solicit a ride; and there were plenty of police cars patrolling the area, making sure no one was abusing Wyoming's hospitality.

I was standing with a young guy who had made it this far from Vail, Colorado. He said that he had been chased through the hills by rednecks, and barely escaped with his body undamaged, but without any of his possessions. There was a rumor going up and down the road that a hitchhiker had died under mysterious circumstances in the Kirkland jail. I was rapidly coming to the conclusion that I was not welcome in Middle America.

I looked at the map and measured the distance I had to travel to get back to Oregon. I had traveled forty-six miles that day, about a half-inch on the map. It was about six to nine inches to the Oregon border. Oh shit. Just as I had reached the depths of despair, a van pulled up and picked up all the hitchhikers and drove us to Pocatello, Idaho.

It was getting late in the day, so I started to look for a place to crash. Although the area around the interchange was fairly well populated with small businesses, I spotted a small grove of trees and brush a couple hundred yards from the road. I ambled slowly and seemingly aimlessly toward the grove, taking surreptitious glances to make sure no one was watching me. I saw an opening in the thicket and dove in.

There was a clearing in the middle and I set up camp. I had my Primus stove and cooking gear, a gallon of water, and some food. I spent a very comfortable and satisfying night within a couple hundred yards of civilization. The first ride I got went all the way to Oregon. A week later I got back home and scratched Middle America off my list as hitchhiking destinations. I pretty much stayed next to the Pacific Ocean after that.

9

Gunsmoke

One of life's greatest fantasies for redneck country folks was to be on a Western movie or TV program, like *Gunsmoke*.

I do not necessarily use the term "redneck" in a negative sense, though I have been known to do so on occasion. Hell, I'm a sort of redneck myself, my family having settled in the northern Sacramento Valley in the 1870s and stayed there logging, farming, and rural- and mountain-living.

I suppose there should be a distinction made between rednecks and good ol' boys. I think Billy Carter, that great poet of the dirt south, may have defined the distinction for all time. As I recall, he was asked what the difference was between a redneck and a good ol' boy. He responded with, "A good ol' boy drives around in his Ford pickup, with the gun rack in the cab and the CB antenna sticking up, drinking a can of beer. Now a redneck drives around in his Ford pickup, with the gun rack in the cab and the CB antenna sticking up, drinking a can of beer; when it's empty, he throws the can out the truck window."

In my experience, most country people are very gracious and hospitable, generally more so than their city counterparts. They seem to try to live up to their Christian ideals more than most people, and they seem to be quite tolerant of others. Because I grew up in a rural community I sympathized with the fear and confusion these people experienced as an aftermath of the hippie migration to the woods. Some local people, however, were mean and vicious rednecks, the relatively rare breed around which that stereotype of the rural Southerner evolved. After having said all that, I myself usually use the term "redneck" in the more generic form to identify hard-working rural people who have lived in the country all of their lives.

When *Gunsmoke* came up from Hollywood to do an episode on location on the Rogue River, a few miles west of Grants Pass, and advertised for extras, you can bet rednecks came out of the woodwork. Somehow the word got down to the lower valley, to the hippie and white trash part of the county, and a bunch of the bush hippies decided to audition.

Allen obviously yearned for the spotlight. He was a Leo, and he walked around with a pained expression on his lean aesthetic Jewish face, from the first time he heard the news. He couldn't imagine a locally made movie or TV program without him being in it, so a bunch of us took off for Grants Pass, where they were doing the casting in the Holiday Inn parking lot.

By the time we finally managed to hitch to town, there were hundreds of local rednecks milling around with short hair, cowboy shirts, boots, and sideburns. On the other side of the lot were all these bearded, grubby, tattered hippies.

The *Gunsmoke* story was set in a frontier mining and trapping tent city along a major waterway. So here were all these clean-cut rednecks, who might have looked just fine in a Roy Rogers movie, but they didn't look like miners and trappers. We looked a lot more like the real thing.

We got the job. The rednecks were not happy. Getting this job almost cost me my life, as you will subsequently find out.

The ones from our area who got jobs as extras were Allen, the Mayor, Harold the Healer, Virgo Jack, and me. For the duration of the shoot I decided to stay with the Harold and his wife, who lived on River Road, halfway up to Grants Pass. The reason I stayed there was because I didn't have a car, and Harold could drive us to town.

The time of year was around August, and let me tell you that there is a lot of misconception Californians have about the weather in western Oregon. It can get hotter than hell in southern Oregon in the middle of summer. During the shooting we had to get up at 5:00 a.m. each morning and drive about thirty miles (nine down the River Road, a one-lane dirt road) to get to the National Guard armory in Grants Pass in time to get issued our costumes and get dressed.

To show you how authentic we were, the rags they gave us for costumes were mostly in better condition than the clothes we were wearing. After dressing we were taken by bus to the shooting site, Indian Mary Campground on the Rogue River. We're getting up at 5:00 a.m. and getting on the job at 7:00 and out to the site by about 8:00.

On location, hundreds of people were constantly milling around the campground, which had a long sandy beach. The set consisted of a tent city, with tent houses for the store, saloon, gambling hall, and whorehouse. It was really neat, complete with a Chinese laundry on the beach, equipped with washtubs, clotheslines, and real Orientals. I won't say they were all Chinamen. The grocery store had a deer hanging outside. It was a good authentic set. It reminded us a bit of home.

It was interesting how we were all cast for the production. First of all, Allen and Virgo Jack were slender, dark-complexioned, with long black hair and black straggly beards. They were perfect French trappers. They got to paddle around all day in a canoe. And smoke pot. And keep cool in that horrible heat. Needless to say they got a ration of shit from the rest of us when they finally beached for the day.

The most poignant casting, the thing that really got us off, was what happened to the Mayor. The Mayor was a rather corpulent guy, with long straggly hair and a floppy hat; he owned a small bit of land at the edge of town.

He was a Class A, No. 1 wheeler-dealer, and was making a pretty good living, by our standards, in the firewood business. His home was the first establishment you encountered when you entered town, and the first place some zoned-out refugee would stumble onto when he wandered into town.

The Mayor sometimes snagged some cheap labor. He would rub his hands with glee, and say, "Why don't you stay here with us? I'll put you to work. Free room (back in the shed), and I'll pay you to split firewood. And pay some of your meals." Try splitting knotty oak sometime. That'll put muscles on ya', boy. You can work on one of those rounds of dry knotty oak for a day, and end up with nothing but a big pile of toothpicks. Needless to say, most of his workers didn't exactly prosper. I guess it was a pretty good education as to what life is actually like in the country. A lot of his workers high-tailed it back to the city after about a month with the Mayor. Most of the people around town thought the Mayor's attitude was just a tad mercenary.

So what did the Mayor get cast as? Since he was so big, and this tent city was supposed to be river port, with riverboats and Indians and trader canoes coming and going constantly, they decided to cast him as a stevedore, hauling boxes and bails up and down the beach all day. For three days.

The Mayor actually had to do hard manual labor for a day and a half, in the sun, at around a hundred degrees. At the end of the first day he came up, red as a beet and sweating like one of his woodchoppers, and said, "Jesus Christ. I never worked so hard in my life."

Harold and I spent the next several days being extras. He was somewhat older than most of the hippies, in his forties, with no teeth and a straggly gray beard. But don't let that fool you. He was a very tough individual, who could walk miles with a sixty-pound pack.

As it turned out he had to be tough, because he had to wear a buffalo robe. He had to wander around all day in a buffalo robe in hundred-degree heat. So I guess with the exception of the Frenchmen out in the canoe, I had it the best of them all. I just wandered around when they needed someone for a street scene.

We got to know some of the crew. Their work is usually filmed in the studio in LA, so being out in the woods was like a holiday for them. After the shooting was finished, a couple of them came down to the lower valley to check us out. We took them to the swimming hole, and we all stripped down and had a great afternoon.

The TV crews were just regular folks doing a job and doing it quite well. It was a great shock for me to see this level of technical competence going into the production of this crap. The set designers were right into 1873, the costumes, everything. I think the authenticity was what I always liked about *Gunsmoke*.

That was the most boring job I've ever had. I don't know how the stunt guys stand it. The stunt guys are all honest-to-God cowboy types. One of them was a champion bull rider and had his big belt-buckle. The stunt men spent most of the day in the tent drinking beer and playing hearts, waiting for the crew to start shooting some violence or danger. They might get a short speaking part, if they didn't want to pay someone else scale. We all needed a beer, but I don't think anyone was up to stealing it from the stunt guys.

One actor spent three days riding around on a horse, wearing a Union Army uniform, and I mean all day for three days. I'd really like to see that show again to see if I could remember some of the background stuff that went on. I figured that for the invested twelve hours we spent each day we probably got six minutes of final film. There were actually some very good scenes shot on the set, one of them getting applause from everyone watching the scene. But when I watched the show on television, it seemed that most of the good scenes ended up on the cutting room floor, as the saying goes.

The entire process was eye-opening for me. The whole purpose of the media is to make the viewer think he's watching something that is really happening. Once you've been a part of it, you realize that you can't trust anything you see. Time is dilated and reality is cobbled together from pieces. You must abstract yourself from what you are viewing.

Although Ms. Kitty, Festus, and Doc weren't in this episode, it was made up for by the fact that a couple of my childhood heroes of grade-B Westerns, Slim Pickens and Jack Elam, were there.

James Arness appeared to be a very gracious individual. Harold the Healer was a member of the Rainbow Family, and a moving force in the first World Gathering of the Tribes in 1972 or 1973, after staging the Vortex Festival a year or so before. We were in a cowboy tent, and Harold walked up to James Arness and handed him an invitation to the Gathering.

Arness read the proclamation, thanked us for the invitation, and said that there should be more cooperation happening in the world, and wished us good luck. I can't say that I was really taken with his professionalism as an actor, considering that he was rumored to be getting three hundred thousand dollars for each episode he condescended to appear in. At that time it seemed like an incredible amount of money. But he seemed to be a nice, gracious individual.

They would fly him to the site in a helicopter when it was nearing time for him to be in a scene. He wouldn't have read the script, didn't even know what the story was all about. Neither, mostly, did the stunt guys, who played small parts in the production. The guest actors, however, like Jack Elam and Slim Pickens, had their parts down.

Arness not knowing his part meant that we would have to do several run-throughs of each scene's dialog before we could shoot. Matthew liked to entertain us by ad-libbing funny lines during the run-throughs.

In our valley there was some slight friction between the vegetarians and the meat eaters. In most cases this was not a significant quarrel, just something to bicker about if all other lines of social contention were played out. Among some of the wilder meat eaters, the term "veggie chump" became a half-affectionate, half-derisive nickname bestowed upon their brother and sister vegetarians. The term was used on more than one occasion as a put-down, sort of like calling someone a wimp.

The gist of this particular episode was that the Marshall was on some official trip down (or up) river, looking for a couple of run-away kids. He comes ashore at the tent city. For the local extras this was really intense, being right there with Matt Dillon. The town was being introduced as it looked to the Marshall as he walked through. I had my big scene, my fleeting moment of cinematic glory, take place as he walked past the restaurant tent.

You could see that this town was really happening. The streets were flooded with all kinds of people from Indians and mountain men to soldiers, gamblers... a real frontier town. Two miners were arm-wrestling in the café tent. There were burning coals in dishes, to burn them if their arm got put down, and gamblers were sitting on the benches making bets. I was sitting next to the arm-wrestlers, gulping down a plate of beans with a slice of bread, not paying any attention to all these people next to me yelling and shouting and running around.

The Marshall's next stop was to banter a bit with the local hooker, and peak into the gambling tent at the end of the street. There was a dude in the street wearing a vest, string tie, and derby hat, hustling the shell game. And on the other side of the street down by the water was the Chinese laundry.

In the story, the local trappers had caught a French fur robber, Jack Elam, and they were in the process of stringing the dude up, when the sheriff arrives. In the rehearsal of the scene he says, "No, I can't allow lynch law in my territory."

The head of the trappers says, "This isn't lynch law, Marshall, this is trapper law."

"How many of you think he's guilty?"

Well, everybody on the set was in this scene; they even called in the Frenchmen from the canoe in the river. The Takilma-ites were all standing around the confrontation, and when the Trapper leader asked, "Who says he's guilty?" we all jumped up and down and waved our guns yelling, "Guilty! Hang 'em!" Meanwhile, we were in the back yelling, "Hang the veggie chump!"

At this point in the first run-through, Marshall Dillon responded with, "Well, I guess we better hang the mother then." That broke up the crowd.

Of course, now with the confrontation, a fight was inevitable. This was a glorious fight for the medium, because it went all over town. They fought through the whorehouse tent and several other tents. There was supposed to be a lot of scurrying around, so to get it going they ran a bucking horse through the town. They had those hamper wires, or whatever they are, tied to their leg. I didn't get close enough to find out how they did it. I was much too busy trying to get out of the way. When you see those panic scenes with wild horses, sometimes it's the real thing. They don't know what those horses are going to do.

We made friends with some of the bit players. I remember one pretty young girl who was playing a B-girl in the saloon. She was looking at a bunch of the bush hippies, with their matted long hair, matted long beard, layer of dirt, and just general laid-back attitude, and she said, "Oh, you all look so real. The rest of us look so phony."

One of the mistakes the prop people made was giving some redneck kid, about eighteen or nineteen, a cap-gun replica of a Colt revolver. He went around for three days thinking he was Billy the Kid, and drawing his pistol at everyone on the set. Finally the stunt guys, along with the rest of us, got fed up. James Arness' double and the leader of the trappers worked out a plan.

We all knew that Billy the Kid would eventually draw on one of the stunt men. So when the Kid drew on the leader of the trappers, James Arness' double, who can draw very fast, drew his pistol and fired a blank into the ground just as the kid fired off his gun. The trapper dropped like a rock. The Kid's mouth flew open, and he actually looked in the barrel of his pistol to see if he could have shot the guy. As I recall that was the end of the dry-gulching.

There was a very real human drama being enacted on the set. Not too long before the *Gunsmoke* thing, the sheriff and DA had cooked up a plan to really put us out of commission. They sent an undercover agent to try to make some busts. And he did.

He cut a swath through the local marijuana industry, such as it was. This undercover agent was so zealous in his job that he even busted his brother-in-law, after a little entrapment. Or so I heard. The perfect type of man for the job the police felt had to be done. There was a furor for quite a while after that.

Where does this agent surface in all of his county sheriff regalia? On duty as a guard at the *Gunsmoke* set. That was also a little poetic touch by the sheriff's office. It didn't work out too well for them, as it turned out. It was obvious that the cop wasn't comfortable in that close proximity to the hated foe. Harold had to assure him that no one wanted to kill him. We heard stories that most of these sheriff officers hated the guy.

He liked to strut around and hobnob with the stars and starlets, and anyone else who looked like they had anything to do with TV production. At least he did until we told everyone that he had busted his brother-in-law. After they found that out, no one would have anything to do with him.

We finally finished the gig and went back home. Several days later we had to hitchhike back into Grants Pass, to pick up our paychecks. They amounted to forty-eight dollars. Sixty dollars minus twelve for OASDI. My original plan on getting paid was to cash my check, buy a bottle or two, and go back home, get a good night's sleep, and then hitch to Eugene for the Country Faire, with my pocket full of cash.

Once I saw the amount of the check, however, I was so despondent that I bought a number of bottles of Majarishi Martinelli, being our local name for Martinelli's Hard Cider, and some bottles of other potables.

A bit of explanation. The Martinelli's apple juice company made some wonderful hard cider. It became the local Takilma rage. Since the cider was something of a specialty drink, Andy at the store got a letter from Maritnelli's asking why the Takilma store was one of the top retailers of their product. The Majarishi part was a sort of sendup of the Maharishi Mahesh Yogi, who had a wide cult following. Some of the locals were under-appreciative of the solemn nature of these spiritual practices.

I finally arrived at my hitchhiking spot, and popped a bottle of Martinelli's, sat down, propped myself against a tree, and waited for a ride. It was ten miles from Cave Junction to Takilma. There were three turnoffs on the way home.

I'm not really sure how many rides it took to get home that day, because by the time I arrived I was too drunk to remember. I know it was several. I think the first ride took me to the Holland Loop/Takilma Road turnoff.

It was really beautiful there, lush green fields, cattle and sheep grazing, wildflowers, bees, cotton-ball clouds. I noticed that the Indian was standing by the road, also waiting for a ride. He was a blond-haired Cherokee, who lived across the river from the Funky Egg. He was guzzling from a recently opened quart of gin.

As I recall, we had to wait a long time for a ride. I think someone else may have been let off at the same corner later on, but I was too far gone to be sure. I think the Indian and I had some deep philosophical discussions. I do remember that at one point, as we were alternately passing the gin bottle, and another bottle of Martinelli's Hard Cider, he said, "Indians are the only ones who appreciate alcohol." I think he was probably right.

We finally got a ride to Four Corners. Almost, but not quite home. Someone drove by, but they would not pick us up. Finally, one of us said, "Fuck it. We'll sit in the middle of the road and they'll have to stop for us." So we sat cross-legged in the middle of the road passing the gin and Martinelli's back and forth. That really could have been our last moment. Pretty soon, the Mayor came roaring down the road, with a load of firewood in the back of his truck, the truck with the lousy brakes. Hell, no problem. He climbed on the brakes and the truck finally came to a halt with at least five feet to spare.

Somehow he got me home. I dimly recall standing on top of the load of wood in the back of the truck, drinking Martinelli's. I got to the homestead with no further mishap that I recall. It seems like there were a lot of people hanging out at the Funky Egg, and I broke out the wine and ale. Quite honestly, I don't remember anything after that.

The next morning I woke up with my body half in and half out of my van. Looks like I almost made it home. I painfully got my gear together then fixed breakfast and coffee to try to ease my poor state of health, and was ready to hit the road for the Country Faire, about two hundred miles away.

10

The Freeze

It was mid-November when The Freeze came to southern Oregon, as it did to the whole northern Pacific Coast. I had spent most of two winters in the Northwest, so I thought I was an expert on climatic conditions in that part of the world, and I was sure that it didn't usually get very cold there. Wet and miserable, yes. Co-o-o-o-l-d, no. According to the locals, the coldest it had been in years was about twelve degrees above zero.

Mara's kids were off visiting somewhere, and our house was really cold. It was a huge one-room with a loft. There were cracks and holes in the walls, and it had a totally dysfunctional stove. When you stoked it enough to do any good the roof would catch fire and I'd have to scoot up the ladder with buckets of water, if I could find any water. Ice doesn't do much good. Mara and I got so cold that we retreated to the Little Funky Egg Company. There was an easy and a hard way to get to the Funky Egg, across the river from Canaan, from where we lived.

The shortest and most direct way, a distance of about two miles was to walk to the river with your packs, guitars, and what all. If you could find enough rocks to jump to easily, you were across and on your way. If not, you would have to take off your boots, roll up your pant legs, and struggle, through the icy water and sharp rocks, carrying all your gear, to the other side.

If you couldn't cross the river you had to walk south about one and a half miles in the opposite direction from the Funky Egg then cross the river at the green bridge and walk all the way to town, several miles. The Funky Egg was full of crashers when we arrived, and we began thinking that it would be nice to get away from people for a while. Part of the reason that the Egg was so packed, was that four or five folks from down the Illinois River had been staying for a couple of days, and the rest of the place was filled with everyone in town who had run out of firewood or companionship. The threat of cabin fever was real; let's go to the Egg and party on, dude.

The folks from down river were ready to go back home to the Carrot Claim, a beautiful meadow on Soldier Creek. My girlfriend Mara and I decided to hitch a ride with them, to visit friends who lived on the top of Horse Mountain, a half-mile above the Claim. This would be an adventure because this is rugged mountain, deep canyon country.

The reason we decided to make this journey was that Mara was especially close to her Aquarius sister, Rebecca, who was living with a notorious outlaw named Donnie. The desire to visit her, combined with the social pressures of hanging out waiting for the end of the current cold spell, probably shoved us over the edge. So Mara decided she wanted to visit Rebecca. It was the middle of winter, snow on the ground, and we were going twenty-six miles down the River Road, a dirt and mostly single-lane track along the steep Illinois River canyon wall. We didn't know how we were going to get back home, but it seems that we trusted our karma a lot back in those days. We knew we might have to make the return on foot, when it came time to go back home and pick up the kids.

The decision to make this trip seems especially strange to me now. It was snowing, cold as hell, we were hippies in redneck country, and we didn't have any money. We had the slightly dubious prospect of getting down river by riding in the back of an open pickup with a bunch of deep-woods maniacs, being driven by a major lunatic by the name of Big (and big he was, indeed), at night, in a snow storm. Why were we doing this? To go visit some more really crazy lunatics; cabin fever must have been a terrible thing that winter.

We loaded our packs, containing among other things three gigantic Buckwheat Bob's buckwheat pancakes for emergency supplies, sleeping bags, and my guitar into Big's pickup. Then we wedged ourselves in among three other people and all the freight that could be stowed into the back of the truck. Part of their trip to town had been to get supplies. We started our fifty-mile sojourn.

As we started down the road it started snowing for real. Big drove until the snow got so deep that we were losing traction. After we almost slid off the road into the canyon, he stopped and put chains on. I felt slightly reassured, seeing that we actually had chains. Then I saw Big tighten the chains with a length of binder twine, and my newfound confidence evaporated. However, there's not much you can say to a longhaired, six-foot, two hundred and forty pound mountain man except, "Right on." Also, I was not into piling off and walking thirty miles back home. So we took off.

Now, the road down the river is one lane of dirt and rock. And mud and snow. But at least it gets a lot of vehicular use, and has a pretty solid bed. However, when you get near Briggs Creek, about twenty miles down the road, and make the 270-degree turn onto Old Glory Road, you start up a steep grade of soft mud. Not many people use this road, especially in the winter. At this point the anxiety began. It was still four miles to Soldier Creek and you couldn't forget the binder twine holding the chains on. Big gunned the engine and slewed around onto Old Glory Road, with those wheels whining. It took us almost five minutes to pull up that 300-yard grade.

I certainly was not looking forward to having to abandon the dubious shelter of an open pickup bed and try to push the truck the rest of the way up the hill, knee-deep in mud. But we finally made it to the top. After that it was a fairly easy drive to Soldier Creek and the Claim, whereupon the pickup gasped its last breath (drive shaft or something), and there she may be to this day, for all I know.

This abrupt arrival signaled the end of the good part of the trip, though of course we didn't know it at the time. We got there feeling just a little bit colder than an iceberg after dark in a snowstorm, but in one piece. The news that greeted us was that there was no one at the Claim. Everyone must have gotten tired of the weather and/or run out of firewood, and decided to ride it out in town or visit people who had firewood. I guess it is time to explain how folks lived (or managed to survive) in the bush back then.

Before I moved to the mountains, when my thoughts turned to fantasies of living in the woods, I thought that once you got out there you were there. I soon learned that there were actually various levels of "out there."

First off, there were the people who moved to a small town, rented a motel room on the highway, got welfare, probably dealt a little marijuana now and then, and partied and had a good time. This would seem like the bush to someone who was from, say, Culver City, California.

The next level would be people renting farms and having extended families, communal situations, a bit away from town. Although the communal groups worked very hard, both at keeping the physical trip together and avoiding killing each other during the long wet winter, their community social activity was recognizable as somehow related to Western civilization as we know it.

The next level involved mostly squatters who lived near the communal groups and either camped or built shanties out of whatever they could scrounge or steal. They pretty much lived a life of non-comfort, but expended a minimum of sustained physical labor for profit.

The last group included people who, for one reason or another, wanted to live way out in the boonies, where they might have to walk a number of miles to the closest store and then back home, carrying a lot of weight on their backs, in sometimes very hot and sometimes very cold weather. Some of them had vehicles, which made things a little easier, but many of them did not.

These bush hippies were a mongrel horde: some were escaped city hippies, some city street punks who somehow strayed into the woods; the latter were mostly invited by the escaped city hippies who were trying to straighten them out and show them the good life. Some were paranoid survivalist types, some fugitives from justice as we know it. Some were old-time miners. This was a strange but generally fun group of people. On occasion they could be dangerous.

The folks we were visiting fit well into the latter category of types. We had never made this trek in winter before, so it was a new experience. The Claim was along Soldier Creek, which joined Briggs Creek about a quarter mile downstream. Briggs Creek fed into the Illinois River. There was a small, reasonably flat shelf on the side of a mountain ridge, with fertile soil for growing, and of course there was plenty of water. Up the side of the hill was a frame house constructed by some miner long ago, and several people currently lived in it. This time it was in a bit better state than it was the last time I was there. Betty and I slept (or tried to sleep) inside the cabin one rainy summer night, under a leaking roof. I mean really leaking. Everywhere.

Two couples had built shacks near the creek. Pete had built a pretty nice, small dome structure, while Tim had thrown up a dirt-floor shack. We learned that Donnie and Rebecca were not in their cabin on Horse Mountain, as we had thought. They had evidently run out of firewood and come down to spend the winter in an old shack, a short way down Soldier Creek. We found them just about frozen to death, with an inadequate stove and no room for anyone else to stay. Rebecca had blankets hanging from the ceiling in a vain effort to hold some heat near the stove. After we visited a while they suggested that we go stay in Tim and Carla's cabin. They had gotten smart and gone to town.

As we entered Tim and Carla's shack, it was evident that the owners had been gone for some time. The place had holes in the walls, of course, no insulation at all, dirt floor, and the stove was a squat half of a 25-gallon barrel, cut off and stuck in the ground. And no firewood. Obviously we would have had trouble getting warm, even if we managed to find wood in the dark. The only thing to do was to take off our boots, climb in bed, and pull the covers over our heads. The bed was a plywood sheet on a board frame with unrecognizable pieces of foam here and there. The whole thing was really clammy and vile, with about twelve blankets of various lineages piled on the bed. They obviously hadn't been washed in a long time.

We spent a miserable night, but at least we didn't freeze. Looking back it seems that over the last couple of years, I had spent several miserable nights at the Carrot Claim.

In the morning we got up, chewed some frozen pancake, and discussed how we were going to get the hell out of there. While we were musing about this, Pete and his lady arrived in his jeep. Pete and I had never been friendly but I sure was happy to see him. We lived our life by choice and I would not expect anyone to help us unless it were an emergency. Pete poured us some coffee and we warmed up a bit before starting back to town. I learned a bit about woods plumbing from Pete that morning. His exposed plastic water pipe was frozen solid where it was above the ground. He got a can of white gas and poured it generously on the pipe. He said, "I've heard that gas will thaw water in a pipe." He lit the gas and sure enough, within a few seconds the water started running, a trickle at first, then completely free. White gas is so volatile that it combusts right away, and will not melt the pipe. I was impressed. Several years later I heard of someone who tried it on pipes under the floor of his house. It didn't work quite as well. I don't know if he had insurance.

This was the second time that Mara had been down the river. Last summer we had walked the whole way, the weather had been near a hundred degrees, and she had just about died of heat stroke, struggling down the road. Now it was just the opposite. Although in later years Mara earned her living as a tree planter, which is one of the toughest and most miserable jobs there is, at the time of this story she had been in the woods for less than a year. She was in terrible shape, and could see no reason to change that condition.

Before we left home, one bone of contention I felt very strongly about was that she should wear pants when we were in the woods. There are too many problems with skirts. I had been very insistent that she wear Levi's on this trip, but instead she wore a long Levi skirt, slit up the sides so that she could stride normally. This is fine for walking on flat surfaces, but it ain't worth a damn for climbing over rocks and logs.

We decided that we would just have to walk back to town, and hope we could hitch a ride somewhere along the road. There was about two feet of snow on the ground. Our destination was Mar, Walt, and Cilla's place, about nine miles back toward town. If we followed the road back to Briggs Creek and then up River Road, the way we came in, we would have to walk about eighteen miles, but at least the pickup and Pete's jeep had cut a trail coming in. Three miles back down Old Glory Road, then three more miles just to get back parallel to where we were now. There was an old logging skid trail that cut from the claim to the River Road, which would cut about six miles off the trip, but it would mean breaking trail for about two miles. I finally decided to cut across rather than going back and around, mostly because I really hate retracing steps. And there I sat so patiently, waiting to find out the price I had to pay to get out of going through all these things twice. Thank you, Bob Dylan. This philosophy has gotten me in trouble more than once in my life.

We started across the meadow, with snow up to our knees. Mara got stuck, trying to get over the first log we had to cross. I was reflecting on that goddamned skirt and gave her butt a little kick. Not hard, just a sort of nudge. She turned around and shouted, "What the hell are you doing?" I said that I was just getting it out of my system early, and hoped she would listen to me next time. Fat chance.

We struggled through the snow. I was able to find the way easily, because of course there were no trees in the middle of a skid trail, which had at one time been a road. We finally staggered onto River Road and took a little rest. The sight that greeted us was really beautiful, with the canyon and trees covered with snow and ice. The Illinois River way below us was frozen clear across in some places. The sky was leaden, though there was a bit of sun shining through. The fact that there was some sun bothered me a bit, because it doesn't take too much sun to go snow blind, or so I'm told, and we didn't have sunglasses.

We discovered that we had another problem, potentially worse than cutting trail. The wet surface of the road had melted and re-frozen, which left a layer of ice. This made it almost impossible to walk without slipping and sliding and expending a great deal of energy. Mara was at a particular disadvantage, because she was wearing her only boots, cowboy style, with no tread. That plus a skirt frozen to the waist must have made it a particularly unpleasant walk for her.

Soon after we started down the road, a redneck and his wife came slowly by us in a jeep, on his way back to town. He must have taken a Sunday drive to see the sights. We stuck out our thumbs, and he drove right past. That was the last car we saw that day. I was really angry with that citizen. I told Mara, "If I had a gun I would shoot out his tires, then we could all walk back to town."

Somehow we made it to our halfway point, exhausted, cold, and tired. We found our friend Mar and a lady we had never met before, named Ginger. Ginger had on a thin coat and was really in bad shape. She had arrived recently from Montana with some dude named Cosmic, who seemed to be absent. They got blown away by the cold in the Big Sky country and headed for the coast, shedding their cold weather clothes along the way. She said it was colder here than Montana.

I still believed the temp was in the teens at night, and maybe the high twenties during the day, but it sure seemed colder than that to me. Of course no one had a thermometer, telephone, radio, or TV, so we had no idea how cold it really was.

We spent that night in Walt and Cilla's cabin, a dome shake house that had holes in the walls. Having holes in the walls seemed to be getting a little repetitious. But by staying close to the tin stove until bedtime we kept reasonably warm. When we awoke in the morning, I volunteered to start the fire. The stove was about five feet from our pad on the floor, so I got up, naked, and started getting the paper and kindling together. I would do this any morning, all winter long, even if there was ice on the floor. It was kind of macho fun seeing people freak out watching the lunatic. However, this time there was obviously something wrong. The cold was terrible. Halfway through the job I shouted, "Jesus Christ!"

and jumped back under the covers. I must have been an icicle. I guess I got even with Mara and her skirt that morning. I would get warmed up a little then jump out of bed and work some more on the fire. I finally got it going, on about the fourth trip out from under the covers. When I finally warmed up a bit, I got dressed and stepped into my gumboots. I almost fell on my nose when I took the first step. My boots were frozen solid to the floor.

We made a breakfast on almost the last of my giant pancakes, and started on down the road. Only twelve miles to Selma, and civilization. The traveling was slow that morning, obviously. I had to wait for Mara quite a bit, and encourage her to keep going. I forgot to relate that along with the other problems with that road, it did a lot of up and down. It starts at river level, and then goes up about seven hundred feet then back down to river level. It does this several times. Just how many I could have told you that day.

We finally stopped to rest at the last big turn before descending from the mountains into a long, lush valley several miles short of Selma and Highway 199. We sat down on a couple of rocks and finished the last of the pancakes. I struggled up, but Mara was about at the end of the line. She said she couldn't go any farther. I got to play John Wayne. I shouted at her, "Get up and start moving or I'll kick your ass up through your mouth every step from here to Selma. I mean right now." I always wanted to say that to somebody. It worked, she struggled up and we slipped and slid for about a mile more. We stopped and looked down into the valley and saw a fox bounding along in the snow, a magical moment.

Miraculously, a man and his wife stopped and let us ride into Selma in the back of their pickup. By now, even in the horrible cold, riding in the back of a pickup was luxury.

When we finally reached the Selma store, we jumped out of the truck. Actually, we didn't jump. We stepped very carefully to the pavement. If we had jumped just then I think we would have shattered into a million pieces. We thanked the good Samaritans sincerely and trudged into the store's coffee shop and ordered coffee. Hot. We looked at the clock and it indicated that it was 3:45

in the afternoon. As we were savoring our coffee someone walked into the store and said that it had just gotten up to fourteen degrees above zero. Startled, I queried further and they told us that it had gotten down to negative sixteen degrees the night before. Then I understood why we had such a miserable time.

We now had a good news bad news situation. True, we had escaped the jaws of discomfort in the dreaded canyon and made it to Selma, Oregon. Selma, however, would never be mistaken for Los Angeles, for example, when it comes to settlements. The commercial district consisted of the store we were in (which fortunately had a lunch counter), a post office, a Laundromat, and a Chevron gas station. Home for us was still about twenty miles away, only ten of which were on the main drag, Highway 199. So now it was about an hour before dark, and we certainly didn't want to try to hitch after dark. Among other things this was redneck country, and Takilma was far off the main track. Our situation was still precarious. We walked out to Highway 199 and stuck out our thumbs. Luck seemed to be with us and we got a couple of quick rides. We reached the Funky Egg, our original starting point, before dark, just about forty-eight hours from the time we had left.

The party and wall-to-wall people were still going on when we arrived, and we discovered that the kids were still off visiting and wouldn't be back until the next day. We were just about beat, but we felt much better after several hours of heat and various intoxicants provided at the party in the Other (the other house at the Funky Egg). There were two houses, Robert's home, the Nebulous of Andromeda, and the Other, which was home for everyone else. Mara and I woke up refreshed the next morning. When the temperature finally got up to zero degrees, everyone went outside and we had a small ceremony. After leaving a message for the kids that we would be home, Mara and I walked and hitched to Black Michael's mining claim the next morning, about four or five miles, and couldn't make it any farther. We walked through his door and caved in. Michael didn't do things by halves. He had the Franklin stove cranked up max and it was like an oven in there. Several of the Godzilla Wrecking Company, Michael's extended gypsy family and performing company, were in the room, as well as three or four of the Gunslingers, .357 magnum pistols and all. Everyone, it seems, had been driven indoors by the weather.

Michael smiled and waved us in. We told him about our journey, and he started pouring water pans that had been boiling on his stove into his oversized tin bathtub. He told us to strip off while he got the water together. To get us started, he poured us each a mug of peyote tea he had brewing on the ubiquitous stove. We complied with his order to drink up. As we sipped the brew and luxuriated in the streaming tub, finally getting the freeze out of our bones, it seemed well worth the misery to have this kind of comfort and hospitality at the end of the trip. I wish I could elaborate on what happened next but I can't remember. Well, you gotta play hurt. Later that afternoon we walked the road about a mile to our cold, cold house.

The weather finally broke and it started raining, but it took several days for our cabin to become unfrozen. As I said before, our dysfunctional wood stove was inadequate to deal with sub-zero temperatures, and the propane stove fittings had frozen and had gas leaks. We couldn't use it at all. The most discouraging sight, however, was the sink full of dirty dishes in the frozen dirty water we had left behind at the time of our flight. The whole mess was frozen solid and we had to look at it until it finally got warm enough to melt the ice in the sink. Gross.

11

Love In Vain

If you have a lot of money it's pretty easy to delude yourself into believing that you can protect yourself from nature. Buy property, build a big house, whatever. If you cannot, or choose not to protect yourself from nature, you must learn to live with it, use it as a partner in the enterprise of life. You are at the mercy of the earth. You do not take it for granted. The old cliché "one with nature," I believe, is our natural state. There is a feeling of being blessed to be allowed to be in this place at this time. There is a great bond formed among people who live with nature, unlike those who *think* about being one with nature.

The first couple of years the whole Takilma community celebrated each full moon with a gathering, most often in the Meadows. In honor of the occasion someone usually managed to come up with some hallucinogenic substance, to assist with the general purpose of communing deeply with our brothers and sisters of the valley community in the woods and sharing a lot of love.

This is not to infer that everyone got along all the time. No, no, no. But it would have been difficult to live in the valley if you were unable to see and accept the humanity of everyone. There were many different types of people and trips going on, and a lot of them manifested traits that were annoying. However, they were seldom malicious. That wasn't what we were doing back then.

One of the foundations of the hippie generation was the ingestion of LSD. During the summer of love, at any given time in the Haight Ashbury a very high percentage of the denizens were stoned on acid.

Acid is a very powerful drug, as the whole world knows. It heightens our senses and lowers our psychic defenses. Seemingly not the best condition to be in when you're among five thousand weirdoes together in a "ghetto" in the city, but it worked. For a while. When groups of people share the experience, they communicate on an entirely different level. All in the group become unique human beings to each other. There is no hiding from the group. It is all there for everyone to see.

This can be good or bad. If the energy is positive, the shared high is incredible. If the energy is negative, that's an entirely different story. One thing is for sure; sooner or later you will meet your true self, and that is not always a fun experience. This loosening of the defenses has made LSD a good psychiatric tool. It was seen as quite promising in the 1960s but, of course, its use in therapy stopped because of the politics. I noticed recently that psychiatrists in Switzerland have been studying its use again. Back in the day, at gatherings like the one for the full moon, there were several hundred people on psychiatric drugs at the same time.

The first time Takilma became an identifiable community was in the fall of 1970, when Allen called the peyote meeting. Full moon celebrations just happened. There wasn't much planning or responsibility. We'd ingest whatever we had at the time, most often LSD. We were too poor to be able to afford liquor, which was probably a good thing.

Many of us were squatting somewhere in the area, so little groups of people would emerge from the woods from all directions. The punch, or whatever, would go around and pretty soon we were flying. My main job in the community was playing music. That is not a bad gig.

Sometimes we played all night, one of the few times a musician gets to play as long as he wants. Picture a beautiful meadow, it's getting dark. There is a bonfire and everyone is in a circle around the fire, light from the fire is shimmering on the trees and bushes and reflected from faces, the magnificent moon rising, all feeding off the vibes of the music, soft rapturous faces of love. Music was usually supplied by Robert, Gemini Bill, Medicine Man, and me, and whoever else was around with an instrument. Always plenty of drums and flutes, of course.

At one of the parties we were feeling this soft warm glow, then an alien spirit entered the group. His aura of evil was tangible to us, in our altered state. He had a red head with a red beard, clean cut, and reasonably short hair. He didn't belong there. No one knew him. I have no idea how he found the place. He started trying to take over the energy by trying to disrupt the music. We had a little energy war going on. Here we have about seventy-five neighbors enjoying themselves. There were many different types of people living in the valley. As mentioned before we had a couple of psychopaths and a couple of I don't know whats, and gunslingers and vegetarians and drunks. Our tough guys were capable of taking this guy's head off, which was what Red really wanted. Kill the energy at any cost.

I was playing music and watching this saga unfold. I looked around the group. Let's see, there is Donny, and there is Long Larry and Suzy Creamcheese, and Big Steve, Rebecca, the Meadows people, Romaine and Mark. I felt this huge surge of love energy coming out of the group. After a short while Red left. As far as I know no one ever saw him again. He had lost.

Before he left he sang an amazing version of "Love in Vain" at the top of his voice. I don't know. I felt like this guy was the devil, sent to test our strength. We were mighty folks that night.

12

Speed Trap

As mentioned before, Takilma Road was (and is) a rough narrow road winding through the forest. There were (and are) numerous houses and shacks along the road, and many children and sundry pets played on or near the road. Vehicle speed was always a concern of the locals.

Sometime around 1973–'74 there was some logging going on up near the headwaters of the east fork of the Illinois River, and the trucks were barreling through town. Drivers were paid by the number of loads they carried so they were not too careful about their driving habits. There were several complaints made to the sheriff's office, primarily asking that the road be posted at twenty-five miles per hour, but the cops were not sympathetic. The natives were getting restless and the cops seemed to be enjoying the situation a lot. It didn't take too much to amuse those folks.

One day Lance was riding his horse on the road, the horse spooked and was hit by a truck. Even though it was not actually the driver's fault, the community became extremely upset. Takilma Nick and Hope Mountain Michael decided to apply frontier law to the situation. They got a couple of tree limbs and tacked on hand-painted signs saying "Speed Limit 25 MPH" and stationed themselves at opposite ends of the populated area. Oh, I forgot to mention that they were carrying loaded .30-30 rifles in case of argument. It is amazing what effect a loaded rifle can have on a tough ol' country boy.

When the Mayor got wind of what was happening, he called the sheriff and said, "You know, Lance's horse got hit by one of the logging trucks and the folks out here are pretty mad."

The dispatcher said, "Well, we sympathize with your problem, but unless there is an incident there is nothing we can do."

The Mayor replied, "I think we are about to have an incident because we have two guys with rifles standing by the side of the road ready to shoot the next guy they see speeding."

The dispatcher said, "We'll have someone out there right away." And they did. All of a sudden the loggers were driving their trucks through town at five to ten miles per hour and waving at everyone they saw.

Robert at the Funky Egg stopped one of the carefully driven trucks as it drove past and handed the driver a beer and waved him on his way.

I can't remember if this event caused a change in the speed laws, but there were no further incidents that I know of and boredom had been thwarted for a time.

13

The Tomasson Creek Massacre

There was lots of music happening in the valley in 1972. Most people didn't have electricity, so pretty much all the music you heard was live. Music mostly associated itself with parties and get-togethers. This was a very good deal, especially when you were one of the music providers. I know.

I met David a year before this incident, when I was living with Betty at the Wilderness Lodge. There were various hippies living one way or another down the Illinois River, just out of Selma. David and Rusty were camped on the south side of the river, across from Selma and River Road, just west of Selma.

They used a hand-pulled cable car, for their food and other supplies, to cross the river. One time they were loaded on acid, and Rusty fell out into the river and broke his leg. The environment we lived in was dangerous.

So here they were, Rusty's leg broke, with nowhere to stay, and totally without funds. Betty and I let them stay at our room at the Wilderness Lodge for a couple of days, and we helped get Rusty to the doctor, and otherwise assist them in getting their trip together. I think Rusty went back to Canada after the leg healed.

A couple from New York, Rick and his girlfriend Willie, showed up sometime later. Rick was a great musician, as was David. They formed a folk duo called The Miracles of Wonder and were a real treat.

For some reason they decided to have an outdoor party at Lake Selmac. We would listen to a lot of The Miracles, partake of some electric cool aid, hang around the bonfire, play music, whatever. It was guaranteed that there would be memorable events at any wild gathering that involved LSD. A bunch of us from the Funky Egg family piled into Robert's truck, the Blue Heron, and we drove the twenty-five miles to the lake.

We had gatherings quite often. We usually held our parties in Takilma, in safe territory. Selmac is right in the middle of enemy redneck country. Some (most) of these parties were mellow and lacked much stress. Some, however, well let's just say that a Scorpio full moon party could get lively.

We arrived, commenced to drinking cool aid and listening to the band. They were plugged in and got pretty trashy. Rick was playing his guitar with a beer can for a slide. It was good but jangly; that should have indicated to us how the night was going to go.

Some people get jealous of musicians, because they get all the energy. It's tough because that's what they're supposed to be doing, focusing good energy. After it got dark I was standing by the fire and playing songs, when all of a sudden I heard this shriek and Aries Jerry comes tearing out of the woods, runs right at me and tries to take my guitar away from me, then runs back up into the woods. After a while he repeated the raid, and tried to grab my guitar again. I decided that if he did that again I would grab a rock and hit him over the head. Well, I couldn't hit him with my guitar, could I? I wasn't operating too well at that point.

At about this time half a dozen loggers showed up. Not just loggers, but Terry Cox, a psychotic badass who in the future was to bash a guy's head in, then bury him in the woods, and then go to jail for a long, long time. Terry was also famous for whomping on a few law officers, or anyone else he could find. Not a fun person.

Fortunately, all they wanted was to smoke some weed. Unfortunately, we didn't have any. In the meantime they were imbibing of the cool aid. And we were drinking their beer. So after a while I guess they started coming on to the cool aid and getting paranoid. They got aggressive and started a fight but we had a few bad boys of our own there, chief among them being Donnie, and they worked the loggers over pretty good. Terry said, "I've got some guns in my truck and I'm gonna shoot all you bastards." Rainbow Bob ran to Terry's truck, took all the guns, and hid them.

Not only did they get beat up but the hippies stole their guns. Man was Terry pissed. He yelled "I've got a .51-caliber machine gun buried at home, and I'm gonna bring it back here and shoot all you expletive deleteds." I can't remember the exact words he used but let it suffice that they were not complimentary. Loggers have a tendency to talk dirty. I didn't believe that there was a .51 calibre gun but I didn't want to wait around to find out. That about ended the party.

I have to say that Robert is in his glory under pressure. We were very stoned, but he loaded us up and got us home. I heard late that night a couple of officers came into the cop shop laughing. The cop at the desk says, "What's so funny?" One of the cops said, "Terry Cox just got his ass kicked by a bunch of hippies. Ha, ha ha."

14

Hep-A

This is my take on events that I tell about in this story. It would not be an exaggeration to say the Josephine County, Oregon, establishment was not happy with the influx of hippies. The cops were jumpy, but there wasn't an awful lot of law-breaking, setting aside the fact that almost every facet of our existence was unlawful in one way or the other. Their main gripe was the bane of every law-enforcement officer anywhere in the universe: they didn't know what the hell was going on. The FBI probably came by on occasion. All kinds of government agencies drove by on many occasions, but they never stopped.

It wasn't long before the county health department began interacting with us, especially the nurses at the V.D. clinic. Dr. Wall (we called him Hole in the Wall), really, really hated hippies. He was brutal when taking swabs, etc. I went through that once. The nurses had it harder. I really felt sorry for them. They tried. Some lady would come in and test positive and make a two-page list of contacts. Blew their country minds. I guess it all seemed like fun back then.

Then the hepatitis epidemic hit. When we went to the county health department, Dr. Wall would not release gamma globulin that they had been given by the state. At this same time there was an article in the Grants Pass newspaper stating that the hippies were swimming in the water up stream and they were going to infect everyone downstream with Hep-A. Serious stuff.

John, member of the Magic Forest commune, contacted a doctor in the state health department. The doctor came down secretly, and we had a meeting. We told him what had been going on and he was really pissed. He took off for town, and the next thing we knew there was a cavalcade of doctors, nurses, and reporters. They pulled right up to the Funky Egg farm. They were going to immunize the whole community with the press right there.

Their misfortune was that their first contact was with Mara and I. We worked together pretty well as a team. We told them that there were some things that had to be done before we would consent to the inoculation program. They had to publicly deny that Hep-A was transmitted by water, and therefore inform the folks down the river that they were not being contaminated. The county health guy said that of course the newspaper article was all bullshit. He knew that, but it was a press matter, and not something that he had control over.

Mara jumped in and told him that she had worked in the news media in LA, and that what he had said was not true. They could force a retraction if they wanted to. He said, "Yeah, we'll publicize the story." The newspaper did run a retraction of the scare story. One small step, etc.

That contact with the state health department was the very early beginning of the move to start the Takilma People's Clinic.

15

Run, Hippie, Run! Redneck's Gonna Get Ya!

In the middle of the winter of 1972 I had decided to hitch down to Ft. Bragg to visit some of my old-time Sacramento friends. It's a little bit tricky hitching from Takilma to the Mendocino coast. You'd start in Obrien, Oregon, on Highway 199 south to Crescent City, then Highway 101 from Crescent City to Ukiah. The hard part was getting over to the coast on Highway 20.

I managed to get to Ft. Bragg easily from Ukiah, and stayed for a couple of days. As soon as I arrived I got a terrible allergic reaction to something in the air, and my eyes were almost puffed shut. I grabbed my pack and guitar and hit the road north, along the desolate and lonely Highway 1. I got a couple rides about twenty miles to Westport, then got stranded. There was another hitchhiker, so I had company. It was starting to get dark and I was thinking about finding someplace to toss my sleeping bag for the night, when a man with a pickup and camper stopped. He had a couple of hitchers with him in the cab, but I could ride in the camper, and he was going to Grants Pass. Hallelujah. I slipped in my sleeping bag, and slept till the truck stopped in Cave Junction.

I got out and put on my pack and picked up my guitar. It was about 1:00

a.m. and freezing, probably about twenty degrees above, clear, stars pulsating, absolutely quiet. No sounds, no cars, no radios, no dogs barking, nothing. Bliss.

All of a sudden I had a thought. "It's got to be about closing time, and I'm not sure I want to get caught out in the open at night when the loggers are driving home from the bar." Shit. As I was thinking this I heard a car start, way in the distance. Man, that cold really propagates sound when it is otherwise quiet, so the car could have been at least two miles away. I looked at the road ahead, in the semidarkness I saw that both sides of the road were cleared fields for almost a quarter of a mile, then there was a wooded brushy area. I started walking fast, and listening. Yes, the car was going south on 199; oh, oh, he's turning onto the Caves Highway, which, by some great coincidence, happened to be the road down which I was currently walking.

The next maneuver I pulled I had been training for since I started hitchhiking. It's that upcoming Olympic event, the 75-yard dash with a forty-pound pack slung over one shoulder and guitar case in one hand, running like hell to reach the guy who stopped way down the road, before he changes his mind and takes off again. Sometimes they take off anyway. Great fun. Sense of humor. This time, however, the goal was not a waiting car, but to find some cover.

To my advantage, I had all that practice, and I also had my pack properly balanced and strapped to both shoulders. I ran as fast as I could along the road toward the trees, hearing the car getting closer and closer. They were close enough to see me in their headlights as I reached the stand and darted into the trees. I hoped they hadn't seen me. Then brake lights came on. They had seen me. The car made a U-turn, another misdemeanor you understand, and drove verrrry slowly past where I was hidden. They were about a quarter of a mile away when they U-turned again, and slowly drove past. Then they took off.

After I got to the trees I really wasn't too worried. They had just gotten a fleeting glimpse of me, and they knew that most woods hippies carried knives, and some of them carried guns, and all of them where drugged crazies. I would be able to see them, but they would not be able to see me.

I'm probably lucky they hadn't gotten a little drunker at the bar. No telling what they might have done. I can just hear the conversation, "Hot Damn Leroy, had one a them sumbitches right in the headlights and let him get away. Shee-it."

I walked carefully to where Caves Highway and Holland Loop Road meet. I dropped my stuff on the hard ground, spread my ground cloth, got my sleeping bag out, climbed in, and slept very well. When I woke up in the morning the sleeping bag and cloth were frozen to the ground. It got a tad cold that night. I wasn't afraid to hitch during the day, and I got a ride home. Ah, the beautiful green valley narrowing to a canyon about four miles down the road that went nowhere. Home.

16

Battle of Hogues Meadows

Nick and I had set up a camp at the headwaters of Cedar Creek, for purposes we will not get into here. I always liked playing in the woods when I was a kid and this was even better. I was living in the woods.

Fortunately the camp and trail were not needed by mothers and children, but occasionally it was a hiding place for low-level fugitives like Big Steve, who was wanted somewhat on a marijuana cultivation case. Or at least he thought he was wanted. Mistaken identity, of course, but best to lay low for a while. Sooner or later they will forget about it.

During his stay, Steve would leave camp for a couple of days and then come back. He was very gregarious and had to visit friends. He said that another reason he left for a while was to flush his system of Nick's "crude oil" coffee. Nick never cleaned out the coffee pot. He just added more coffee grounds and water and an occasional egg shell and then boiled it all up. When he thought it was done he would hold up the pot, pour a cup while looking at the sun through the liquid stream, and if he could see anything but black he would put the pot on the fire to boil for a while longer.

The story we had circulated while he was staying at our camp was that

Steve had skipped town. I was miffed, therefore, when I ran into Cleveland Bob and he said, "Guess what, I saw Big Steve last night."

I said, "No you didn't, he left town."

He said, "Yes, I did, I ought to know."

I said, "No, you didn't!"

He replied, "Yes I did; he was at the pizza parlor. They have a deal where if you can eat a whole pizza by yourself you get it for free. He won the pizza, easy."

I could see that my argument was losing traction. I replied, "Steve could be in pretty big trouble if people talk about him. I will admit he isn't making it real easy for us to cover for him if he's hanging out at the pizza parlor, but we should keep that information to ourselves; that way if anything happens, at least we won't be responsible."

He thought about it for a while and said, "I guess you're right."

At the time of the shootout Steve was staying in camp with us. The Gunslingers were living by the green bridge in Hogues Meadows, about a half-mile from our camp.

Nick was the commanding general of the Takilma Rifles, as well as the sheriff. If you didn't believe it, all you had to do was ask him. He was definitely on a Che Guevara trip. Late one evening Nick, Steve, and I were sitting around the campfire, passing a bit of controlled substance, and BSing. Nick was forging the lead balls for his .36 cap-and-ball revolver over the campfire. I always told him that it was ridiculous for him to use a .36 cap-and-ball on game because no one else anywhere near had such a weapon. My argument was trumped by the fact that it was cool to forge your pistol balls over a campfire. Enough said. All of a sudden we heard "blam blam, blamety blam blam" from the direction of Hogues Meadows. It sounded like several guns of different calibers. Ominously the shots sounded like different guns the Gunslingers carried. "Oh, shit, we must go to the aid of our brothers."

Nick was in a quandary. Speed was of the essence, but décor was also important. He always carried a pack with him, and he assumed his most martial air as he began picking through the stuff in the pack, selecting a shirt, military jacket and beret, and leather gloves. I looked for a swagger stick but I didn't see one. He tried to stand at attention the whole time as he dressed for coming engagement.

Our arsenal was somewhat limited. Nick had his .36 cap-and-ball, Steve had a .410 single-shot shotgun, and I had a machete. Luckily there was a bit of moonlight, not much, but there was no cleared trail from our camp out to the road (intentional), and there was a lot of old logging slash everywhere. Also we weren't walking too steadily right then. We were stumbling through the brush and slash trying to be silent raiders, with very little success. Needless to say I was not happy with this turn of events, but what was an officer of the Takilma Rifles to do but answer the call. We finally made it to the main house, where the Cedar Gulch landowners lived, about a quarter-mile from Hogues Meadows.

It was totally quiet both at the house and the meadow. We rapped on a window and Jack lit a lamp and poked his head out of the window. "What the fuck's going on out there?"

Nick said, "We don't know, but we heard a bunch of shooting, sounded like down at Hogues Meadows."

Jack said, "I didn't hear anything. We've been asleep."

We still couldn't hear anything, so it became obvious that whatever had happened was over, and we didn't want to get involved at this point, so we decided to go back to camp and call it a night. I for one was mightily relieved that it was over.

We found out later that Bud Short, a redneck neighbor and part owner of the Short-Ormsby ranch, had been out shooting his rifle. Evidently he had been shooting in different directions and with the canyons in this area shooting caused the gun echoes to differ significantly.

17

Citizens for Reforestation

By 1973 the socio-economic face of Takilma had begun to change from the totally anarchistic philosophy of the '60s. Nuclear families were beginning to emerge, people were beginning to purchase property, and welfare was beginning to be an important factor in the stability of the community. The Takilma People's Clinic was well on the way to establishment, and some of the locals were beginning to work on government contracts in various phases of forest management.

Some of the old hard-liner anarchists still existed in the area, however; and I was among this group. Takilma was my home and still the best place to launch the cultural-spiritual revolution that some of us still hoped would come to pass.

The marriage between the Nixon administration and American free-enterprise larceny began to come between the Takilma efforts to seek employment and the issuance of government contracts. Some contractors were able to low-ball tree planting contracts by using illegal Mexican labor and bypassing many of the requirements of the process. This fact enraged a number of locals, including (Funky Egg) Robert. He began to address a letter to the forest service generally stating that here the poor hippies were trying to make citizens of themselves, get off welfare, and find meaningful employment and the government was not giving them an even break. When I heard about the letter I approached Robert and asked if I could work on the project with him. He readily agreed.

Now, anyone who knows Robert knows that there is no deviousness to his soul. He meets all situations head-on, as for example that time that his head met Mad John's tamping bar during a dispute over a dead chicken in the yard of the Little Funky Egg. I, however, considered politics to be a major energy rip-off, and if effort were to be made in this area, a good guerilla will find his enemy's weakness and exploit it with wanton ferocity.

A committee was formed consisting of Mara, Black Michael, Sheila, and I. I explained my ideas on the subject. Associating ourselves with Takilma would be the kiss of death. The government knew perfectly well that there were no Republican votes amongst our constituency, and furthermore the decent citizens of the area had no sympathy with us low-lifes. We needed to create the impression that we were a group of responsible Josephine County citizens concerned about the economic welfare in the area as a whole. Of course, this was true. We needed to convey the impression of competent professionalism in whatever communications we had with any outside agencies. We had to be proactive in our approach.

Our first problem was finding an address to use for our correspondence. Michael took care of this by volunteering his Cave Junction P.O. box. Our group had various skills that were not generally bruited about. Sheila was a skilled typist and secretary, Mara was a public relations specialist, Michael was a professional troublemaker, and I had been a professional systems analyst in one of my previous lives. In fact, I had worked for several years in the Systems Analysis Office of the California State General Services Department, which was responsible for the control and coordination of all data processing in state government, so I was familiar with report preparation.

As we discovered in our general research on reforestation, I can't remember the details of the research, not all of the provisions of the Knutson-Vandenberg

Act seemed to have been complied with by the government, and this gave me an opening to work it into the report we were compiling. The final copy of the report with the cover letter read like this:

Citizens for Reforestation

Josephine County

P.O. xxx, Cave Junction, Oregon 97532

Dear Sir:

It has come to our attention that although money is available through appropriation and special funds from timber sales, replanting of our precious national forests is not being fully implemented. According to the U.S. Forest Service and timber experts, if reforestation is not implemented within a short period of time following clear cutting, new trees will not grow.

The area of our concern, Josephine County, Siskiyou National Forest, is a labor surplus area, and the money being withheld would create a reduction in the welfare and unemployment rolls. We cannot stress the need for action too strongly, and we trust that you will give this matter top priority.

Sincerely,

Mara _____ (Mrs.)

Secretary

Attached report

MD/jmk

SUBJECT: REFORESTATION

Recommendations:

- That the U.S. Forest Service be directed to release the FY 1972/73 funds held in reserve from timber sales (as directed by the Knutson-Vandenberg Act of June 9, 1930, 46 STAT. S27; 16 U.S.C. 576)

- That the Office of Management Budget be directed to approve release of funds allocated by the Congress for reforestation during the FY 1972/73.

- That all money already collected for brushing of clear cuts, to reduce fire hazard and allow for reforestation, be released for implementation.

- That the proper authorities be directed to order the Forest Service, whenever possible, to award contracts to the lowest bidder who resides in and hires labor from local labor surplus areas, if trained and available, as is now the case in Josephine County.

Background:

For a number of years the Bureau of Land Management and the Forest Service have allowed logging contractors to clear cut vast areas of our National Forest. In recognition of the potentially dangerous ecological problems caused by clear cutting of timber areas, forest fire hazards implicit in the slash left behind, the Knutson-Vandenberg Act, along with other legislation, was passed by Congress to generally provide a policy of reforestation of these logged areas. In our area the reforestation program has been carried out mostly by outside contractors who hire labor from other areas and move from area to area.

Facts bearing on the problem:

- During the FY 1972/73 funds for reforestation and brushing have been drastically curtailed; even though the funds are available, partly from timber sales and partly from allocation.

- Some areas, if not replanted within the next year, will no longer support trees.

- Many experts in the field believe that clear cut logging in mountainous areas, such as ours, is completely unfeasible if rebuilding the forest is contemplated.

- The local Ranger District (Illinois Valley Branch) feels that their hands are tied in regard to use of the funds supposedly available.

- Our area is a labor surplus area. Some of our lower income citizens have formed tree-planting groups and are certified trained and competent planters by the Forest Service.

- Of the few contracts let this winter, most were awarded to outside contractors who, in some instances, hired labor from other states.

Alternate Solutions:

- Stop clear cutting entirely.

- Allow things to proceed as at present.

- Release all funds now available and adopt a policy of local employment and initiative in areas where this is possible.

Discussion:

- Stop Clear Cutting. Although some members of our organization believe this is the most acceptable solution to most of the problems in the National Forest, we realize that logging is an integral part of the economy in this area, and any change in these policies could take too long to implement to help our immediate concern, reforestation.

- Allow Things to Continue As They Are. What bothers us about this solution is not so much that the local economy is being hurt, or that our forests are being endangered, but that the present policy of reforesting is being tampered with, and we don't know what this thinking might bring in the future.

- Release Existing Funds. This solution would appear to be the most feasible because it would partly help solve our local unemployment problem and keep the Government's promise to reforest. This could all be done at no additional cost to the tax-payer and no change to current policy or procedure.

Copies of this letter and report were sent to the following committees, persons, and groups:

Richard M. Nixon

Senator Robert W. Packwood

Senator Mark O. Hatfield

Congressmen: Herman E. Talmage, Chairman Senate Agriculture and Forestry Committee W. R. Ponge, Chairman House Agriculture and Forestry Committee William D. Ruckelhaus, Administrator Environmental Protection Agency Earl L. Butz, Secretary U. S. Department of Agriculture John R. McGuire

U. S. Forest Service

San Francisco Sierra Club

Seattle Sierra Club

Oregon Environmental Council

Joe Walicki, Wilderness Society

The Oregon Journal

The Grants Pass Courier

Margaret Wood, Josephine Conservation Council

Notably absent from the distribution list was John Hoffman, chief ranger. He had seemed to be a stumbling block in the contract award process, and we wanted to try to blind-side him. If the first hint he had that a game was afoot were questions from his superiors, he might begin the process on the defensive. This is more or less what happened. After we sent out the letters we waited to see what the lure would catch. We got a number of responses, most of them positive, but the prize was from the Office of the Chief of the Forest Service, which read as follows:

United States Department of Agriculture

Forest Service, Washington, D.C. 20250

Mrs. Mara _____, Secretary

Citizens for Reforestation

Josephine County

P.O. Box xxx, Cave Junction, Oregon 97523

Dear Mrs. _____:

Secretary Butz has asked us to respond to your letter concerning reforestation in Josephine County, Oregon, on the Siskiyou National Forest. This will also respond to your similar letter to the Forest Service.

The restriction on the expenditure of funds was made to combat the inflationary effects of Government spending. The Administration established a level of spending at $250 billion in FY 1973 and proposed a slightly higher budget in FY 1974.

In order to maintain a given level of spending, some programs no matter how desirable must be eliminated or reduced. The President in making his recommendations to Congress, and Congress in acting on those recommendations must consider all national priorities in determining which programs should be funded.

In order to control inflation, restrictions were also placed on the expenditure of cooperative funds. Monies collected for reforestation and timber stand improvement under the Knutson-Vandenberg Act are cooperative funds. We have been given relief from some of the restrictions, and according to our records at this time all requests for use of cooperative funds for reforestation and timber stand improvement have been approved for FY 1973.

Our contracts for reforestation and other cultural work are put up for competitive bid to give everyone a fair chance at the work, and to assure that the Government is accomplishing the work at the best price. On the surface it would appear that local labor should be able to compete with out-of-state labor. If there are some specific circumstances that preclude local labor from entering the market, then you should present these to the Ranger or Supervisor. Sometimes the size of contracts or other requirements can be changed. However, we cannot confine competition to certain areas.

The Ranger and Supervisor will be pleased, as we are, with your interest in the activities on the National Forest. Your views will be considered in the future development of our programs. Thank you for your letter.

Sincerely,

JOHN R. McGUIRE

Chief.

Bingo. We were elated at this letter for a number of reasons. The first statement that caught our eye was the first sentence, stating that the letter had been directed by Earl (the Butt) Butz personally. The second, and most significant point, as far as we were concerned, was the next paragraph implying that money was being withheld because of the potential inflationary effect it might have on the Josephine County economy. At last we had something to take to the local press.

We worked with the *Grants Pass Courier*, and they published a generally positive story about our efforts, with some emphasis on the withholding of funds mentioned above. Of course our cover was blown at this point, and Citizens for Reforestation, being unmasked as a bunch of hippies, albeit clever hippies, went out of business. Over the course of the operation the only person whose name ever appeared was Mara _____, Secretary, and the only materials used were a P.O. box, a typewriter, paper, and postage. I guess we got the most bang for our buck.

One of the results of the operation was that the government, at least the Forest Service, realized they would have to take us seriously. A short time after the operation ended, John Hoffman contacted several Takilma citizens who had previously participated in contract work, requesting a meeting. Mara and I volunteered to host the meeting at our home, across the river at Canaan. I prepared a Mexican dinner for the group. The meeting was mellow and facilitated by the consumption of "seeds 'n stems" tea that was described as herbal. Mrs. Hoffman found it quite good.

The upshot of this meeting was the establishment of the firefighting crew, and was the beginning of a close working relationship between the Forest Service and the Takilma hippies. This was to change the entire socio-economic landscape in the valley.

I can't say that this was the result I foresaw when we began our street theater. We moved the town closer to the establishment. I've heard that the Lord works in mysterious ways.

18

Duel at the Funky Egg

I have heard that nature abhors a vacuum; I sometimes think that it abhors moderately long periods of tranquility as well. It helps somewhat if you see tranquility and turmoil as yin and yang, as a part of a whole . . . something.

A group of Moslems ended up in Eugene, looking for someplace to live in the woods. Eugene was a popular feeder of people and V.D. to our valley. One of our citizens, (I'm told it was C— Bill), invited the Moslems to Takilma. The band consisted of about ten men and several women, veiled of course. The leader was a black ex-Berkeley activist who named himself Abdul, or Abdullah, as I was informed by Arizona Don, who was an expert at correcting people. There were several Jews and God knows what other racial and ethnic folks. The only thing I am sure of is that there were no Arabs included. They had instituted sharia within the group.

Their stated purpose was to go into the woods, find their chosen spot, and start a tribe and live off the land. Well, they were city people so they didn't know how difficult and labor-intensive that would be. To facilitate this goal they purchased horses, mules, and .30-06 rifles. When they arrived in Takilma and were looking for a temporary place to stay, Black Michael offered to let them use his mining claim.

Michael was a Vietnam vet, Berkeley and Oregon graduate, and the wacky leader of the Godzilla Wrecking Company. The name came from his huge truck, which he named Godzilla. The wrecking part was proved later when he tried to pull under the overhang at the gas pump and tore down the overhang.

Ordinarily this would have been discomfiting, but it was made worse by the fact that the store was owned by Andy, who was probably the poster child of the hippie/nigger-hating faction of Josephine County. Luckily he didn't shoot Michael with his .357 magnum, only shot into the street. His torment was delightful to everyone but the hippie winos, who needed his wares, and one time would even stand being shot at, just as long as he kept his cooler and shelves stocked.

The Godzilla Wrecking Company was known for its weird people even for the Takilma valley. One member was Mobile Michael who looked a lot like General Grant with a black beard and he wore a confederate officer's uniform complete with saber. There was also Butch the bagpipe player. It's not fun as an acoustic guitar player to try to jam with bagpipes. This can be a very discouraging situation.

I think Michael was from a middle-class family (never got the whole story), and he felt he had never paid his dues to the "hood." This got him in trouble more than once, with streetwise black brothers trying to hustle him. Abdul fell into this category. Michael invited Abdul to camp on his mining claim, after the folks downtown objected to the Moslems carrying their rifles everywhere and shooting them off, including shooting behind their mules when they wouldn't move. They were also constantly intoning, "God Is Great and there is no God but God." Over the course of time several locals joined the group. Hey, it looked like a fun new game.

The Moslems were not well thought of in Cave Junction. They took their rifles to town and intimidated everyone. They would enter any business establishment, including the bank, with their guns, so that their women could cash welfare checks.

They got along tolerably with the Takilma locals, though they were not shy pointing out our shortcomings, such as nudity or anything else that offended sharia. One interesting confrontation happened just after they arrived. The Gunslingers came down from their claim to find out what the big deal was all about. It was not a confrontation actually; both sides were just interested in checking out the other guys. You had the Gunslingers, with shotguns on one side, and Moslems with rifles, on the other. You could almost see the Moslems looking at the shotguns and thinking, "If we go to war with these guys we definitely have the wrong weapons unless we can pick them off at long range." Of course the Gunslingers had rifles too, they were just not part of their everyday apparel.

Things on the mining claim deteriorated rather quickly, over who was actually in charge of the claim. Things came to a head one day while Michael was in town. Michael's girlfriend was working in the garden, topless. Abdul saw her and entered the garden shouting that she was a whore. He then proceeded to hit her several times and escorted her off the claim, saying it now belonged to him. Someone went to town and told Michael what had happened.

When Michael got back to Takilma, he arranged a meeting with Abdul. Abdul told him that he no longer owned the mining claim. He then hit Michael and knocked him down (Michael was about half Abdul's size), and told Michael if he didn't like it they should shoot it out right there, and offered him a gun.

Michael told him it wasn't happening with Abdul's gun, but it would happen, then he left. Michael went looking for a weapon and ended up borrowing a shotgun. Meanwhile, Abdul left for Cave Junction. Michael joined a rather large gathering at the Funky Egg. We all waited to see what was going to happen. I could see that our record of no shooting injuries might be coming to an end.

Michael was near the road with his shotgun waiting for Abdul. Sure enough, a car came by with Abdul in the back seat. When he saw Michael, the car stopped, he jumped out and started waving a pistol around. Michael had the shotgun at the ready. Men, women, and children lined the street to watch the spectacle. Not me. When he waved the gun at the crowd and said he was going to kill all the white M– F–ers I ducked behind the house. Maybe I'm a coward but I don't like loaded guns pointed at me. I don't even like unloaded guns pointed at me.

Shotgun Paul was sort of moderating the discussion, positioned between them with his .16-gauge shotgun at port. Abdul swung his pistol at Paul, which I thought would be the end of Abdul. Paul rounded on him but didn't pull the trigger. At this point Abdul may have begun thinking he had overplayed his hand a bit. I couldn't hear what was said, from my perch behind the house, but Michael fired the shotgun and Abdul fell to the pavement. With that the crowd began to disburse. Dr. Jim was called from the clinic and they hauled Abdul to the hospital where he died. Michael left. Sometime later he flagged a sheriff down and turned himself in.

There was a lot of tension in Takilma, because what was left of the Moslems started talking about Jihad and a holy war with the Christians. I guess everyone but them was a Christian. However, having seen what happened to the tough leader they eventually left for . . . somewhere.

There was a lot of fear and anxiety about Michael's fate. Many of us saw this as excellent opportunity for the legal establishment to railroad the only other black person at this end of the county to jail for the rest of his life. It was somewhat ironic that the only two blacks in the area had a shootout.

As far as Cave Junction sentiment was concerned, there was no lynch mob. In fact Michael became something of a hero, especially with the bank employees who no longer had to process transactions with rifles in the background.

Sometime later I attended an angry local gathering at the Funky Egg, after the news went out that the DA and sheriff were coming to issue subpoenas for the coroner's inquest. The two showed up exhibiting nervous good cheer. The crowd was sullen; things did not look good. The DA called out several names from his list, being handicapped because most of them were nicknames and aliases. He looked down at the stack and he asked, "Is Crazy Jim here?"

Someone said, "No."

Then the DA asked, "Why do you call him Crazy Jim?"

Shotgun Paul said, "Because he's crazy."

Just at that moment a pickup came down the road doing about twenty miles per hour. Crazy Jim was standing up in the back with a beer in his hand. He saw the sheriff and pointed at him and yelled something. I turned around to tell the DA that he had just seen Crazy Jim. I heard a thud and looked back and saw Jim rolling on the roadway with his beer held up in the air. He got up, brushed himself off, and said, "Didn't spill a drop. I'm Crazy Jim. I heard you wanted to talk to me." That ended the tension. Everyone, including the DA and sheriff, cracked up. I can just see him at the DA convention. "Ha, you think that story's good? Let me tell you about Crazy Jim."

The grand jury verdict was justifiable homicide, and Michael went free. Some years later he had another run in with a bad black dude that could have been ugly but the guy took off. Michael was a good brother and I still miss him. He died of more or less natural causes a number of years ago.

19

Why I Went to Lasqueti

Growing up in the country, weather and climate were important topics. The prevailing "civilized" opinion about weather and climate was that it was in a steady state, with some aberrations here and there. Folks who lived in the woods knew; Christ, we grew up counting tree rings. Long periods of moderate weather and long periods of harsh weather. Nothing steady about it at all.

My country sensibilities were mightily offended in the cities with all types of pollution, including noise, and I had no desire to live like that. I understood that by the time I was twelve years old. I remember my dad driving us to the Bay Area. We seemed to pass huge numbers of cities, Alameda, Richmond, Albany, Berkeley, and Oakland, all cramped together. I felt claustrophobic; my ego was being tattered to shreds. How can there be so many people? Although I'm sure I enjoyed the trip to the city, when I got home I said that when I was grown up I would buy a huge piece of property, fence it in, and get a shotgun.

In later years with all that Tore-ass-idness (Taurian inclination), I spent a lot of time thinking about the probably inevitable environmental disaster ahead if we were to keep living on the same heedless scale. I didn't understand how we could think we could keep degrading our nest and not pay for it somehow.

I didn't know what the climate was going to do, but thought it would be pretty spectacular one way or the other.

Around 1968 I decided that we had maybe five years to turn the system around. That was the way I had it figured anyway, but when I tried to use it as a conversation starter it wasn't well received. It even freaked out one of my hippie friends so bad I had to talk him back. So I kept my mouth shut. Mostly.

I had never been a "thing" person. Stuff was not ever important to me. During my working years I lived a very sparse and frugal life. During my last working year I was making a fair amount of "escape money" for the future.

Interacting with the hippies, I sensed that maybe, just maybe, a new social paradigm was developing that could spread around the world and save it. Yeah, right. But it was coming together physically and spiritually, and I got as involved as I could, while still working for several more years before totally dropping out.

I felt this incredible energy in the Takilma valley. There was nothing we couldn't do. I will admit that I was pretty impatient in some ways, when not blissed out, and to me this movement was going to save the world from my disaster model.

Having grown up in the sierras and traversed its canyons and mountains almost from the time I could walk, I was out of sync with my Takilma neighbors. I talk a lot more about that in the story "Walking." My world view was fairly unique in that I was considerably older than most of my peer group, and I had been a successful professional, a programmer and systems analyst, before dropping out. I began to realize that these kids (who were originally middle class, young, and from the cities) were beginning to move back toward the establishment and the dream, at least my dream, began to fade.

The mantra for the time was, "Do your thing." There were the communists (people who live in communes are comm-u-nists according to Archie Bunker), the folks who just wanted to hang out, those who wanted to farm and live off the land. Also there were those who wanted to play in the forest. The Gunslingers were somewhat of this persuasion, and I think that is one of the things that attracted me to them. I had no fear of the natural environment. There were bears, cougars, and rattle snakes around but I was used to them from my childhood experiences. I really ended up playing in the woods like I had as a child. I loved exploring and building trails and living in a camp, though much of the time I was living in a sort of real house with Mara.

My first fantasy, as I made my way to Oregon, was to live on a commune and contemplate life. After living for a short time in Takilma, I harkened back to my hereditary roots, grandparent pioneers, me climbing around in the woods. I realized that the pioneers could teach me how to live. I could live like that, too. I had gone through huge changes in all aspects of my consciousness. I had believed, somewhat, that everyone was capable of comprehending the same concepts. I found that to be totally untrue, and I began to see that each of us has our own karma to work out. You cannot live someone else's life.

The Carlos Castaneda's teachings of Don Juan were an important part of my education at that time. They still are, as a matter of fact. I realized that I was capable of following the warrior's way, gaining understanding and control of my life. I honed my skills in woodcraft and learned to live my life strategically. I was preparing myself to survive in the wilderness.

At some point, I had a feeling that I had been inhabited by the soul of an old Indian sage. There was no incident, it was just that I realized that I saw the earth as the Indians see it. I hated the idea of private property. Not politically, but psychologically. We are chained to our property. I realized that the reason aboriginals are difficult to "civilize" is that the goads for those from Western Europe, greed and fear, are totally missing from their psyche. They were quite happy just being. Of course, they didn't realize that they had a choice. They also felt that the intentional desecration of the earth was a sickness, a disease. Now who wants to contract a disease?

I didn't do air traveling until late in life, and precious little after. I do re-member one time flying across the Midwest and thinking, "They've divided the whole country into squares." How ironic. The ultimate insult. This was worse than stealing their land, killing their animals to starve them out, giving them smallpox-infected blankets, and the general policy of extermination. The circle is the holy aboriginal symbol. It represents completeness and purity. The square is the anti circle, the symbol of evil. That is the ultimate blasphemy, turning their sacred earth into squares.

I first got the idea of moving to Canada when Homer and Loretta, my first wife and her husband, and our two children, picked me up in Takilma. We explored the gulf coast of Canada for a couple of weeks. We ended up backpacking across the wild northern end of Quadra Island. One night we camped by a little bay. When we woke up in the morning, we found that the tide was out and we had an oyster bed about thirty feet away. We picked a bunch of oysters, threw them on the fire, and had breakfast on the beach. YES!!! This is the place I want to live some day.

I hadn't realized how much my spirit had been invested in the hippie movement, and I was devastated when it began to fall apart. My vision had been the total restructuring of the way we view ourselves and the Earth. It was an attempt to develop worldwide consciousness in order to save the fragile but strong eco-structure. I felt we were very close to being doomed.

I remember one time Mara and I were discussing the community and I said, "It seems like everyone here has brought their -isms with them."

She asked, "What -ism did we bring?"

I replied, "anachronism."

I went through a major brain fart, and hated nearly everyone for nearly everything. Goddamnit! They didn't live up to my expectations! Black gloom. At this time, I recalled the stories Harold the Barbarian told about squatting on one of the islands in the Gulf of Georgia in Canada. God, I wanted to get out of the U.S.

20

First Border Crossing

My first foray into Canada was probably the spring of 1974. I had some connections in Hope, B.C. I had known Cindy in southern Oregon; she was married and living in Hope. Shawn had spent some time in Hope the year before, and stayed with Cindy and her husband and daughter. I got rid of everything I owned but could not carry, which wasn't a whole lot at that.

My outfit consisted of my old Kelty pack full of several changes of clothes, foul weather gear, a Primus stove, and as much food as I could cram in the sorely overloaded pack. I had a hatchet, a small frying pan, and several nested coffee cans with wire bales for cooking pots, all hanging from the back of the pack. I had two knives, an Old Timer and a Case sheath knife. I had a sleeping bag and ground cover also. I was wearing a homemade leather belt pouch containing dried herbs—I know that wasn't too bright. And my guitar. In my mind I was immigrating to Canada, never to come back.

The first leg of my journey took me about a half-mile to the Illinois River west fork bridge, where I stopped to rearrange my load. I got a ride to Cave Junction before I realized that I had left my knives at the bridge, so I had to hitch back and get them. I got back to CJ, and noticed that the lid on a molasses jar had gotten loose, and the pack had a lot of gunk in it. I had to go to the Laundromat and wash everything. So far the trip hadn't gotten off to a very good start. I had made the first ten miles anyway.

Thumbed up to Portland and visited my friends, then departed for the north. I got a ride to Lynnwood, Washington, and decided to call it a day. I found an abandoned house close to the freeway and spent the night. The next morning, an older woman gave me a ride to Blaine, Washington, on the Canadian border. Now here's where the gig becomes sticky.

I was a longhair, long-bearded dude, with all my patched-up gear and forty dollars in my pocket. I don't know what the hell I was thinking. I was quickly ushered into the Immigration room, where I had to provide some identification and fill out some forms. I had already filled out forms at Customs. One of the questions was whether I had ever smoked pot, and of course I said no. They gave me a five-day visa. I figured that would be the best I could get for the forty dollars in my pocket.

The commander, or whatever he was, came into the room. He was about thirty-five years old, with his polished shoes, his knee-length socks, and navy blue shorts, his white starched shirt with epaulettes on each shoulder, and a crisp peaked hat. I knew I was in for it. Now the search. Of course he looked into everything. I forgot to say that I was in possession of a stone pipe, given to me by Harold the Healer. I had smoked some tobacco through it to try to mask out any other substance it might have contained. He asked me to unpack my sleeping bag. I was thinking, "Oh Christ, no." So I opened it to display a Grateful Dead song book, a sheaf of song lyrics, several bow saw blades, about half a dozen potatoes, and a cheap Zebco fishing pole. I just can't begin to imagine what this whole thing looked like to the functionary I was dealing with. "Oh, I'm just going to Hope for a couple of days, then I'll go back home."

"Oh."

He spotted the pipe and sniffed. I was starting to get a tight sphincter at this point. He said, "What have you been smoking in this pipe?"

I said, "Just tobacco."

He said, "There's been more than tobacco smoked in this pipe. You signed a document stating that you have never smoked marijuana. If drugs have been smoked in this pipe you will be jailed and fined two thousand, five hundred dollars. What have you been smoking? Pot? Hash?"

Oh boy, this game's getting rough. I was outwardly (hopefully) relaxed, but I can't say about the inside. I replied, "I don't know about Canadian law, but in the U.S., the fact that I had in my possession a device, a pipe, that has had oh, shall we say marijuana? . . ."

He interjected, nodding and saying, "Yes, we're not children."

Honest to God. "That doesn't prove that I had smoked anything through that pipe."

He picked up the pipe and said, "I'm going to have this analyzed."

A little bit later he returned the pipe and walked away. I fidgeted for about a half hour. The commander came in several times, he'd stare at me and then he'd leave. He came into the room one last time, looked surprised, and said, "Are you still here?"

I said, "Yes."

He said, "You can go on through."

I asked, "To Canada?" and he nodded.

Then he said, "You'd better wash that pipe out with hot water."

I did better. I ditched it.

The bastard had kept me sweating for a half hour. I went outside, and after about ten minutes, when my heart had gotten back to normal, I stuck out my thumb for the first time in Canada. Two big guys in a hot pickup stopped and I climbed in. They asked where I was going and I said Hope. The driver said, "That's where we're going." Oh joy. But. . . . These guys took off down the road going about eight-five to ninety miles per hour, and all the while passing the hash pipe. I thought, *Oh shit. Here we go again.* But I smoked some hash. These were not guys you would like to be pissed off at you.

But I'm thinking, *Crap.* Two bad things looked like the only possible outcomes of the caper. Either we got in a crash and I got killed—no problem—or we got pulled over; then I'd be in deep doo-doo. Just a half-hour earlier I had sworn that I had never done drugs. I was in a quandary. I really, really wanted out of that truck but I couldn't give off any paranoid vibes. I told them that I had a friend in Chilliwack, just ahead in the road, so I would like to be dropped off there.

OK, done. I got out at the interchange, in this beautiful farm land; it was a wonderful day so I sat down and again waited for my heart rate to go down. I soon got a ride into Hope, the gateway to the mighty Fraser River canyon.

As I walked into town along the sidewalk, I encountered some narrow strips of gardens with well-kept grass, between the river and the highway. I was to learn that this strip was tribal land. There were several Indians lying on the grass with a jug of wine. They invited me over and I had a great time. Five days later I would have to be out of here but for now I was in Canada. In retrospect, that seems to have been one hell of a day.

21

Ross Lake

I banged on the roof of the pickup that was carrying me west on Highway 20, the Cascade Highway in Northern Washington State. We had just approached Ross Lake, which runs north–south on the border between the U.S. and Canada. A few minutes earlier we had stopped at a ranger station, and I got a map of the area. I needed to get adjusted to this new country, because I was going to walk across the border back into Canada.

The pickup pulled over to the side of the road and I jumped off. One of the other people riding in the back handed me down the battered remains of my heavy Kelty pack and my battered guitar case. I thanked the driver, who had picked me up when I had jettisoned my first ride at the junction of Highway 97 and Highway 20, just south of Oroville, Washington.

It was getting late in the afternoon at the foot of Ross lake, so I knew I had to get moving if I wanted to find somewhere to camp before it got too dark to see. I looked at the tourist map of the area, and could see no campgrounds marked for a long way down the trail. I pondered briefly about the bizarre five days I had spent in Canada. I had walked across the border looking something like a trapper out of the 1837 Rocky Mountains, with a guitar, long hair, long beard, and forty dollars in my pocket.

I had gotten a five-day visa, and for some reason was allowed to cross the border at Douglas, B.C. Five days later, at the forced end of my stay, I decided to use my last seven dollars for a bus ticket to Osoyoos, British Columbia, then to cross the border into the U.S., load up my pack with food purchased with the last of my food stamps, and try to hitch up the North Cascades freeway to Ross Lake. I would then sneak across the border and walk or hitch back to Hope, B.C., where I had started just this morning, and then I wouldn't need no stinkin' visas no more.

So here I was, ready to start on the last leg of the rectangle, which would take me back to what in five short days I had learned to regard as home. Attached to my belt were an Old Timer knife and a leather pouch I had made, which contained many spices in plastic Baggies. The contents of this pouch had caused a major misunderstanding at the border, when I crossed back into the U. S. It was finally sorted out after everything had been carefully examined. It's amazing how much oregano looks like a controlled substance.

My biggest problem was that I was carrying a fire-starting kit that contained some old man's beard moss, and a sticky cube of fire starter about the size and shape of a sugar cube, probably consisting of sawdust impregnated with pitch. It was pointed out to me that it looked an awful lot like a gram of hashish. I would not have known that if the border folks hadn't told me.

What made the situation worse was that there was no one else crossing the border at that time and the Customs people were very bored. Oh, well, all's well that ends well, or at least that's what I have heard. It was somewhat ironic that I almost had more trouble getting back into my homeland than I had had getting into Canada.

It was a good thing that I had done considerable packing over the past several years, lacking a vehicle and carrying my world pretty much on my back. Unfortunately, I hadn't had much in the way of food stamps when I had walked into that store in Oroville, so I had loaded up with a lot of heavy food, especially potatoes. I was now totally broke, no money, no food stamps, and no prospects, but I did have several days worth of food, so not to worry.

I hiked to the edge of town, about quarter of a mile. I like small towns, especially when I have to walk to the edge of them. I laid down my gear, stuck out my thumb, and had a ride almost immediately. The country around here was middle Washington, mostly grassy foothills and volcanic ridges. I gazed fondly northward, getting the lay of the land. Of course, like an old outlaw, I was constantly looking for good places to sneak across the border.

So here I was, riding in the back of a pickup on a beautiful day, admiring the countryside as it changed from the brown hills then wound up through the green cascades, jagged mountain peaks with heavy timber, and through the Pasayten Wilderness, where the Pacific Crest Trail crosses the Canadian border. This is the mount doom country, made famous by Jack Kerouac in the *Dharma Bums*. Kerouac was a major influence on my life.

I hoisted my fifty-pound pack, picked up my trusty guitar, and then started the 28-mile trudge along the east shore of Ross Lake, north into Canada. The trail was pretty flat in the beginning, and would continue along the shore of the lake for about eighteen miles, then uphill for several miles, circling east, then back west, down and . . . the dreaded border. I trucked along the trail as fast as I could, until it started to get dark, and I was getting tired. I hadn't encountered anyone to this point, and there was no place really suitable to camp, so I just threw down my plastic ground cover, pulled out my sleeping bag, and sacked out right on the trail. Nothing stepped on me during the night, so I guess it was a good choice.

The next day I hiked to the first campground, threw down my stuff, sat down, wished I had a cold beer, and just kind of lazed for a while. The previous thirty-six hours had been pretty intense. There were a couple of neat girls in the campground, so I decided to rest up the next day, do a little fishing, and cook a good meal.

The morning of my third day, I packed up and started the last leg of the trip. Sort of. As I said before, the trail rose into the mountains, circling around going east of the lake, about six miles up the trail I reached a beautiful wooded area that contained a campground named Deer Lick. I rested for a while and watched a group of young people working around the area. I learned that they were students and Junior Sierra Clubbers, who were doing volunteer work getting the camp ready for the season.

I had a conversation with some kids, who invited me to hang around, so I said, "What the hell?" I really felt funny, being with these clean-cut young people who would end up yuppies in a few years, though I didn't know it then, and they were fun to watch. I couldn't believe it when the leader of the group said that they were going to have a campfire that evening, and discuss how they were going to organize. This was pretty bizarre stuff for on old bush hippie. If I were with some of my friends, we would throw up some kind of shelter and sort of hang out and party. We would do music, but not at a "campfire." Oh to be young and eager again. When I pulled out some whole potatoes, instead of dried stuff, to fry up for dinner, I caught some of their looks, which seemed to say, "Why do they let people like this in our wilderness?"

The next morning I continued climbing the trail. After a couple of hours I ran into a young, long-blonde-haired dude wearing shorts and a cowboy hat; he was being pulled by a dog who was almost dancing he was having so much fun. This guy looked a lot like a friend back home, named Hope Mountain Michael. He was the first cool looking person I had seen for a couple of days. He looked me over, said, "You look like a far-out dude, do you want to turn on?"

I said, "Sure," so we sat down, smoked a joint, and then split our separate ways.

The trail started back down and circled west toward the lake, and I started getting a little apprehensive. "That border crossing feeling makes a fool out of a man," according to Billy Joe Shaver. I know that feeling very well. I noticed on the map that the trail ran next to a ranger station, right at the border. There probably wasn't anything to worry about. I doubted that they would check the stream of hikers walking along the trail, but after all this work I didn't want to take any chances. I looked around at the heavy undergrowth and took off across some really tough country, circled behind the ranger station, and ended up in the campground at the north end of the lake. I evidently hadn't been spotted by any agents.

It was obvious that the easiest way to sneak into Canada, or the U.S. for that matter, would be to have someone pick you up on the U.S. side in a boat, fish for awhile, get back to the campground, pack up the boat, and then leave. Just as I arrived at the camp, a pickup pulling a boat started to edge its way out of a campsite. I asked the driver if there was any chance I could get a ride with him into Hope. He said sure, and I climbed aboard; he took me to the outskirts of town.

I unloaded my gear again and made straight for the Hope Hotel, which contained the local pub. I left my pack outside, sat down at a table, bought a cold beer with my last quarter, and relaxed with the most luxurious feeling I had ever had to that point in my life. I was totally free. No visas to turn in. I was not a Canadian. I was still an American but that didn't mean anything up there, and I started working on my Canadian accent right away. I was going to stay in Canada, and I felt great.

I spent the summer hanging out and partying with the hippies. There was a vibrant community there that summer. I lived in Cindy and Davis' abandoned chicken house, in spite of their invitation to stay inside. I wanted to accept as little charity as possible. I made most of my spending money collecting beer bottles at two cents per bottle, and toting them around in a gunny sack. I lived mostly on hot dogs, cooked on my Primus stove, in my comfortable new digs. I tried picking ornamental boxwood for wreaths, but without a vehicle it didn't work out. At the end of the summer I decided to return to the U.S., even though I was offered a room with Cindy and Davis.

22

The Island

Lasqueti Island is about the size and shape of Manhattan Island and pointed northwest to southeast. It is eight miles east of Vancouver Island and between it and Texada Island. The passage between Lasqueti and Texada is the beginning of the inside passage to Alaska. We used to watch the *Princess* (the *Love Boat*) on its way north.

When I first arrived at French Creek dock I was walking, of course, looking for the Lasqueti Ferry chute. I walked to the end of the wharf and saw a sign that read "Lasqueti Island Ferry." Just a regular boat slot, no car-moving capabilities. Wow. I soon realized that the ferry, the *Captain Vancouver*, was not owned by B.C. Ferries but by a Lasqueti-ite named Ian Cole, one of the many truly unique and outrageous folks who inhabited the fringes of civilization.

The ferry service was financed by subsidies from the provincial government and from Canada Post, for carrying the mail on and off the Island. The ferry service ran Thursday through Monday, and was off Tuesday and Wednesday.

Friday through Monday there were three ferries per day, leaving False Bay at 8:00, 1:00, and 4:00. It would leave French Creek at 9:30, 2:30, and 5:30. The maximum passenger load was twenty-five. This was usually not a problem during the winter, but it could be a bitch with all the summer people staying on the island. That is, it would seat twenty-five if the weather is not too bad. The government wouldn't allow the ferry to be run when the wind exceeded thirty knots per hour. Truthfully, in that wallowing pig of a boat you wouldn't really want to go across in a bad storm, unless you had a very good stomach or a critical need to get across. The seasick people would usually go out to the aft deck in their rain gear, and just kind of hang onto the rail and barf into the ocean. Needless to say, a trip to town during these kinds of storms was a cause for some trepidation.

Ian's agenda for the day was that when they got to French Creek he would send his deck hand to downtown Parksville, to the government liquor store (all liquor was sold through government liquor stores) to buy a box of beers and bring them back to the ferry. He would consume them during the trip. When he got to French Creek from the noon ferry the whole scenario was repeated, as it was at the 3:30 crossing. Ian evidently needed three boxes to make it through the day. He actually handled it OK if he could sleep it off. He'd repeat the same process the next day. But if he was up partying all night, look out.

Several people told me that one time, while the crew was out to the liquor store, Ian fell off his stool and banged his head on the steel bulkhead. When the crew couldn't revive him, they had to call emergency. The Royal Canadian Mounted Police (RCMP) came along for the ride. They took one look at the cabin and busted Ian for driving a ferry while intoxicated. I didn't even know there was such a law. As far as I can remember, that was the only time he had trouble with the law, at least in regards to ferry driving. It's pretty hard to get busted on Lasqueti itself because there are no police.

Since there was virtually no retail business on the island, people had to go to Parksville/Qualicum to shop. This means they needed to have two cars, one on the island and one in town. If you needed to take a trip to town, and if you had your own car or were traveling with a neighbor, you would drive down to False

Bay somewhat early, to be sure you could get on the boat. If you had anything you wanted to take to the other side, you would have to carry it to the boat and stow it.

Trip planning could be tricky. If you leave on the early ferry you have from 9:00 when you arrive in French Creek until about 2:00 to be ready to re-board the boat. If you are without vehicle, which was my usual condition, you would already have a ride into town with someone, and sometimes you might do the whole shopping trip together. That was always great. It is several miles from French Creek to Parksville. The usual first stop for me was the Laundromat. Start clothes then rush off to do shopping, throwing stuff in the dryer and back to shopping. Most of the shopping was at the grocery stores and hardware shops.

If need be you would hit Buckerfields Agricultural Center, get all your business done, then start back to French Creek. There could be a massive scrambling, getting all the stuff everyone had acquired from the parking lot to ferry berth, stack it up and wait for the ferry to dock. If the weather's decent. Sometimes the ferry doesn't run because of weather. I've been stranded in town two times that I can remember. Bummer. After the boat arrives and is unloaded, the scramble starts. There is a narrow passage to the cargo hold, below the passenger deck, so it's pretty much single file. This is the island supply run, so you can see people lugging a lot of different stuff. Unless you hire a barge or have a friend with a fishing boat, this is the only way stuff gets to the island.

When reaching the island and the ferry pulls into the dock, the scramble starts again. A few cars can be driven onto the dock to load up, but access is one way and everyone is in a hurry. Lots of stalls and confusion. We all looked like a bunch of ants as we carried our stuff up onto the dock, waiting for however we would get the stuff home.

People always helped out their neighbors. It was never hard to get a ride down island, and at that time everyone helped each other loading and unloading cargo. The closest I could get to home was to Millicheap Road. From there I had to walk about a half-mile, with a very heavy load. In the winter it might be starting to get dark and I would have to walk through the woods. The trail was intentionally cluttered, so it would look unused. Fortunately, at the beginning of the trail I ordinarily kept a candle lantern (tin can with a candle inserted through the side), and matches, to light the way home.

In the woods candle lanterns are far superior to flashlights. Flashlights send out a focused beam so that you can see what's directly in front of the lens and nothing else. The candle lantern diffuses the light, and you can see a wider path. At this point, this has been a pretty long and arduous day.

Regarding cars. As I said before, in order to have any kind of mobility you had to have a car on both sides, an island car and a town car. Obviously the good car would be the town car, so most island vehicles were junk heaps. Well, who cares? There's only about fifteen miles of road on the rock. I can say that there were a number of dangerous vehicles on the road at that time.

Often there was no regular mechanic on the island. If you had serious trouble and you really wanted to fix it you could hire a barge to take it to the other side to be worked on then barge it back home. Nope. Most of the time, the clunkers would end up near the edge of the road for eternity. It has been an enduring problem over the years.

The government requires that you separately insure each car, and there is no island discount. Good luck. When the RCMP would send patrols of Mounties, they originally sent them on the ferry. Their proximity made some folks a bit uneasy. They would set up road blocks and check for valid driver's license and insurance.

If someone was able to alert the island that the cops were coming, the telephone tree would start working, so everyone with or near a phone would know. Later, as the raids became more elaborate, the RCMP would barge a pickup across and deliver the troops with a hovercraft or helicopter. Funny, they always waited for the day the store sold gas to raid.

I remember one time I walked home from False Bay with a very heavy pack and I didn't want the Mounties to see me. Every time I heard a car coming I'd dive into the woods. When I reached the corner of Lennie Road and Main Road, I saw about six cars parked on Lennie just short of Main. Access roads were private property, so the RCMP couldn't do anything but glare. Good citizens and bad citizens were waiting for the Mounties to leave, before they got on the road.

There were things that the Mounties had against us other than driving without insurance, or putting boat gas in our cars. Marijuana and illegal Americans were also on the agenda. Good citizens and hippies shared a dislike for the police.

Lasqueti had a telephone system donated by B.C. Tel., from the obsolete equipment inventory, which had a few numbers and five or six party lines. They only had four-digit numbers like 8843. That worked for us on the island, but when someone off-island tried to make a long-distance call, there were problems. You'd tell friends, "Now, you will get an operator in Vancouver who will tell you that there are no four-digit numbers in B.C. Tell the operator to put the call through to Nanaimo, who will then complete the circuit." You had to route your own calls. There was no government-supplied electricity (hydro, as it's called up there), and no public water system. There was a two-room school that had a principal and two teachers; a post office; and a two-man road crew who tried to keep the dirt and gravel road in some kind of shape. There was also a government wharf, with the wharfinger hired usually from the local populace.

Many items that are not considered important on the mainland were very important on the island, among them newspapers. Paper was always scarce, so newspapers were very precious. Really good as fire starter, good for insulation, garden mulch, and wrapping stuff. Nancy Varney had the *Vancouver Sun* mail her large quantities of old papers. She doled them out to anyone who wanted some. It was also fun to find out what was happening in the world three months ago.

For entertainment that doesn't require strenuous effort, reading was the favorite. Books were very valuable. You read whatever you could get your hands on. Everyone on the island was well-read. Nancy Varney had hundreds of books, and she acted as a sort of lending library. The provincial library had a lending program through which you could order books by mail, and they would be delivered and returned, all for free.

We were a real pain in the ass for pretty much all official entities. There were many islands in the gulf far more primitive than Lasqueti, but we were up to three hundred wild people who did things our own way. Whether it be the school administration or the constabulary, they didn't know what to do with us. One potential problem example was that at one time the local school principal and the local B&B and bakery queen were living together, and the principal's wife was living with the primary school teacher, stuff I'm sure the district didn't want to know anything about. They did, however, accomplish amazing things at the school.

As noted before, the only real businesses were the store/pub/gasoline dispensary, a propane dispensing operation run by Cecil Varney, and the False Bay Inn, a very limited-use facility run by Nancy Varney. That's it folks. One thing conspicuously missing was an RCMP station. That's one of the reasons they didn't like us. They didn't know what was going on.

Pete Forbes and Tom Millicheap had a fishing company in Scotty Bay at the north end of the island. They built and fished steel seine boats that worked the west coast to the Gulf of Alaska.

So the oft asked question, "How do you live?" At the time I arrived, there were very few ways to create capital on the island. As seen, the kinkiness of the ferry system precluded the ability to commute to Vancouver Island, ergo no welfare. Oh, I'm sure there were a few scams going on but nothing major. We were pretty much on our own.

Some people had gigs in Vancouver or Victoria, and made some money some way. Nobody pried too much into other people's business. Oh, we would gossip a bit. The fundamental existential problem for many islanders was that there wasn't much work anywhere during the winter, so moneymaking was mostly during the summer. However, since everyone relied on their garden to keep from starving to death during the winter, they would have to abandon the garden for the summer unless they had partners. Some people worked in various aspects of commercial fishing, some planted trees, some worked in logging camps up north, a few hardy folks, mostly women, worked canning salmon, a really yucky job. Reaching mid to late summer without a winter money stash coming in was a very scary thing.

It was important to have diversified income sources. There was quite a bit of grunt work, and no one bothered to check legality. Actually, most Canadians were sympathetic to illegal immigrants, especially those from the U.S., even though some of us could be jerks. The pay was low but no one noticed. We were just too grateful to get anything at all.

Marijuana cultivation was a viable stay-at-home job. Not capital intensive, at least in the early days. Very labor intensive and very nerve racking. Most growers just used small cultivation as a part of their diversified income. The stress came from the fact that enemies to this endeavor include mice, deer, weather, rip-offs, and cops, in about that order. If you get to cultivation without disaster you need a drying shed, to dry the harvest and then groom the weed. This would have been an excellent time for a police raid but they never did.

The next step was to figure a way to get it to dealers in town. And if you get this far you hope like hell you get paid. Let me state that I don't know anything about this from personal experience. It is information I have been told by others.

You do get to stay home for the summer, which is pretty nice considering the other nine months. Each season has its joys and sorrows.

There were a few professional growers, as there always are, whose life was pretty much devoted to cultivation, and they made it hard on the rest. It didn't help when the dealers in town started advertising Lasqueti Green to their customers, even though very little local stuff got to town. Of course this all took place in the '70s and early '80s.

Many of the islanders were legal Americans. Probably because there were no police, there were a few illegal Americans, as well as a number of other nationalities, including French, Germans, Aussies, Israelis, English, and several from the Balkans. This was true all over the coast but the cops and the media really loved Lasqueti. An island is an easy target because it can't move.

It must be noted that the island had a large population of twenty- to thirty-year-old ladies who were (and are) absolutely delightful. Some in partnerships, some single, who could take care of themselves on all sides. Respect was not gender related. No whining. The only complaint I remember would be some pretty little gal saying, "I can't help it. Goddamnit, men are just stronger." Not a complaint, just exasperation; but none of them shirked, ever.

Mara left Takilma for Lasqueti Island. I left some time later, originally bound for Hope, B.C. I had spent the previous summer in Hope, but my plans changed when I got a letter from Mara implying, in my mind at least, that she was in deep water being illegal with two kids. She wasn't sure how to play the fugitive game. There's very little you can do to prepare yourself for that kind of life. I decided to visit her and find out what was happening, and see if I could help.

When I got to Lasqueti I said, for the second time (the first being Takilma), "Holy shit. This is the place." We decided to stay together on the island. This was about as far from the real world as I was capable of getting at that time in my life.

Although I was disgusted with Homo sapiens in general, I found islanders to be quite interesting. You were either an islander or you were not. The divisions fell as follows: full-time islanders, regular summer people, visitors, everyone else. Some of the semi-locals lived on boats and mostly drank in the pub. But if you stayed for the winter and put down roots, and showed that you were going to be an islander, you entered the community.

Islanders by nature know who they are. There are no suburbs. All those who are bound by the water are islanders. The region was economically poor, and people had to work together and really help each other. There was much work exchange, and not much money was involved.

So here I was, sniveling and hating all mankind, then fate-dragged into this wonderful community. Noooooo. . . .

We started the trip with about seven hundred dollars. Mara and her kids, Bret and Maia, were originally living in Billy's cabin, which was a pole shack covered with plastic. This was a very basic structure that was located at the bottom of a short, steep hill on a shelf just above the high tide line. The only advantage it had was that it was very hard to find.

At this time there were three shacks by the garden. Ron's reasonably nice shack, the log barn that had been somewhat fixed for habitation, and Billy's place. All of us were squatting. Mara and I decided to move to Sandy Point on the south side of Sandy Cove.

There were snags in the building process. We had no money and no place to buy what we needed, so we had to wing it. I built a lean-to for us to camp in and started scrounging. I spent forty dollars for plastic and staples for our staple gun. Mara made the basic design for an eight by twelve kitchen. I devoted myself to gathering materials. Beachcombing was very productive, of course. There were an amazing number of plywood hatch covers that had obviously been left unsecured on their boats. You can use it for anything.

The beaches are also cluttered with lumber that has been lost off the barges over many years. The ends were usually worn from endlessly being tossed from beach to rocks and they were different thicknesses but they were a Godsend. I was also able to acquire some shake bolts so I made a number of shakes. I found an abandoned plastic dome that had a lot of good lumber in it.

The house was pole frame with the poles made from dead fir out on the point. For the south wall I took the wall from the old barn, on the other side of the cove by the garden, which had fallen down. This wall was about four feet high and made up on half-logs attached to a two by four frame. I somehow got it down to the water and towed it across the bay at high tide in my little skiff, *The Banana Boat*. I got it up the hill to the house.

For tools I had a homemade pole ladder, a hatchet with a hammer head, a bow saw, a wood chisel, and a tape measure. I was well-fixed for nails, because my neighbor across the bay used to pick up boxes of discarded nails at the factories on Granville Island in Vancouver. Very handy. Ron had a boat so he could transport stuff from Vancouver to his front door (at high tide), easily. When I finished the kitchen, I started on another pole structure, this time a ten by ten sleeping house. I had to use poles, I didn't have any lumber. It had a dirt floor but it was covered by a carpet so no dust got in. It was very airy and cozy. It had a little loft, which was Maia's room.

These shacks were our anchor. Our first winter on the Island I got a very severe case of the flu. I was in bed for several days and we were running low on firewood. The neighbors wanted to help, but I was adamant that by God I was going to do it myself. They did bring the doctor down to look at me. I was an islander. That term was explained to me by Boho Ron, my neighbor across the bay. He looked at me and said, "Well, I guess we are full-time residents of Lasqueti, meaning that we are too broke to get off island for the winter."

At our lowest that first winter we were so broke that I was trading home-brew beer for kerosene. It was mid-winter, the days were short, and we only had enough kerosene for one lamp, for two adults and two kids.

The island store was at False Bay, which handled a few food and hardware items; it was run by the Louie family, I believe. Louie was the fuckup son of a big Chinese business family, so he and his brood were banished to Lasqueti Island. You can bet they loved being stuck in this God forsaken place and having to deal with these . . . hippies! Overall the store was not a very congenial place.

One time I walked and hitched the five miles to False Bay, with an empty kerosene can and a dollar twenty-five in my pocket. When I told the clerk that I needed a dollar and a quarter worth of kerosene she said, "Our minimum sale is a dollar seventy-five." When I told her that was all the money I had, she told me that I was really something. Wasting her time. Needless to say, the Louies were not considered islanders.

Later that winter Mara got some work on an oyster farm on the bay, donning gumboots and slickers. Hard, grubby work. I did some work for the Varneys, digging out a basement for an addition to their main house. I thought moving dry clay with pick and shovel was bad. I found out wet clay is worse. We shoveled it into the pickup bed then dumped it in potholes in the driveway. This work was hard, but again a Godsend.

Everything on the island had to be shipped from Vancouver Island or the mainland. The Louies would sell small amounts of kerosene and gas at very inflated prices. The poor folks survived by several families getting together and paying a barge to bring fifty-gallon barrels of fuel to the island. The partners would take it someplace, and divvy up the fuel. Just living was a lot of work. One of the positive things about the island was that for weeks I would be without money, or identification. No one to check ID and pretty much nothing to spend money on.

So here we were, down to our last kerosene, and Jody and Heather showed up with a third share of their fifty-gallon kerosene drum, as a gift. Wow.

A while later I told Mara, "Goddamnit, I'm starting to love these people."

She said, "Me too."

23
Food

Food takes on a totally new meaning when you live in a foreign country with no help from the government, unless it's to help you out of the country. Certainly it makes it difficult to afford yourself the luxury of vegetarianism. Not that I am against it or anything, I was practically a vegetarian for almost five years. But the thing is, when you live where there are plentiful fish and wild game, and you have very little money for food or anything else, it's almost necessary to eat whatever you can get your hands on.

Obviously gardening is a way of life in the bush, and gardening when you are poor, on a small island, in the Gulf of Georgia, can be an interesting experience. It's really quite amazing what stupendous lengths some people, like me and the rest of the folks who came through and lived for a while at Sandy Cove, go to for a garden.

When we first arrived on the island, the garden was rather small, probably about a hundred and twenty square feet, which was adequate for the four of us and the Pirate, who was living on the side of the bay near the garden. However, there were some territorial squabbles among neighbors and it was decided (not by me) that the garden should be expanded. That meant that I would expand the garden. I have read a lot about the rain forests of the equatorial region, and the vigor of plant growth, and I suppose it is more dynamic than along the Japanese current up north, but if so, I'm glad I didn't end up there. During four to five months up north you can almost see things growing. It is very difficult to keep berry vines and alder roots out of a garden. As soon as you start cutting down trees to let the sun in, controlling unwanted vegetation becomes a war, especially if all you have to control this stuff is a mattock and shovel.

I guess I should go through the development step by step. It was first decided that we would almost double the size of the garden. This necessitated cutting out countless salmonberries. The procedure was to sharpen the machete and get a good pair of gloves and start whacking at the branches, which, being quite limber, are hard to get a good swing at. After several days of this you can get close enough to the main shoots (you could call many of them "trunks") for the real fun to begin, digging them out one by one. This is hard work, but is nothing compared to digging out the alder roots after cutting the trees down. Roots go all over the place and they don't want to come out. Mattock time.

Now we finally have the worst of the stuff cleared out, but what are we going to use as fence posts? Well there is cedar growing around, and splitting it is not too difficult if it happens to be clear. There is very little clear cedar on these islands because of the difficult growing conditions. So it's ax and wedge and mall, splitting through knots, twists, and what-have-you, trying to get enough posts, approximately eight feet long and triangular, six to eight inches on a side. I finally got that done. I borrowed a post-hole digger (thank God), and started twisting it through rocks and roots about twenty-four to thirty inches into the ground. I stuck in the posts, filled the holes with dirt and rocks, and then tamped; repeat: dirt, rocks, and tamp, etc. Finally the posts were all in. Now what do we use for fencing material?

I forgot to say that since we didn't have any money to buy any wire, these thoughts would ordinarily have been moot, but I remembered that there was quite a bit of old page and barbed wire at an abandoned homestead in the next cove. Dick, a friend and benefactor, and I rowed over to the homestead with a couple of Swede saws and a couple of axes.

My memory about having seen all of this wire was correct, however I hadn't looked at it too closely. It had been there for at least thirty years. The posts were all pretty much rotted away, but the wire was still there, running through jungles of salmonberries and through the middle of many alder trees, which had been small when the fence was first strung. It was a pretty tedious process hacking and freeing up all this wire. We did have an ulterior motive, however, for some of this wire was destined for a garden of a far different type. Getting this wire was a Godsend, no matter how hard the work. If you have ever tried to make a sturdy natural fence, you will understand.

Do you think of this as being theft or vandalism? Probably in a court of law it would be, if anyone wanted to push the point. Certainly, someone somewhere owned this fencing. On the other hand, there are not too many resources in the bush, and if something of use has been abandoned for a long period of time it becomes, in the eyes of the local community, fair game. Things do not last very long in that climate when not looked after. Hardware was a precious commodity. Anyway, only bush hippies would be caught dead with old rusted-out wire on their fences. All them city people like to have everything nice and new and shiny.

I guess you have to design your fence around whom, or what, you want to keep out of the garden. On our island the outlaws were deer, cattle, and chickens. Each of these varmints presents a completely different set of problems. Chickens don't usually fly too much except to roost at night. Sometimes you clip their wings in hopes that they won't be able to get to the bottom branches of fir trees. Anyway, when they're just doing their thing during the day, fighting, fucking, and eating, they're not likely to try to fly over the fence, especially if they've never been in the garden before. For stupid critters they have an uncommonly long memory when it comes to fresh greens. For chickens, fencing doesn't have to be too high. But it had better be impregnable near the ground. They can squeeze through a very small space. Page wire along with maybe some nylon fishnet will work for this level of security.

Cows are another problem entirely. They don't deal with life's subtleties like the chickens or deer, they deal in brute force. There were free-range cattle on the island at that time. Several herds wandered the island. They went where they wanted to go, and did pretty much what they wanted to do. One of the things they really liked to do was get into gardens. In my observation cattle are pretty stupid, but they tend to believe that fences, as well as all other obstructions, are there to keep them out of something good: probably greens or livestock feed, yum, yum. Several cows disappeared mysteriously over the years.

Cows are not by nature your good citizens, nor advocates of law-and-order. Their modus operendi when it comes to fences is that one of the cows will lean on the fence and several others will lean on him (or her), and they will do this for a reasonable period of time until they either knock the fence down, or forget why they're there. So to keep cattle out, the fence has to be very sturdy, that's why the cedar rails for poles. But you also need barbed wire strands. I'm not all that certain B/W works against a hungry cow, but you have to do it anyway. It's really infuriating when they get in the garden, because they only eat about a quarter of it, and they either walk on or shit on the rest. Very depressing.

Deer. Now here's a not-too-bright critter (sorry, Bambi). They can walk right by a garden protected by a four-foot-high fence for years and never even look, and you feel pretty smug. But if one of those bastards should ever find out what is inside, there's almost no way to keep him (or her, in fact most often her) out. One thing that helps is building it high, about seven feet, with either page wire (best) or about three to four strands of barbed wire above the page wire.

So the fence is now one height of page wire (about four feet), three rows of barbed wire (two feet), a little too short to keep deer from jumping over it. Also, a small deer (I am told) can jump between two foot strands of barbed wire. Boy, you talk about paranoia.

One thing that is very prevalent up in the gulf is cedar shakes and laths. The Indians even used cedar bark for clothing. And although the coastal cedar isn't very straight-grained or tall, with a chain saw and froe you can make a lot of handy construction materials. Want a box to put something in? Take out the froe, split several shakes, and nail them together. Cedar laths are used for many things, from sealing walls to threading through fences to keep the holes too small for the deer to jump through. Also, to make pickets so that the deer would think the fence was too high to jump. See? I told you. If you think deer are bad, I'll tell you what my experiences with raccoons have been like.

Actually, for me this whole effort was futile. The first year we were there, and one of the reasons for building a new fence, was that the cows got through the old fence. I built the new fence and I don't think any cows had gotten in for years, but the next year the deer got in. I don't know how in the Christ they got in; I had pointed pickets nailed in all directions and at all angles on the fence poles, but it seemed to be of no avail. Finally I asked one of the neighbors up the road to come down with a gun and try to pop one at dusk but, of course, for the next two nights the deer didn't show up.

I finally made the fence deer-tight and the next year the chickens got in while we were gone tree planting, and wrecked it again. The next year I moved away. However, I hear that the inheritors have had no problems with varmints, so I must have finally done the job right.

Now you have got the fence in and cleared most of the vegetation for a few feet outside the fence. Looking inside the fence you see alder stumps and roots. This is no joke. You have to hack through all of these damn alder roots with a mattock, then pull the roots out. My, my. And salmonberry roots, but these were quite insignificant compared to the alders. Once I worked all day to clear roots out of a four by eight-foot patch. Next problem, soil.

These islands are quite new geologically, and haven't developed an awful lot of soil in most places. Most of the organic material is made up of hardwood and conifer leaf mulch, and moss. I have read that lichen eat rock, and then moss eats the lichen and creates soil. There is a lot of rock, some mineral soil and a little bit of topsoil. Also, the rock is quite porous so it doesn't hold much water. Minerals also tend to leach out with the water, so the soil is usually mineral poor. And very acidic, being created by pine needles and leaves.

One good source of minerals is seaweed, of which there is an abundance; mostly when and where you don't want it. However, it is heavy as hell, mostly water until it is dried out. One time I dried a whole bunch of seaweed on some high rocks in the bay, expecting to take it up the hill without having to carry all the water. We had a high tide and a storm that night and it all washed away. Easy come, easy go. So we used to lug it up the hill (a steep hill, I might add) in gunnysacks slung across our shoulders, or heaped in a large wheelbarrow with one person pushing and another pulling. We composted everything we could find. I dug out the outhouse one time and composted it. Not a fun job.

Build the soil with compost and various kinds of animal shit. Like in India, the cattle are sacred partially because they fertilize the soil. It seems that cattle predated Monsanto. It was convenient if you lived in close proximity to a place where cows seemed to like to defecate. You go out with a couple of buckets and small shovels a-searchin' for cowshit. Actually, this can be kind of fun in the late fall when you're starting to get rock happy. Imagine having one of your major euphoric experiences happen when you open the door in the morning, and see that a whole lot of cows have decided to take a dump across the road.

Maybe, on a cold, clear day, I'd take a wheelbarrow, some plastic bags, and a shovel. I'd probably have a mushroom bag also. You could come home with four to five bags of manure and a pound or so of edible mushrooms from chanterelles, meadow mushrooms, and boletus. All a part of the food trip. It's one good excuse for exploring in the woods.

It took me about five years to learn thirty-five varieties of edible mushrooms. I had a couple of field identification books, but they weren't a lot of help. Fall, of course, is the prime time for mushroom hunting. All organic processes require water, so when moisture is abundant and the temperature is moderate, these things mostly do their stuff. The best varieties for eating (rather than collecting) are the ones that tend to grow in clumps rather than those which are more or less solitary. Takes too long to collect the solitary varieties.

If there is an open field near, you should be able to clean up on meadow mushrooms and puffballs. Some of the books say you should be careful of picking meadow mushrooms in the immature stage because before opening it is hard to tell them from the "destroying angel" amanita. Just make sure the gills are pink or brown. They produce for a long time and a lot of them seem to grow together, so if you want a mushroom omelet, just go out into the field and pick 'em. One of the things that makes life in the country enjoyable.

I never was too good at other types of wild edibles (except berries), but looking for food while walking trails is a very good way to observe the nature as you travel. My personal favorite, because they are a good spring and early summer mushroom, is the oyster mushroom. It grows on dead deciduous trees, mostly alder in the Northwest, and they are large and very prolific. Just after a spring rain, if you keep your eyes skinned you can come up with maybe ten pounds, in a very short time. They are very tasty, though slightly rubbery, and they dry very well. As a matter of fact, if your timing is right, if there is a short rain and then a hot spell, they will dry right on the tree. All you have to do is break them up and you have naturally dried mushrooms.

Well, this does bring up a topic about food in non-electric environment. Food preservation. Because freezing is out, except for short periods in the winter, the methods left are canning and drying. And eating on the spot, of course. I have seen a small deer disappear in a day and a half.

When you are really poor, and living away from civilization, nutritional requirements are looked at differently. If you don't have a local Safeway, regular good-paying job, or government scams, just feeding yourself uses a very large part of your energy. In our generally affluent society, we tend to take food for granted. The only people in our society who go hungry are the homeless, since they can't get food stamps or welfare.

It's too bad that we are able to take food so much for granted, because it decreases our ability to understand most of people and cultures of the earth. We talk about the struggle for survival, but we don't understand it from a gut level. This, I think, was what JFK had in mind in forming the Peace Corps. Giving Americans a way of understanding what most of the people in the world have had to deal with since we climbed down from the trees, or wherever we climbed down from.

So, back in those days a lot of time was spent speculating about what we really, really could do without. Well, there is always something else that you c-o-u-l-d live without. Like butter and cooking oil. Render different kinds of fats, including sheep fat, to eliminate the need for cooking oil and butter. Many bush folks have done this once or twice. Lamb fat does taste a bit strong, but it makes the flakiest piecrust I have ever seen. I think that we won some kind of poor contest, however, by evaporating sea water for salt.

For a winter food stash, our family of four would need oh, about a hundred pounds of wheat berries, fifty pounds of rice, thirty pounds of rolled oats, fifty pounds of whole corn (a bitch to grind up), fifty pounds of beans, five gallons of cooking oil, five gallons of black strap molasses, and twenty-five to fifty pounds of peanuts to make peanut butter. Raw peanuts are best to buy, because I think peanut oil gets rancid fairly soon after the nuts are roasted. However, if you get raw peanuts you have to be very careful roasting them. They singe very easily so there is often a lot of waste. Have to eat the burned ones. Oh damn. Also, don't get Spanish peanuts because the skins are bitter and have to be removed, a very tedious job. It's worth all the effort, though, if you like peanut butter. Homemade peanut butter is better than anything you can get in the stores. You also need a good grain grinder.

That Alberta hard winter wheat has very hard thick hulls, and is very difficult to grind. No need for Nautilus equipment to keep the muscles in shape when you hand grind some good old Alberta winter wheat.

You also need fifteen to twenty pounds of cheese, five to ten pounds of wheat germ, five pounds of nutritional yeast, ten to fifteen pounds of coffee beans

(Columbian), fifty to a hundred pounds of pinto beans, twenty-five pounds of split peas, one pound of bread yeast (if you don't use sourdough), a couple of pounds of baking powder (for the wimps), and twenty-five pounds of powdered milk. This pretty much takes care of the basic necessities. If you have these staples and anything canned up from last summer or out of the winter garden and if you can catch or hunt anything, you can kind of kick back.

Spices. I will tell you that with some spices and imagination you can cook up some very tasty meals. Very important when a lot of what you eat is basically bland. It is very important to learn how to use spices, as any vegetarian can tell you.

Fifteen pounds of hard tack provides a delicious and nutritious alternative to crackers, though it is more enjoyable if you have good teeth. Funny thing. The poorer you are in the bush, the better you eat. You can't afford junk. For my taste, you can add to the basic foods list: five pounds of buckwheat, twenty pounds of lentils would be nice, and smaller amounts of barley, rye, and millet (a delicious grain). "Purty good for bird seed," says Long Larry the Logger.

The secret, of course, is freshly hand-ground flour. There is nothing like it. I used to make a porridge in the morning with freshly ground wheat berries, rice, millet, corn, oats, spices (cinnamon and nutmeg), maybe a bit of vanilla, canned fruit, wheat germ, just a tad of nutritional yeast, some peanut butter (the secret ingredient), and blackstrap molasses, and I had a very tasty meal. You could use the same stuff and add some powdered buttermilk and baking powder to make pancakes or bread. Beats McDonald's anytime, though I'm not sure the kids would agree. Whatever the kids felt about this kind of food, they would eat every bite, none of this, "I don't like that." I was a pretty good cook, which helps.

Most years we could garden through the winter because the ground rarely froze. The winter veggies were pretty much Brassica family, cabbage, Brussels sprout, broccoli, and cauliflower. Now don't get me wrong, but this can constitute a pretty bland cuisine. You really begin lusting for fresh greens. Then, the day after the winter solstice little green heads begin to pop out of the ground. Many of them are stinging nettles. They are very plentiful and very tasty if steamed. You can almost feel the energy when you eat them. Don't touch them with bare skin. I used to go out with a pair of scissors and a bag. I'd just clips the tops off and they would fall into the bag. Meal planning and preparation was a very important and time-consuming part of every day.

24

Fed Up

In the late 1960s, when many young Americans fled to Canada, mostly to avoid Vietnam, they found, at least on the West Coast, fertile ground for cooperative effort. Eventually, Vancouver B.C., had a number of cooperative houses, a radio station, a food co-op, and finally a credit union.

Back in the U.S. the movement was beginning to break up, but of course the Canadians, being usually behind times, were not aware of this. The Canadian west coast infrastructure has always been somewhat primitive due to its vast distances, rugged geography, and relatively small populations. There is one major highway going north–south in the middle of the province and sort of one going west–east. Hundreds of communities are dotted throughout the province, with varying access to commercial centers; and coastal communities are in many places only accessible by water.

Because of the difficulty and cost of transporting food to outlying areas, food was very expensive and variety sparse, especially relating to food groups other than meat, potatoes, and oatmeal. A group of politicals got together in Vancouver to attempt to put a food distribution system into operation. This was the genesis of the Fed Up food co-op.

From the beginning, the obvious two political factions formed. The city people were mostly interested in politically "correct" food, many of them were expatriate Americans; and anything they could do to irritate the American government, e.g., food from China and Cuba, satisfied them. These folks were obviously mostly Americans, since Canada did not see either of these countries as an enemy. The other group was the cheap food coalition. These people, American and Canadian, lived mostly in the bush.

The Fed Up co-op included three to four full-time employees and a warehouse. The model was based on warehousing only, except for one storefront in Courtenay, B.C. Orders were compiled weekly. Each member community handled the details of food procurement in its own way, of course. The operation on the user end, specifically on Lasqueti Island where I was a member, was organized in the following fashion.

The island we lived on, being long and thin with relatively few vehicles, was broken down into three areas. The north end, where the main island commerce was conducted; mid-island, my group; and the south end. From the list of food available from the co-op, and there were impressive choices because Vancouver had many wholesalers, each member family would select the type and quantity of food desired. This information was compiled as a single order for the group, with quantities compiled as bulk rather than individual orders. The three group orders were then put together, to comprise a single island order. Members pre-paid at the cost of the food plus 10 percent for overhead. Frequency of order was up to the main group. We usually ordered four times per year.

Staffing requirements at Fed Up were met by commitments from the member groups, calculated by the average amount of money spent by the group. At the local level, the members who chose to go to town for the current week cycle were given twenty-five dollars and told, "See ya later." Winter duty in Vancouver was a coveted assignment for the dirt-poor islanders. I'm sure that many relationships and lives were saved by this cabin-fever-easing vacation to town.

The twenty-five stipend doesn't seem like much, but the amenities in town were a lot better than that. The worker was responsible for getting to town and getting back home after the week was up. Shelter was provided by rooming in one of several co-op houses in Vancouver. Having to room with several other people was no problem with bush dwellers, and having central heating, hot water, and showers were really a bonus. There was one free mid-day meal provided at the warehouse, which, since we had several tons of food within a few feet of our work area, was not a problem. I still dream about that food. And there was no junk food at all. The work was warehouse work and very hard, but for the bush people back-breaking work was the norm, not a problem.

Another advantage of this work sharing was that it provided a chance to tighten the movement, by establishing contact with people who would not ordinarily meet. B.C. is a vast province, with greatly separated communities. The trip to town was particularly good for musicians. The weather was generally pretty good when I was in town, and I made a good bit of change playing street music.

At the warehouse, the group orders from all over the province and Edmonton, Alberta, were compiled into a single order. Vendors were contacted, the orders placed, and then we waited for the food to arrive. We set up pallets for each group that was ordering that particular week. The vendors generally delivered on Tuesday and Wednesday. The bulk food was broken up to fill the group orders. This could be a delicate operation when dealing with liquids such as oil, molasses, and honey. Bulk dry food, as well as dried fruits such as raisins and currents, also had to be repackaged. If a particular product was unavailable we had to decide upon a viable substitute, which was occasionally a bone of contention when the order got back home.

I forgot to mention that the groups were responsible for transporting the food to the group home location. When the orders were finally filled, they sat on pallets until the group picked them up. This always meant acquiring a truck one way or the other, driving to the warehouse, and stacking the pallet(s) on the truck. Some locations were very difficult to get to. Terrace, up the coast near the Yukon border, was a trip of maybe eight hundred miles; very difficult and expensive miles during the ice and snow of winter. People in island locations had different problems. The Edmonton, Alberta, group had to truck the stuff through the Canadian Rockies.

On Lasqueti we used several methods of transport during the time I was involved. The most direct was to hire a truck to pick up the food at the warehouse, take the B.C. ferry to Nanaimo, and drive to the French Creek harbor. There were several options from there. At least once we hired the ferry to haul the food to the island. This required some coordination. It was helpful if the ferry, with willing hands to load the cargo, arrived in French Creek around the same time as the food truck. This actually happened on occasion.

Step two was to have a truck with helpers at the Lasqueti dock when the ferry arrived. When the food came to the north end, the yellow house, often unoccupied, was usually designated as the staging area for the island break-up operation. The food was off-loaded from the ferry onto the truck, driven up the hill, and then unloaded at the yellow house.

There would be work crews from the three island units waiting for the food to arrive. At this point a breakdown operation, similar to the breakdown into individual orders at the Fed Up warehouse, took place. Each of the three island orders were broken up, and orders, quantities, and prices were adjusted. At this point there was a lot of anticipation and excitement. Most of us had been living on oatmeal for several weeks leading up to this big event.

Each group was responsible for transporting its food to the group distribution point. For mid-island, this was usually at Arnie's Corner (corner of Lennie and Main Road). Again, the food was divided up into individual families, and adjustments made to the original order. There was always a lot of participation at the group breakout. It was important to find out who in the neighborhood ordered what, and who one wanted to visit over the next few weeks at about meal time. Of course, each family was responsible for transporting its food to the home location. In our case this amounted to several miles by backpack or by boat if we were lucky and the weather was good. Talk about pigging out when the food got home. Christmas is nothing compared to the food arrival from Fed Up.

During the winter all the transportation options contained uncontrollable variables. Just because someone, say a fisherman who agreed to haul the stuff from Vancouver to Lasqueti, promised he would deliver, didn't mean that he could or would. Using boats is always iffy. The trip would be contingent upon the weather among other things. If the food was loaded in the hold, you could hope that it had been cleared of fish guts and rats, and the boat didn't leak.

One time a fisherman offered to bring the stuff from Vancouver in his fishing boat. We would save a lot of money and hassle this way. The boat owner had a day job and was going to come across on the weekend. The weather was bad and he couldn't get across the gulf, so he docked in Gibsons, a short way up the coast from Vancouver, and went back to town to work. For a week the boat sat at the dock in Gibsons. Our survival was at stake, so there were some anxious moments on the island. Did the boat leak? God I hope not. We finally got the stuff, and it worked out OK that time.

Another time, one of the islanders offered to ferry the food from Vancouver. The weather was bad, and he lashed the drums of oil, molasses, and honey to the deck. The lashings broke loose and all the barrels were lost. Not so lucky that time. Eventually civilization, as in mass food transportation, caught up with us, and the Fed Up system no longer needed.

Living in conditions like this we really learned the concept of community.

25

Sandy Beach Brewery

When I was in high school I didn't drink or misbehave much. My family was somewhat prominent, with my father being a well-thought-of coach and athletic director at the high school, and my mother an elementary school teacher. I would have a beer with my dad occasionally, but no drinking and partying. I must have had some kind of fascination with alcohol, however, because I remember one of my friends telling me the recipe for homebrew.

No, I didn't drink in my hometown, but when I went away to college I tried to make up for lost time. After supporting college for two summers working in a saw mill, I got a chance to fight fires for the U.S. Forest Service at a station right on the middle fork of the Feather River, my favorite hiking and fishing spot. I really enjoyed the job that summer. I was there with my buddy Don Buchla, who several years later designed the Buchla synthesizer.

For some reason we decided to brew beer in an abandoned horse trailer on the compound. Of course, this was illegal for several reasons. We were under age, for example. As far as brewing beer and storing it on a government compound is concerned—I never read up on the law, but I suspect that it was not highly thought of.

It had been a long time since that friend had given me the recipe. The only thing I remembered was that I needed malt, sugar, and yeast. As it turned out, we put lots of sugar in the crock. When we decided to bottle it, the beer was still very sweet, but we didn't know anything about the dangers of bottling with too high a sugar content. We bottled it and stored it under the barracks. We tried some of it after a few days and got drunk as skunks. It tasted sweet, like cheap Champaign. I vaguely remember driving Don up to Bucks Lake to party. The road was really rough, sometimes a creek bed, and I think I was driving pretty fast, but I don't know. We obviously made it there and back OK but I don't remember much about the trip.

If you have ever made beer, you know what happens if you bottle it when it has too high a sugar content. It keeps working in the bottle, building up gas pressure, and then explodes. It can be very disconcerting and messy.

One night when the whole crew, including both bosses, were lying on our bunks, talking about whatever guys talk about in those situations, we heard "Bam!" followed by a crack. It sounded like a gun going off and then the bullet striking something.

My boss said, "What was that?"

I made a smart retort, "I don't know." I did know, however. That sound was one of the bottles exploding, and the cap hitting the floor underneath our beds.

Don and I hardly breathed until the older folks finally went to sleep, and we snuck out and hid the bottles in the woods, risking one blowing up in our arms.

The next time I tried my hand at brewing came the next year at college. I had several friends, also engineering students, who were brewing beer. I used to visit them to study, while drinking beer and watching their fifteen-gallon-per-batch operation. I found that ingesting copious amounts of beer while studying was not conducive to transfer of information between short- to long-term memory, so I slowed down on the intake after the first few days. However, since my roommates and I liked our beer, and we didn't have much money, we decided to do up five gallons of our own. I can't remember how good it was, but I know that it was better than the stuff we made up in the woods.

Twenty years later, during the first traumatic winter we spent on the island, we were totally destitute, and I certainly couldn't afford to purchase liquor. Homemade beer and wine were an important part of life in the community. There wasn't a lot of money and there was no liquor store on the island. Commercial alcohol was (and is) very expensive in Canada. Also, if anyone bought beer in town to take back to the island, and if they wanted to quaff one on the boat, they were honor bound to share, so it would be hard to get home with any left.

Fruit trees and blackberries flourished on the Rock (our fond nickname for Lasqueti). There were a large number of early transparent apples, which were only good for juice anyway, so lots got converted into wine. Crush the apples then squeeze them with rack and pinion or screw. It was a lot of fun. Sticky juice all over everything. The wasps liked it too, so we would work, while fending off hundreds of yellow jackets.

Winemaking was illegal in British Columbia unless you got a permit from some ministry or other, but of course everyone ignored the law. Everyone, that is, except Ed, a very nice well-to-do American, who was somewhat ignorant of the vagaries of Canadian bureaucracy. Everyone told him he was asking for trouble if he applied for a permit, but he just didn't feel right about the whole thing.

He sent in his permit application, and several weeks later the RCMP came down on him like the invasion of North Africa, trying to find out what the hell he was up to. I'm not sure anyone had ever actually applied for a permit before. Anyway, Ed was not a pot grower, so he was clean, and the cops finally left shaking their heads. Crazy Americans. Permits. Sheesh.

We lived across a small inlet from the Pirate. The Pirate had a checkered past. He had run away from home and joined a carnival in his teens. Later he had lived in Vancouver, and had been a house painter as well as a small-time thief. He obtained a nice nineteen-foot clinker skiff, moved to Boho Island

and later to Lasqueti. He had been known to boost a few things from time to time, and I heard that he had "fuckin' near been lynched" one time up north on Vancouver Island.

He used to make winter raids on summer cabins occasionally. At this time, 1976–'77 it was still possible to run freebooting operations in that part of the world, especially during the winter. That began to end when CB radios became more popular, and civilization and instant communication generally settled in.

I've had a number of people tell me that they had tried to make beer and didn't have any luck. I find that hard to understand. Turning sugars into alcohol is one of the most fundamental biological reactions. If you simply mix a sugar substance with water, at moderate temperature, the sugar will turn into *something*. It may be alcohol or it may be some form of vinegar, but it will turn. If you mix some yeast in, it will certainly turn to alcohol instead of vinegar, simple as that.

From my limited knowledge there are two distinct types of brewing, ale and lager. I have never brewed lager. It requires special "bottom fermenting" yeast, and works for a long period of time at relatively low temperature. It always seemed rather arcane and complicated. For ale, you can use pretty much any kind of yeast, throw all the stuff in water at about seventy-five degrees and let it turn into ale, then bottle it after a couple of weeks. Just my kind of operation.

Don't get me wrong. I like beer. A lot of people drink a lot of products technically called beer, such as Budweiser, but I really like the taste of good beer. It's funny, hops were introduced into ale centuries ago as a preservative. The first people to drink it must have said something like, "Hoot, mon, what ha' ye' put in the ale? Cat piss?" But for some reason, over the years people have learned to enjoy the bitter taste of hops, and for some, the more the better. If you want to tell the beer aficionados from the drinkers, serve thick hoppy brew and see who drinks it.

Malting barley causes the starch in the barley to turn into sugar. In rural areas at times in the past turning grain into alcohol was, and in some places still is, an economic necessity. Shortly after the American colonies federated there was a Western incident called the Whisky Rebellion. The crux of the problem was that the Western farmers could grow grain, but there was no economical way to get the huge bulk to market before it spoiled. What to do? Turn it into whisky. Preserve it and reduce the volume, so to speak. Is that why the process is known as distillation? I don't know. The government decided that the whisky should be taxed, while whole grain should not. The Westerners were outraged and rebelled. It has always been thus between the city and the country. Anyway, barley, corn, wheat, and rice can be turned into sugar if you know how, and have the patience. I tried malting my own barley once. Over a woodstove. Ha.

As I remember the process, you start out by cracking the grain, then put it into a sieve or can with holes in it to keep the chunks out of the mixture; then immerse it in water kept at a constant temperature between something like 159 and 162 degrees for a long time. I can't remember how long. Try that on a wood stove, hanging a candy thermometer from a rafter, and trying to keep the temperature constant. Not fun after the first time. Buying malt in a can is more appealing. Buying hop-flavored malt is even better.

I found bottle accumulation to be a problem also. I didn't have any, and neither did anyone I talked to. The solution was to check out the dump and the ditches along Main Road, walking around with a gunnysack over my shoulder. My God, were some of those bottles grotty. Some had been left with a little beer in them, which got moldy of course. Slugs really like beer, so some of the bottles came equipped with mud, mold, and their own dead slug. Not too much profit in trying to determine the history of those bottles.

You need a lot of twelve-ounce bottles if you are going to make beer. Twelve to thirteen bottles per gallon. So if you make ten gallons, that's a hundred and thirty bottles. I managed to acquire a sufficiency of bottles eventually. The next problem was how to clean them up, given that I didn't have running water at my cabin.

I decided to do a pre-clean in the salt chuck. I knelt in the cold wind and cold water, and cleaned over a hundred bottles as well as I could with a stick and bottlebrush. It was terrible on the hands, as well as on the back and knees. I then rinsed them with fresh water. Fresh water was always a problem, since we didn't have running water. I finally evolved a reasonably efficient system to obtain clean water. The creek was about a hundred and fifty yards across the bay. The Pirate thoughtfully put in a plastic pipe from the dam up the creek down to the bay, and that was a help.

The procedure was to wait for a high tide, put four five-gallon buckets in the dinghy and row across the pond. At high tide I could row right up to the water pipe, pull the bung out of the pipe, and fill the buckets. Then I would row back to my side of the bay. This was where the process got a bit tedious. These buckets were in imperial gallons rather than U.S. gallons, or one hundred and sixty ounces instead of one hundred and forty-four ounces. So let's see. Water weighs sixteen ounces to the pound. So that's a hundred and sixty ounces or ten pounds to the gallon. Five gallons then weighs fifty pounds. Carrying two buckets at a time, or about a hundred pounds, up the hill, can be real heavy. It wasn't a far walk, but you could seriously strain something in your body if you weren't careful. Let us just say that we were quite careful with the use of fresh drinking water.

In wet times we had a catchment system, to get rain water mixed with old leaves, sawdust, and filtered by old cedar shakes and tar paper from the roof. It works for washing dishes OK, but I don't know about brewing beer. It probably would have given it an interesting flavor at that.

Now we have the water, and we have sort of cleaned the bucket we are going to make the beer in, by rolling it around in the salt chuck. We put some cold water in the bucket, then some hot water we boiled on the stove, until it feels like about eighty degrees. Next we pour in some sugar and a can of hop-flavored malt, and I stir it around with a fir branch. I was telling one of my beer making friends about my technique one time, and when I reached the fir branch part of the story, he just threw up his hands in disgust. The last stage is to pour in some yeast and stir it around to dissolve it, cover the bucket with a cloth to keep spiders and mouse turds out and, if the bucket is in a reasonably warm place, it will be ready to bottle in about two weeks.

The rule of thumb about malt/sugar is one pound per gallon of water will give about five percent alcohol, which is a reasonable potency. I guess you tend to use your thumb a lot when you live in the bush. You can go as high as your yeast will ferment before it dies of alcohol poisoning, about 12 percent for bread yeast, but if you make it that potent you had better drink it judiciously if you want to live and not hit the rocks on the way home.

The bottling process is probably where people have trouble, if they're going to have trouble brewing beer. The wort needs to contain .one half percent sugar at bottling time in order to develop an acceptable head. Much more and it will blow up, and too little it will be flat.

There are three ways that I know of to get the proper amount of head sugar in the wort. The easiest, obviously my favorite, is to bottle the beer when you get the proper percent sugar. To do this you need a good beer hydrometer to test the specific gravity. When it is right you just bottle up the stuff. There may be some sediment in the bottle, but if it has sat long enough, when you drink it the sediment will be reasonably solid, so you just develop the touch to decant beer into a glass without disturbing the sediment.

The next two methods are very similar. If for some reason you want the beer to finish working before bottling, let it go until no more bubbles are coming up, bottle it, then add enough sugar to give it a head. Let's try out the old math. Well, I'll cheat on the first method. Simply put 1/2 teaspoon of sugar in each bottle before you cap it. The down side of this is, first, it's a lot of messy work; and second, it's hard to get the same amount in each bottle, so each one will taste a little different.

The third method is to wait until the beer finishes working, decant it into another container, then dissolve enough sugar in warm water to make a head. Lets check out the old maths, eh? Remember this was in Canada. If one pound or sixteen ounces of sugar will give one gallon of beer 5 percent alcohol, how much to make the content .5 percent? Obviously 1.6 ounces of sugar per gallon of beer. You want the sugar in solution to diffuse evenly in the beer. The only time I made a bad batch was when I allowed the beer to work all the way out, and for one reason or another I didn't bottle it right away. After a day or two I tasted it and it was a bit vinegary. I restarted it and bottled it. This was not the best beer I ever made, but no one ever protested.

When is the beer ready to drink? Well, it starts to get a bit of head after about three days. It is acceptable after a week; though it doesn't have much body, it tastes pretty good after two weeks; and from then on up to about three months it just gets better. Some friends I taught how to make beer ended up drinking it all before they got to the bottling stage. One of them told me, "I don't know whether to bless you or curse you for teaching me how to make beer," as he dipped it out of the bucket.

But this was all later. As I think I mentioned, the Pirate liked his alcohol, though he couldn't hold it very well. I don't know if he got into serious trouble on Vancouver Island, but the RCMP knew him, and it wasn't unusual for them to follow him around when he went across. He was busted a couple of times for DUI and at least once for shoplifting. I got the idea that if he could get his alcohol on Lasqueti, rather than the big island, he would have a better chance of staying out of jail.

I didn't have the beer-making equipment or the supplies to make it, at that time. I also didn't have the money to buy any of these things, or the malt and sugar. The Pirate, however, had all the equipment needed, inert siphon hose, bottler, caps, and hydrometer. I broached the subject with him. If he would give me his tools and provide the malt and sugar, I would brew the beer and share it with him 50/50. He really smiled at this, and the ladies up the corner thought that it would be good for him to stay home and get polluted rather than being followed around by the cops on the other side, so the Sandy Beach Brewery was formed, brewing fifteen gallons at a crack.

For a while things went pretty well. I managed to stockpile quite a bit of beer, under the bed in Brett's old cabin, and this was fun. One of the things the connoisseurs who do everything perfectly miss is having differences in the batches of beer they make. It's kind of like gardeners who have to tame everything in their yard; not letting anything get out of hand. I really had a good time pulling a bottle out of a batch and trying it, then trying some from another batch. And think, "Oh, I remember this batch."

One time I had a party with about ten people at the cabin. I kept pulling out different bottles, and telling their history. Blood Sugar Sam was there, and Sam was not shy about his evaluations of people and things. He didn't usually drink too much, but he seemed to be into it that day. His father had been in the military, and Sam had grown up in Europe. He kept sampling my beer, and comparing it to various European brews. Mostly mine didn't fare too badly by comparison. One batch he tried, however, reminded him of a particular French brew. "That is not good," he remarked.

I had enough beer that I was able to trade for some saw blades and kerosene, so I guess I was a bootlegger for a short time.

Well, the Pirate spent a lot of time being drunk, and pretty soon he was drinking up his share of the brew, and occasionally sneaking over and getting into mine. All the neighbors were getting alarmed at this turn of events. No one thought he could drink that much. Finally he started worrying about his liver, and decided that he didn't want to play anymore. As I recall, I kept the tools, but Sandy Beach Brewery went out of business.

26

The Great Tree Planting Venture

Summer was coming on, and as always happens, a group of the less responsible bush hippies just hadn't gotten their summer money trip together. In the North Country you have to get your money for the next winter during the summer. For one reason or another Mara and I weren't fishing, or working in a food booth at the craft fairs, or growing illicit herbs, so we were feeling a little glum and contemplating another winter of oysters and beans. I must admit, though, that it had been a fun summer so far. Then David B came along with his big plan to start a tree planting cooperative.

He came to the island and called a meeting for everyone who was interested in making big bucks planting trees up north near the Yukon border. All the down-and-outs came to the meeting, of course. Even if it didn't pan out, it seemed like a good excuse for a party. I took my guitar. I think the meeting was at False Bay on the nice hillside between the yellow house and the False Bay Inn.

We were sitting on a hillside on a beautiful day, probably partaking of some exotic herb or other, and listening to David present the lovely vision of each of us earning two or three thousand dollars, and at the same time communing with nature in some of the most beautiful and primitive country in the world. His plan was that everyone who joined the venture would put up a hundred and twenty-five dollars to front for food and equipment needed for the trip. We would hire a cook, and everyone would be responsible for their own shelter, transportation, etc. Mara and I pungled up two hundred and fifty dollars, that totally exhausted our money supply, and signed on.

We didn't know at the time that David had come in with a ridiculously low bid, which was the reason he got the contract in the first place. Usually, in contract situations, you have your crew trained and ready to go before the contract is obtained. If you're lucky, it isn't unusual out there to be able to clear two thousand dollars or so in three to four weeks, and that amount of money will take care of quite a few groceries, barrels of kerosene, and bottles of propane in the coming winter. A part of the allure of this kind of enterprise is also the sense of adventure and travel. And you're not signing your life away, it's only for a few weeks. If you were really lucky you could actually make enough to spend the winter in Mexico.

We were a mixed group. Some of the folks in the venture were the drifters, who winter in Mexico and summer in Canada and other places. Several people were Yanks visiting the island, and it seemed like a good way to have an adventure and make some money at the same time; illegally, of course, but on our social level that was neither here nor there. But most of us were the indigenous poor folk who maybe had not been off the rock since last summer. I almost forgot, of course Mara and I were illegal too, but we had been in Canada so long that we kind of felt like we belonged, and we had many friends who felt the same about us. I suppose that having lived illegally for so long, being slightly on the outskirts of the law was just a way of life. It sort of added some fun to life. Sometimes, but definitely not always.

David was a Scorpio with a long line of bull, and although we were pretty aware of that fact, and since he was an off-islander we were naturally a little suspicious of him, we decided to take the plunge and sign up. Hey, what did we have to lose except a hundred and twenty-five dollars? What's the matter, no gambling spirit? Actually, we should have been a little more suspicious of him, if only because of the fact that he was willing to hire us.

We started making preparations for the great expedition. The first thing we found out was that he was a vegetarian. That should have been the tip-off. Pardon to any vegetarians listening, I used to be one myself. But there are vegetarians, and then there are Vegetarians.

David was a Capital V vegetarian, as he was a capital anything he was into at any given time. This was not an unusual thing, a tree planting camp being divided by food preference. We seem to need to be divided by something, so I guess food is as good as anything else. But I doubt if you will ever see a logging camp divided between vegetarians and meat eaters. Naturally we had a big squawk about it and he finally allowed us to buy some meat. Since meat doesn't keep very well without good refrigeration in the middle of summer, and all kinds of varmints including bears like it a lot, he probably had a point. At least for practicality. But the real point was that we weren't acting like proper city Sierra Club hippies, as far as he was concerned. We had a couple of mountain types in the group like Hawk, who fancied himself as a mountain man á la Grey Owl, a famous Canadian mountain man during the first half of the twentieth century; and Heather, who built wooden boats; and an Indian, Haida Bob. To them, saying they couldn't eat meat was like saying they couldn't have sex. So the deal started to sour from the beginning.

Mara and I got lucky and were promised a ride all the way up the interior with Darryl and Loretta, who had a Volkswagen bug. We started planning what to eat on the way up since we were pretty broke.

Haida Bob and Heather were going planting also, so we decided to try to get a young sheep for meat to take along for the trip. With a .22 rifle in hand we started to look for the sheep herd. Although there are a lot of feral sheep on the island, it is axiomatic that when you want to get a sheep, all the herds are either up on the bluffs or at the south end of the island; but we got lucky and managed to sneak up on a herd just on the other side of Conn Bay. Bob shot a yearling and we skinned and butchered it on the spot. In approximately an hour from the time we started to hunt we had a butchered lamb in a plastic bucket in the creek. Indians from the north don't waste a lot of time when it comes to harvesting wild game. It is interesting that it is not a macho trip for them, instead it is a job, a necessity of life, and Bob prayed to the soul of the sheep, and apologized for having to take its life. This looked like it was a good omen for the trip.

I don't remember too much about the trip north, except that where we spent the first night, a lake someplace between 100 Mile House and Williams Lake, where we encountered some mosquitoes. It seems that the farther north you get the more bugs there are around, and at the summer solstice they really start coming out.

The next day we started getting into the foothills of the northern Canadian Rockies. These are not like the ones eight hundred miles to the south. Up there they are much smaller and smoother from millions of years of being blown by the constant Arctic winds. This is the Peace River country. High, rolling peaks and fertile valleys. I suspect it's really a bitch around there in the winter.

Sometime in the afternoon we pulled into a small meadow valley along a fairly substantial river. We saw some other vehicles parked, and a bunch of our fellow planters plus some Forest Service people (with a helicopter) were conversing. David came over and told us that the weather had been especially wet that spring, and they were a bit slow about site preparation in the consequence. They had been trying to get a road through to the site, about ten miles in the interior.

There had been a fire road up there a number of years before, the Peace River fire being the reason we were up there to plant trees. That fire was pretty famous in its time. From traveling most of that fire track, I guess you could get an off-road vehicle in to the site without too much trouble if you were so inclined, and could even get one into the camp, with great difficulty. Two jeeps did make it up to camp, but it was much too soft for a D9 Cat, as they found out. They had tried to cut the road through so they could communicate by truck rather than helicopter, but the Cat had gotten stuck, so they sent in another one to pull it out and of course he got stuck too, so enter the valiant tree planters.

The plan was to stack all of our belongings in the center of the meadow and the helicopter would fly us and our gear to the site. Most of the folks thought that was OK, but a few of us idiots thought it was kind of incongruous going to commune with nature and flying in a helicopter, and hell, it was only ten miles, we could do that on a ROAD, too. Several of us started out hoofing it, Mara, Loretta, and me. Darryl, Loretta's boyfriend, was and probably still is a Leo. You couldn't have kept him from a helicopter ride with a dozen horses.

We told the rest of the crew that we would meet them at camp, and started walking through this beautiful country. We walked about four miles, until we came to a fair-sized stream bisecting the road, and it was roaring. I said, "Uh oh." I had grown up in river country, but the girls hadn't, and the immediate future didn't look so good. I took off my clothes and started into the stream. I noticed that about a hundred and fifty yards down the stream it flowed into the main river, and if you floated that far it would be very grim.

I got about a third of the way across the stream, and the water was up to my ass and really swift. And cold, but that didn't matter. I'm just being factual. I realized that it was no use trying to get the girls across, so I came back to shore. We got a little anxious because it was getting late, and if we went back to the staging area, and if we missed the last helicopter out, the three of us would have to spend the night without any warm clothes or sleeping gear, and it was still freezing up there at night.

While I was contemplating our predicament, Kim, who in a previous life had been the official Fool for the city of Vancouver, and Hawk, our resident mountain man, showed up. Hawk asked what was going on, and I told him we were having trouble crossing the river. He looked at me with disdain and said, "Don't you know how to cross a river?" I said I had thought I did, but I could be wrong. He rummaged around and found a tree limb to use to help brace himself, took off his clothes, and started into the river. Hell, I'd never studied river crossing, I had always just done it, including the time I crossed numerous creeks and river when I hiked the 211-mile John Muir Trail. I was kind of interested in finding out how it should be done. He got about a third of the way across, and I could see that he was having a real tough time of it. Barefoot in freezing water with millions of sharp rocks can begin to make a person think. The only good part is your feet get numb after a short time, and then it is up to your imagination to figure out what kind of torture they must be going through.

When he decided he couldn't make it, he worked his way back onto shore and put his clothes back on. I said I thought I was going to cross by myself and get help, but he and Kim wanted to go upstream and try to find a good ford, or maybe find a fallen log over the river. The canyon got steep and narrow and rough above us, and I was not interested in any of that, so they took off. I learned later that they found a place to ford the river and threw their boots to the other side. Two boots were lost and they were both for the left foot. They ended up with no usable boots. They seem to have managed to borrow footwear, but Hawk's mountain man mystique was temporarily blunted.

My idea was that I would swim across the stream and hustle up to the camp as fast as I could, we'd come back with ropes, and get the girls across the creek. It didn't seem like a great idea, but I couldn't seem to come up with anything better. I knew I could make it unless I got waylaid by a bear or something.

Actually, there was probably at least some chance of this happening, because later one of the Forest Service guys told us that there was an average bear population of twelve grizzly bears per square mile in the area, which is quite a lot. There may have been a dozen bears but I doubt they would all be grizzlies. He was probably just having fun with us.

I took off my clothes and bundled them up and left them with Mara and Loretta. I tied my sneaker laces together and hung them around my neck. I went about a hundred yards up stream and did a shallow dive. Man that water was cold. I drifted with the current diagonally down the stream and came out about across from the girls and quite a way above the junction with the river below.

I put on my shoes, and started trotting along the road to the camp. I must have looked a little funny out there, miles away from a human being, bare-assed naked running along this old fire road that ran more-or-less parallel to the big river below.

The next part of this will show you how technology will jack with your head. Here I was in the Peace River country about seven miles northwest of the Alaska Highway on a washed-out logging road. The highway was on the other side of a major river, and there was no help unless I went all the way back to the meadow and tried to stop someone on the highway. At night. What I mean here is that it almost could have been a hundred years ago. The only reality was that I had to walk and run to the camp, and see what we could do about rescuing the girls. This is primitive country, low mountains, but not too much timber or high brush because of the fire.

I was trotting along the fire road on the river bank, with my head totally in the here and now of the wilderness. About ten minutes later I hear swish-swish-swish above me. I look up and there, hovering right over me, is this helicopter full of people, with their eyes about as big as saucers. They landed right next to me. Those jet copters don't make hardly any sound.

This was a real jolt. All of a sudden I wasn't in the wild north anymore, but might as well have been in downtown LA. The pilot, wearing his uniform (shades and a baseball cap) shouts, "Hop aboard."

I yelled, "There are two women across the creek back there. I'll just go on if you will go back and get them."

Now you may not believe it but I was not into this scene with the helicopter. I was partly relieved because I was worried about the girls, but I was quite content to play Nanook of the North without the intervention of this fucking helicopter. I think that this might have been a significant event in my life, because I had moved north trying to get away from all technology, and live as our ancestors had lived, and had been accomplishing this for quite a few years at this time, with a fair degree of success.

The helicopter pilot answered, "We'll get them, climb in." I climbed in, under the somewhat bemused gaze of the other passengers. About five minutes later we set down at the landing wc were going to use as a camp. A pile of our personal belongings and food were in the center, but our gear had not as yet been brought up, so I didn't have any clothes to wear. Someone gave me a beer though, so all was not lost. I think I needed it. I had just gone through about a century of evolution in ten minutes. I don't know what Mara and Loretta thought about hanging out by the river all alone. I guess it could be a little scary, but they were bush ladies and were awfully good at taking care of themselves.

The camp was on a shelf on the side of a mountain. Jack the cook had already set up a parachute for a cook tent cover and managed to cobble up a few tables, and he was in business. He was already kneading a big batch of bread dough. After all our stuff arrived we started to make camp.

Mara and I slept on the ground in Darryl and Loretta's tent. I can't remember too much about the tent except it did a pretty good job of keeping the mosquitoes and black flies out. For the uninitiated, black flies are a tiny bug that seems to live in low vegetation, and swarms of them fly out when a potential food source appears. The only good thing I can say about them is they make you forget about mosquitoes. They tear the flesh from exposed skin. They are tiny, so no single bite is noticed. Then you wipe your face and your hand or rag is smeared with blood. The wounds can get infected. It's just a miserable experience.

David tried to organize the camp like he usually did, with the Sierra Club crews he was used to dealing with, and we just looked at him like he was from another planet. We set up our camp like any group of crazy anarchists would. I heard David say, "I just can't believe the lack of camp discipline in this group." He was not happy. He should have been happy then, because things were soon to get much worse.

I should talk a bit about tree planting. Reforestation, of the areas turned into moonscapes by logging or fires, was one of the few fairly lucrative occupations for people who lived in the bush. If you didn't mind traveling to the job, you could sort of pick your spot. Even though logging was on the wane, there was no competition from loggers in the tree planting game. Planting was considered below their sense of dignity, and they would rather collect unemployment. There were two general flavors of planters: those who worked as a co-op, and those who were paid by the tree. The government pays by the tree and they don't care who gets the money. Contractors were the main providers of tree planting labor, and of course they would pocket a lot of the money coming in. Good planters could make a lot of money in a good day on good terrain. The co-ops deducted expenses and split the money more or less evenly. The crews were mostly friends and neighbors, so they didn't need too much managing.

For this job the two tools being used were the dibble, used to punch a hole in the ground, into which a live tree (with soil and roots in a little plug) was inserted. Just step on foot lever of the dibble, pull it up, insert tree plug into the hole, tamp the soil a bit, and go to the next spot. The other was called a hoe-dad in the U.S. and a similar tool in Canada was called a mattock. It was like a one-tined pick, but the pick had a flat, narrow blade used to dig the hole, so the dry-root tree could be planted. The procedure was to locate the spot to put the tree, raise the mattock, and then drive it into the ground all the way to the handle; pull back on the handle, which opens a V-shaped hole, pull a tree out of the container on your belt, place it carefully into the hole, pull the mattock out, tamp the soil, then move off to plant the next tree. The major problem is J-root. This happens if you don't dig the hole deep enough or you didn't notice that the root got jammed and planted it with the bottom of the root pointing up. This will kill the tree. They probably let a few J-roots pass. One bad planter can ruin a whole crew.

Tree planting is very hard work, requiring great skill. The managers of the forest decide how densely they want to plant, quite often ten by ten feet. I have heard that some contractors and planters stashed a lot of trees, so the government did a lot of inspecting. They would throw out a string with a weight on the end. Wherever it landed was the spot for the inspection. The inspectors would make a circle around the spot, inspect the area, and dig up all the trees. The inspectors would say, "There can be eight to eleven trees within that circle, otherwise you flunked. So you have to be fast, and careful when planting.

The traditional way to plant ten by ten is to line up a group of people, say six, sideways and facing the direction they will be planting. They space themselves ten feet apart, then start walking down the line and planting a tree every ten feet. You have to learn to pace ten feet, so you don't have to measure how far you have moved since the last tree. A problem that you don't have on a recently logged site is natural reproduction. Unfortunately, along with many other problems with our Canadian expedition, the Peace River fire had occurred a number of years before. Trying to see these hidden little trees, in all that brush was tough, but they will count against you in the inspection.

Really crack crews don't stay with the alignment, they kind of meander up the mountainside, but they can only do this because by now their whole world is marked off in ten by ten squares in their head. They know the forest. You can add to the terrain problems the fact that most planting happens in the off-season, winter/spring, and it can be a bit uncomfortable working outside in the Pacific Northwest. You spend a lot of time in snow and freezing rain, slogging up mountainsides, usually steep, with boulders and partially burned trees and stumps and brush all over, and then you try to locate the next tree spot. Regardless of rain and snow you've got to keep production up. You probably work six days a week, of course daylight till dusk, sleeping on cots in tents, often with snow on the ground. The job could go on for a month or more. My hat is off to tree planters, especially the large number of women who do this job. They are generally just not as strong as men, so the toll on their bodies is greater. For us, planting in July, cold and wet was not a problem.

Needless to say, we were not crack planters. In fact only two of us, David and Kim had ever contract planted before. I had done specialized planting for the Forest Service, so I knew the rudiments of planting, but had never done this kind of work. David tried to organize crews and spend a couple of days practicing before we actually started work, but most of us were all primed to make some money. We practiced for a short while then started planting for real, or something reasonably like real.

The inspectors where watching us and they just shook their heads. "Haven't you folks planted trees before?"

"Well, er . . . ah . . . no."

"Holy shit."

The whole thing was brutal. The inspectors tried to help us, to no avail. There is a time limit in the contract and obviously we would have a hard time meeting it. We were just a mite perturbed.

After another day or so, a helicopter landed and out jumped two well-dressed guys with ball caps, wrap-around shades, and clipboards. There was a big private conference. Oh, oh. I mean here we were, ten miles across that raging creek . . . what the hell were we going to do? I asked one of the inspectors what we should do. He replied, "I'd get on down the road as quick as I could."

We gathered in Dave's teepee. He pulled out some peyote buttons and we partook of them. I got my guitar out and started singing. I had been the backup and house band for a couple of years in Takilma, and I knew how to set the vibes with the music selections I used. It's sort of like the old theater organs before the talkies came in. Their job was to set and augment what was happening on the screen. My grandmother played theater organ. The point is, I could see that we were hurting on a number of levels, and I had to bring the energy together. The mood became a very mellow, semi-meditational. One of the crew, Rick, came up to me later and asked, "Do you know what you did in there?" There was a look of awe on his face. I sort of mumbled something, not wanting to tell him that I did know what I was doing in there. If he wanted to feel it was a small cosmic event then let it be.

The word came that we were cancelled out, and they would take us and our stuff out to the meadow in the helicopter. Everyone raided the kitchen, taking everything they could carry, then on to the copter and down to the meadow. Our belongings were in a huge pile in the middle of the meadow, and people were milling around aimlessly. David flew into Chetwynd with the Forest Service, to get the business straight. Sometime later they flew him back to the meadow. To show you how good David was, he talked the Forest Service guys into guaranteeing a check that was able to pay each of us twenty dollars for the road. They were really nice people. David also purchased a bunch of beer and wine. We scrounged all the wood in the area and lit a bonfire. Everybody unloaded their stashes, I took out my guitar, and we had a joyous party. The next morning twenty or so people walked to the Alaska Highway, to hitch back home.

A side bar to this story is that a couple of the crew had been picked up by an earnest young American who was on his way in his new jeep to "discover Alaska." The guys managed to talk him into joining the planting crew. His jeep was the only vehicle that made it up to the site and back. I have often wondered how he saw the whole trip. He'd started to Alaska, met and had been camping out with these really weird people for several days, then he was back on the Alaska Highway going north, and probably wondering if that loop he took with the Lasqueti crew had really happened.

Mara and I got a ride to Prince George, the hub of the middle of British Columbia. There was one highway going from Alaska to Vancouver and one going west to the coast at Terrace and east through the Rockies, and south to Calgary. We had been dropped off downtown by the McDonald's golden arches, and we sat on the curb trying to figure out how to get back to the highway. If a person is trying to hitch through a city, the worst place you can get stuck is downtown. Almost all rides are local and we didn't even know where the highway was.

After a short while a young guy, who was obviously a straight business type, came by and asked us our story. We gave him a short sketch and he said, "If you want, I will drive you to my condo and we can smoke a joint and I'll take you out to the highway." We couldn't refuse an offer like that so we went to his condo building, took the luxurious elevator, went into his swanky digs, and we smoked some very good stuff. He then drove us outside of town, where we could hitch or camp for the night. That encounter improved our morale more than somewhat. We had a bit of a rush, however, when we drove around a curve and saw about fifty RCMP, all decked out in the red uniforms. It was obviously a Mountie wedding, but for a few seconds we were sure we were going to get busted for something.

Our benefactor left us with a wave, and I scouted a nice little campsite away from the road and beside a small stream. We ate and had a good sleep and were back on the road early in the morning.

We got a ride from two women who were coming down from Alaska. Their carryall was pretty beat up by the time they got this far south. Up north the highway was much worse than it is today. They took us into Vancouver and dropped us off on Hastings Street, the heart of skid row. Mara went back to the island to take care of the homestead, and I headed south to Portland to try to get work and salvage our summer.

27

Goldendale

It wasn't actually Goldendale, it was Maryhill, on the Washington side of the Columbia River, about fifteen miles east of The Dalles, Oregon.

Following an abortive tree planting adventure in northern British Columbia, after losing the two hundred and fifty dollars representing about all the capital Mara and I had in the world, I struck out south to try to find some other work. Our situation was really serious. If we didn't get some money together pretty fast, we would be totally destitute the next winter, suffering our usual fate of semi-starvation. Just kidding, mostly. During all the time I lived in the bush I never missed a meal, though many of them were skimpy.

I hitched to Portland and stayed with friends there, looking for employment. I first went up the Columbia River gorge to the Hood River area, where I had picked before, but nothing was ready at the moment. It was too late for cherries and too early for pears.

Going to the Manpower Hall in Portland was the first time I had encountered indigent employment in the cities, and it wasn't a whole lot of fun. No matter how early I arrived at the hall, there was always a long list already up, and new job listings were not posted very often, so I became somewhat discouraged.

If you don't get a job by early afternoon, you will probably only get a couple of hour's work. That just would not cut it, so I was at least mildly interested when a new job notice went up.

About the third day I spent in the hall, an employer, a Japanese named N-----, put up a notice that he would transport several people to his farm, about fifty miles up the Columbia gorge from Portland. The laborers would work for two weeks at two dollars and sixty-five cents per hour, a nickel below minimum wage at the time, but hey, we were farm laborers, dig? Workers would be allowed to live in cabins, and would be furnished with food. The cost of the food would be deducted from pay upon termination of work. There was no way N---- was going to give cash to a bunch of winos.

It didn't sound great to me, but at least it was steady work, and I would have a pretty good idea how much I would make, better than waiting in the Manpower office for a miracle. I told them I would take the job and they told me to be back at the office at 11:00 p.m., when the truck would pick me up.

When I arrived at Manpower, I discovered that I was the only one who had volunteered. The driver, who I at first took for the boss but later found was just a worker like me, told me that the work place was a truck farm. The owner would take orders from distributors in Portland, pick what was ordered, then truck it into town. They had just completed their daily delivery.

I loaded myself, my guitar, and my pack into the back of the truck, laid out my sleeping bag, and slept all the way to the farm. Although the drive through the gorge is beautiful, there is not much to be seen at night from the back of an enclosed truck.

When we arrived I discovered that all the cabins were full, so I sneaked across the fence to Maryhill park, on the Columbia River, threw out my sleeping bag and went back to sleep.

At dawn I took stock of my surroundings. When you go east on the Columbia River Highway, the gorge is a beautiful conifer forest along craggy rock walls, very lush. After leaving Hood River it becomes very dry and arid in the summer.

However, along the river there are some rich loam shelves, facing south on the north side of the river, some of the best growing conditions I have seen. This was to be my new home for the next two weeks.

The shelf was perhaps a quarter of a mile deep and half a mile long, with the park between N---'s farm and the river bank. This was a gorgeous spot, and hotter than hell.

Later in the morning I started working. We got orders to pick some pears, and after that I worked with several of the Mexicans picking tomatoes. The work here was a lot different from any other picking I had done. Since I grew up in an agricultural community, I had done my first picking as a teenager: peaches in hundred–degree-plus temperature, and believe me I didn't like it. The fuzz got all over me and itched like hell, and you really had to work fast and smart to make any money at all. I didn't mind hard work, but this type of work didn't appeal to me. Actually, to be truthful I have always hated hard work but I have done a lot of it. It didn't kill me and I have always satisfied my employers, including myself.

In later years, after I dropped out of the white-collar world, I picked apples and pears in Oregon and Washington with some success, but there was no peach fuzz, and the temperatures were less than a hundred degrees. Mostly I found picking to be fun. Although the money is not great at best, the job doesn't last too long. Of course, in order to make any money you have to work as fast as you can, taking minimal breaks. I was always being humiliated by the Mexicans, who appeared to be working at a leisurely pace, but out-picking me about two to one, though I didn't do too badly for a gringo.-

But here I was being paid by the hour, and I really didn't know how to do this. When I started picking the tomatoes I straddled the row of plants and stooped over, and just started almost running down the row. I looked up and saw the Mexicans watching me like I was a lunatic, while they were just ambling down the rows. I finally realized what was going on. No one works faster by the piece and slower by the hour than a Mexican. Labor was all these workers would know for their whole lives, and there would be no surprises for them. There is no nobility in labor, it just is. If you can stretch out a job, so much the better.

Most of the workers in camp were hoboes, and a few bums. Hoboes are mostly rural folks, many of whom have some fixed address, at least a post office box somewhere, and many get minimal money from the government, maybe military retirement or disability. They ride the rails because they like to. One of the reasons they work is so they can go to town and get drunk and laid. They do tend to have an affinity for alcohol of any kind. This farm was particularly popular with the hoboes, because the Wishram, Washington, freight switching yard was within walking distance. Hoboes on their way to party in Portland would drop off and pick up a bit of change, then head out.

Bums are usually city people who end up on skid row, and panhandle for money. Hoboes don't beg, or at least they don't cop to it. In the pecking order the hoboes are on top and the bums are on the bottom. We had some of both in camp.

Hoboes are interesting people. During WWII my father ran some Forest Service camps during the summer, after school let out. Sometimes, with the worker shortage during the war, he would hire what we called "pogies" from skid row in Sacramento.

The first guy I met at Manpower, who drove the truck back to the farm, was recently dubbed The Buffalo. This I found out from his partner, Red, was because he looked like a buffalo going up and down the ladders picking fruit. Red had a red nose, and he told me that he was given that nickname by the singer Teresa Brewer, whose father had lived in the same old soldier's home or hospital as Red, in eastern Washington. Red and the Buffalo had their trip pretty much together. They always traveled together, and they carried a shotgun with them. They said that there were jackals around the jungles, and they would roust you, especially if you were drunk, a pretty probable condition.

Another interesting character was Cherokee Slim, an Indian who was tall and slim and of reasonably fair complexion, who looked a little like Gene Autry in his younger days. For some reason, maybe because I was packing a guitar, Buffalo and Red invited me to move into their cabin.

There was also a young semi-hippie, who had wandered into the job from somewhere. He was a city kid named John and pretty much out of the loop in the camp. I liked the kid OK but he was pretty cynical and negative about most things.

The Japanese N----- and his wife had a going operation on the river. They had a produce shop on the property, so they had customers coming and going all the time. They had a mutt dog named Tiger, who would bark at all the trash (workers), but never at the customers. Somehow he knew. The owners hated the workers with a passion. Someone asked N----- why he didn't have animals on the property. He replied that he didn't need to, because he could hire all the animals he needed at Manpower in Portland. There was a very chilly vibe going on there. The Mexicans referred to him as the Chinga Chine, roughly translated as the fucked Chinaman. I don't know if he understood Spanish, or much cared.

The foreman was an early middle-aged, Eastern European with a mussed up face and flat nose. He looked like he had participated in a confrontation or two. He wasn't too bad to work for, though. During the day we would sit around until an order came in, we would pick however much of the fruit or vegetables were needed, then wait for the next job.

At night we would sit in the cabin and BS. I would spend the evenings strumming and playing guitar. I found out that Cherokee Slim played and sang Jimmie Rodgers tunes. Most Indians love Rodgers best and Hank second best, so we would trade songs. Slim said that he had run into Johnny Cash one time, and John wanted to take him home and record him. Slim said the deal fell through when he hocked his guitar, got drunk, and ended up in detox. I suppose for many of these folks, the concept of responsibility and success is terrifying. I came up with the idea of hopping a freight with him to Portland and having my friend Gaddis record his music. He said he would do it.

There must have been some beer and wine around, but since no one had been paid, and wouldn't be until they left the job, we stayed sober. One night I was telling the guys about Lasqueti and life up there and ended with, "I really love those people, but somehow there isn't a complete connection." Red looked at me and said, "I can tell you what the problem is in one word. You got a streak of wild in you." Well, that was more than one word but it started me thinking.

Although we were living in a forced temperance camp, you must remember that we were in an apple and pear orchard, so it wasn't too long before buckets of fruit were fermenting. Looking back on it, I guess these work shifts ordinarily went in two-week cycles, just long enough for the first batches to be ready to drink.

One day John and I were bitching and moaning about the job, but he observed, "Yes, this job is the pits, but where else are you going to run into Jimmie Rodgers?" He had a point.

A couple of days before the job was up, Slim walked up to me and said, "I'd like to go to town with you but just like an old hobo I've got to go." We shook hands and said good bye. I never got to ride the freights. Buffalo said, "If you ever ride a boxcar you won't be able to stop." I don't know if this is true, because I never got to test it out.

I finally had to get to town, so I went into the market to get my paycheck. Tiger barked at me, and the wife sneered at me, then she finally gave me a check. I had a hell of a time cashing it because I didn't have a bank or a bank account. I had to go all the way to Vancouver Washington to cash my pay. Things had changed since I left the real world. I talked to one of the bank officials on the way out. I said, "You know, there used to be someone in the bank whose job it was to handle the odd cases. I guess technology has pretty much eliminated the weirdoes and losers." He regretfully agreed with me.

28

Rocking Horse

I had been alone for about two years and came to the realization that I had nowhere else to run; civilization had caught me and I had to find a new direction in life.

I was sitting in a cabin on someone else's land, forty-three years old, no electricity, no vehicle, no visible means of support, not legally in the country, and virtually no money. In recompense, I was surrounded by some of the most beautiful scenery in the world, if I do say so myself. I thought I had escaped the technological realities pretty well. Sanity began creeping into my life when some evil person gave me a battery-powered radio. Plugged right back in to the big world. Shit. I was still dreaming of going to the real bush, to really try to live a "by necessitated" self-sustaining lifestyle.

I was listening to a CBC information-talk program, the topic of which was the controversy between various Inuit Indian tribes about what native language the CBC was going to use to download television into their igloos or whatever. I was dazed when it finally hit me. Holy shit, no matter where on earth I go those satellites will be up there, two hundred miles away.

I could tick off any job skills that would be legally available to an undocumented worker, and they were sparse. I was pretty well bushed by that time, and I realized that whichever direction I chose to go, I would have to deal with a lot of people, many of them reasonably sane by their standards, and also have to deal with bureaucracy. Bummer.

The decision was pretty easy, the execution less so. I still wanted to perform music, and needed to engage it full time in order to really progress. So . . . Why not?

Well, several reasons. The best way to get started would be to play at open mikes on Vancouver Island. I lived on Lasqueti and my cabin was five miles from the ferry terminal, I didn't have a vehicle, and the ferry didn't run at all on Tuesday and Wednesday. So if I went to Vancouver Island on Monday, I would have to wait until Thursday to get back, unless I was able to hitch a ride on a fishing boat. I felt I needed to be on Lasqueti at least a couple of days a week, to keep my island trip together. Much work and little compensation.

I could have worked around the ferry problem except that the only open mike I was aware of at that time was at the Frontiersman Tavern in Coombs, the self-proclaimed capitol of Vancouver Island, on Monday nights. I felt I had to use open mike venues in order to build my performance skills to the point that I could get paying gigs. I had two gigs within the next couple of weeks. I played once at the Frontiersman open mike. The other was a showcase put together by John White, a drifting musician who had been living on Lasqueti for a few months and played regularly at the False Bay Restaurant. He also played some on Vancouver Island. The showcase/ review was held in Errington, B.C., and he invited all musicians who were interested in becoming a member of a performing cooperative to come over and play. HELL YES! We had a nice evening. I don't think we had much turnout, but I got to do a set and I met Julie, who joined me later, as a duo— we become Redbone Hound.

Typically, the performing co-op never got any further, but at least I had gotten my toes wet in my new venture. I was back on the island sometime later when I heard there was a Cowboy Open Mike every Thursday night at the Rocking Horse Inn. Ideal. I decided to attend that week. The only problem was that the ferry happened to be in Vancouver for inspection for a week or two, and I was stuck on the rock.

At this point I ran into Dazy, and I explained my plans, lamenting that I could not go over this week because of the ferry. She thought for a while and then said, "Well, I'd like to go across. Got some stuff to do, so why don't I take you with me in my herring skiff?"

The next morning she looked out and decided maybe she didn't want to go across. We had some coffee and she said, "What the hell, lets go."

It was blowing some, but not too bad. After we docked she drove me to the edge of town, so that I could hitch to the inn. It was about 7:00 when I finally managed to make it to the pub, located on a back road about five miles from Parksville. It was in the woods off the beaten track. As a matter of fact, it was a riding horse ranch with real horses, barn, cowboys, etc.; hence the name, I guess. The English pub was beautiful, and that's where the action was.

I stuck my nose through the door and looked in. There were about ten people sitting around, drinking and eating. There was a drop-dead gorgeous barmaid, of course. I looked around the room and there didn't appear to be any musicians. I said, "Where's the music?" The barmaid looked at my guitar and said, "Looks like it just arrived."

Turns out the Rocking Horse had a built-in sound system and two microphones. I was too dumb to realize how unusual that was. I set up and started singing, and singing and singing. I had no program, but I knew a lot of songs so I just kept singing and waiting for another singer to drop in. Finally I took a break, and got a beer from the barmaid. She said, "You're pretty good." I didn't really believe it. I was pretty wobbly that night and for some time after that. I said, "Thanks."

She asked me if I played for money and I said that I couldn't think of anything I'd rather do at the moment. She asked if I would like to play at the Rocking Horse.

I said, "When?"

She said, "Starting tonight?"

This, honest to God, happened; I'm not making it up.

During the next set a huge cowboy, with a dark complexion, fancy cowboy boots, and a ten-gallon hat came in, sat down, and listened to the music. Now, neither my wardrobe nor my appearance bore much relationship to the norm. I had long straggly hair, long beard, and an old beat-up goat roper's hat. I felt a bit intimidated. After I finished the set, the cowboy called me over and ordered a drink, and started to talk.

He introduced himself as Ian Dewar from Montreal. The ranch was in receivership, and Ian had been hired to be interim manager, to try to salvage the business. Since the bar was pretty far out of town, he was trying to promote the place by having special theme nights. He was just out of the big city, and was really excited about becoming a cowboy. He said his recurring dream was to ride a horse into the bar.

Obviously I was on good ground here. He said the idea of the open mike was to audition for a musician to do Thursday Cowboy Night. He said that when he first saw me playing, he went back out and tried to find my mule.

"I'M IN!"

Ian was very good at promotion and I had a huge crowd on Thursdays, which is a tough night in the nightclub business, especially when you're so far out of town. If the cops had wanted to make some easy busts, they could have waited till the Rocking Horse closed and then stop everyone coming out. Thankfully they never did; though on the last night I played, four cars ran into the ditch.

When I arrived at the pub, my first task was to go into the yard and tune my guitar to my harmonicas. At that time, especially on the street, I played primitive harp in a holder. I remember one time I started my first set, and when I played the first notes on the harmonica, I realized I was about a quarter note off in tuning. Embarrassing. I had to apologize, go into the yard, and retune.

Before I started playing, I remember asking a young performer acquaintance if he had any advice for an aspiring performing musician. He replied, "Always remember that you are not the most important thing in your employer's life at any given moment." This always stood me in good stead. I always arrived early, prepared with a song list, in tune, steady and as sober as necessary, worked as hard as I could, and took short breaks. As in any job, reliability is the most important attribute.

When I met Julie at the showcase I invited her to visit me on the Island. Several young ladies had been interested in visiting me in the recent past, but the rigors of the trip intimidated them and they ultimately declined.

I was in False Bay to meet the ferry, when off walked a very pretty black-haired young lady in gumboots and cutoffs; she had a pack, guitar, flute, and a black lab retriever named Pekoe. Wow. She stayed for several days and we played music, of course. It turned out that she was twenty-eight years old, Gemini, had a B.S. in music from the University of Michigan, had studied lute under a master in Basil, Switzerland, and classical guitar from some dude in Spain. At the University she was a member of an early music ensemble called The Jongueliers, or something. She also played several different finger and flatpicking styles on the guitar. The only thing I taught her was how to flatpick fiddle tunes, which are very difficult. Of course, she figured it out in about a week. Bitch.

We decided to try to perform together as a duet. How was this tough old mountain man dealing with the situation? I was terrified. Reflecting on the past it seems that whenever I had to make a lifestyle change, fate or something seemed to throw me into the middle of the lake to see if I could swim.

Julie and I became Redbone Hound, a successful acoustical duo. We split up, for the usual reasons, love stuff with band partners, later in the summer. At the end of the summer when I decided to go on south to the States, I settled up with Ian. He thanked me for the effort. He said that before I started playing he was taking in five hundred dollars per Thursday and by the time we quit it was pretty consistently a thousand. I got thirty dollars per gig, as was our original agreement. This wasn't bad, since the least I could make on a weekend was thirty dollars. On a number of weekends I was able to play Friday and Saturday in pubs. The least I made for a weekend if I worked three days was a hundred and thirty dollars, which is not bad for a musician.

29

Rodeo

I think the climax of that summer happened the evening after the rodeo at the Rocking Horse Inn. I had been playing music at the Rocking Horse on Thursday nights (Cowboy Night) all that summer, part of the time with Julie when we were Redbone Hound and the rest of the time doing a solo show. The place was a beautiful English pub that was part of a horse ranch out in the woods. There were a lot of wild nights that summer, but none like that Thursday night.

Since the foot ferry to Lasqueti Island didn't run on Tuesdays and Wednesdays, my routine was to cross on Thursday for my Rocking Horse gig. If I had Friday- and Saturday-night gigs on Vancouver Island, as I did about half the time, I would stay around and perform, otherwise I would hitch a ride to the B.C. ferry to Vancouver and spend the weekend playing music on the street. I had several U.B.C college friends I had met and played music with at various music festivals. I would spend the weekends with them, then return to Lasqueti on Monday to do gardening and other chores until Thursday. Truthfully, this was not the worst summer I ever spent.

A Texan buddy of mine named Larry, who I knew from my days in southern Oregon, came to visit shortly before one of my gigs at the pub. When

Larry saw the island he said, "Shit, man, you've got the kinda place most people would kill for. For free."

Larry hadn't seen me perform for money before, so going to the Rocking Horse was a lot of fun for him. The last time he had heard me play music I was sitting on his back porch, about six years earlier, and my music had hopefully progressed some since then.

That young Texan was right at home hanging out with the goat ropers, drinking it up in the pub. I really like playing for cowboys. Provided they don't start fighting. That is a bummer. Anyway, you'll probably have a lot of fun before the fight starts. Being the evening after the rodeo, I didn't have to work the audience to get them started. They had jump-started long before we got there. I just had to get their attention. The first thing you have to do is ingest a little alcohol, not enough to lose control of what you're doing, but enough to try to get into the spirit of the gig, and, as important, to be seen getting into the spirit of the gig.

For me, after I get my sea legs, I can drink a bit. If I get too high I know it, and slack off. But as the evening wears on, nobody really cares. We're jamming.

This night I had the distinction of having the bull riders, from the rodeo, sitting at the table right in front of me. That is a very strategic spot in an entertainment room, because the behavior in the front table really affects the musical environment for the musician.

When I started my program, with "Gotta Get Drunk," as I almost always did back then, the goat ropers started overacting a tad. They started badmouthing the hired help, even though they liked the music. I noticed that there were four to five young (eighteen to twenty-two years old) cowboy lads, and one who looked about sixty but was probably about thirty-five. He was grizzled, had about two days' whisker growth, and looked like one of the priceless cowboy cartoon characters in Williams' old *Out Our Way* comic strip that used to be in the Sunday papers. The older folk probably know what I'm talking about.

I soon discovered that this old gent was, in fact, the champion bull rider from somewhere, and these crazy kids were his bull-riding students, and they worshipped at his feet. You understand, these young folks come from places like Nanaimo and Port Alberni, and in these surroundings this dude takes on awesome proportions. So these young guys were trying to figure out how a red-hot bull rider is supposed to act, and they didn't have a clue, except that they figured they were a pretty bad bunch. The old pro kind of laid back and stayed cool, so the younger ones got cool, and we had a real good time that night. I think I had about six beers (5 percent), four to five shots of Cognac, and I don't know what after that. One thing about playing music, you really use up a lot of energy, so if you don't go overboard with it, you work a lot of that alcohol off. I played for almost three hours, and four-hour gigs occurred regularly.

If you're trying to justify the boss hiring you back, and if you want to feel that you earned your money, and if you really want to get the audience high and have a good time, which is the only thing that is important to me, then you will use up a lot of BTUs in those three or four hours.

After I ended up my Rock 'n' Roll set with "Chattanooga Shoe Shine Boy," "Rock Around the Clock," "Ghost Riders in the Sky," and a real hallelujah version of Hank Williams' "I Saw the Light," I had a couple of drinks and greedily accepted the small amount of adulation and congratulations on a good show. Ol' Larry was just having a great time. We soon disengaged ourselves and walked down the driveway to Larry's truck. I loaded my equipment and lit up a joint, and pretty soon the bull riders showed up with a bottle. We passed a joint, and when it got to the champion bull rider, he threw it on the ground and stomped on it and said, "I hate that shit." Well.

One of the problems I have had in the past when mixing certain liquors is becoming stupidly brave. Or bravely stupid. Whichever. This night I was evidently doubly so. The tailgate group consisted of the four to five goat ropers, Larry, me, and a rather large young friend of mine named Rich. Not good. What happened next I couldn't swear to on the witness stand; I was a bit under the weather at the time.

About six months after the rodeo, when I returned to Canada and was shopping in the Overweightea Grocery Market, I ran into one of the old regulars at the Rocking Horse. The first thing he said to me was, "Buckwheat, I never will forget that night of the rodeo when that cowboy stomped on your joint." Six months later, mind you.

I said something like, "Yes, I get the shakes over that every once in awhile myself."

Then he said "Wow. What you said to him really cracked me up."

Perplexed, I said, "OK, I'll bite, what the did I say to him?"

He said (and I don't believe a word of this), "You said, 'Hey, that's my joint. What would you think if I pissed in your beer and make you smell like a goat?'"

I do not believe I said that. I can imagine myself equating his stomping on my roach to me pissing in his beer, irrespective of the difficulty of accomplishing this feat, but what that would have to do with smelling like a goat I haven't a clue.

This is a ticklish spot for a man. A challenge has been issued. Certainly not too many men relish the idea of getting the shit kicked out of them. At the same time, they cannot give in without giving up some of their feeling of self-worth. Sometimes you shrug it off.

So here we were, kind of eye to eye. I saw my big buddy Rich drift away from the group and over to a pile of old fence posts, trying a couple of the smaller ones out for size and heft. The problem wasn't really with the champion bull rider and me at this point. I think he made his statement and I made mine. But the cubs didn't know how to act. Their leader had been challenged. Shouldn't we go to war? Isn't that what bull riders do?

Fortunately, they let it set and so did we. As a matter of fact, Larry and I were so quick to get out of there that I left my pack with my microphone and mixer in the parking lot. One of the goat ropers found it and returned it to me.

For the next year and a half I bounced around playing music in Oregon during the winter and Vancouver Island in the summer. At some point I crashed and burned, and returned to Lasqueti Island to live. This time I was a much higher profile in the community.

30

Hay Run

Got up about 6 a.m., had a cup of coffee, maybe a slice of toast, then walked out to the corner. Feel the wind. Westerly. Far out. A westerly wind is a change wind. The weather was in transition between . . . what? Another storm? A high-pressure area that causes fierce northwest wind and can be stronger than the southerly storm winds? The important thing was that because it was blowing westerly we would have a few hours before what was going to happen next would actually happen.

The reason I was freezing my butt off at 6:30 or so on a November morning at the side of the dirt/gravel road worrying about the direction of the wind was I was going on a hay run. Now, you might ask, why was I doing a hay run in November? Go ahead, ask. Well, now that you ask, it wasn't my idea.

When you live on an island that lacks vehicular ferry service, it is a major undertaking to transport large quantities of goods. There were freight services available, and some of them were quite reasonable, but it cost a lot of money to bring a barge load of anything across the gulf. There were regularly scheduled freight runs, but they were taken up with islanders' smaller orders, and weren't really up to including two hundred and fifty bales of hay.

If you knew that you were going to have to hire a barge, the best way to cut costs would be to partner up with one or two other people who have to do roughly the same thing, have them share the loading and unloading, and split the cost of the run. Now, this sounds fine, but when you let other players into the game difficulties seem to arise.

Consider. If Karl had decided to make the run by himself, the only major impediments to completing the project on time might be: He got sick and had to cancel the run; his truck broke down; the barge had sunk; the supplier wasn't able to make it to the dock at the right time; the supplier couldn't get the hay from his supplier; the barge had sunk again; a big storm came up and you couldn't get across. There are a lot more things that could screw things up, but I think you get the idea. If Karl had done it alone it might have taken about a month for all the pieces to come together. Karl added two partners to the deal, so instead of a month delay, and making the run in August or September, here we were making it in November.

I was working for Dick and Karl. Alf and his son made up the rest of the five of us who gathered at the government dock and boarded the *Palaquin*, Peter Leroni's barge. It was a wooden, flat-bottomed barge with a pilothouse at the stern. As we approached the wharf, we could see smoke coming out of the four-inch smoke stack, from the wood fire in the tiny boat stove. The barge had a loading ramp held tight by guyed five-eighths-inch steel cables, operated by an electric winch, which also operated the freight booms. Peter built the whole thing himself and it was funky, but quite functional, as things have to be in that part of the world.

As we stood on the dock and talked, while waiting to get under way, things looked promising. The last storm had ended the previous evening, and it was now blowing westerly, which meant that we probably wouldn't have a storm before this evening.

That was the good part. Also good was the fact that a last-minute phone call had confirmed that the truck with the hay would definitely be at the French

Creek dock at exactly 11:00 a.m. The sort of bad part, if you have any kind of queasy stomach, was that a westerly swell would take us on the bow quarter, and the boat would buck the whole way across.

As soon as the boat cleared the bay it started bucking like a bronco. Remember that this was a flat-bottomed barge. It was very hard to stand up on deck without holding tight onto something. And it was cold. So we all congregated in the pilothouse and sipped on coffee. It was a bit snug with all five of us. So after a while I decided to go down into the living quarters. Peter lived under the pilothouse. He had a boat wood stove with a rail around it above the top, to keep things from flying off. He also had a bed anchored to the bulkhead. I personally didn't have much seasick problem as long as I didn't try to read. Reading a book had been my original idea in coming down here, but it didn't work so I more or less contented myself by looking out the porthole at the violent sea, instead.

We were in the inland waterway. The deep-sea swell is broken by Vancouver Island, so sometimes, especially in the summer, it was as calm as a lake. Not even a ripple. However, when the wind picked up it could create chop up to six feet with waves no more than ten feet apart; so a boat could not ride them, it was battered by them.

I finally decided that looking at the ocean wasn't doing it for me, so I went back up to the pilothouse to BS with the guys. The trip across took two and a half hours. We finally entered French Creek estuary and glided up to the dock . . . and guess what. The hay truck was waiting, and it was equipped with a loader to help us with the bales. Unbelievable. It was all working.

We decided to load the hay on the barge, lash it down, then go into town for some breakfast. With that in mind we busted our ass for about two hours loading the hay. As we finished loading, however, the weather didn't seem to be cooperating. The wind had picked up and turned southeast, so we'd be bucking again in the other direction. We covered the load as well as we could with plastic tarp, lashed it down, and started back across the gulf, as a light rain started to fall.

To tell you how serious we thought the situation was, we didn't even have time to drive the two miles to buy a case of beer to drink on the way back. Two and a half hours back across the gulf, pitching and bucking, with nothing to eat we finally entered the final haven, False Bay. The wind miraculously ceased, and we pulled in to the dock. You can plane a bit in the ferry, but not in a hay-laden barge.

It was near dusk when we arrived, and we still had to get all those bales off the barge and onto the three trucks we had left parked on the government wharf. Some of the better government docks in Canada have power winches, donated and maintained by Environment Canada. Needless to say, False Bay was not one of these. We had winches, all right. Hand winches that probably got lubricated with grease at least once every five years whether they needed it or not. Things corrode quickly near the sea, even without great amounts of precipitation, so just raising an empty palette could sometimes be a real chore. However, Peter's homemade power winch saved us. It was able to lift the two-layered hay palettes onto the dock. Then we hand-bucked the bales onto the truck beds. I say the winch got them to the dock. The first thing that had to be done was that one of us would have to horse about eight bales onto a palette. Then we would attach the winch cables to the palette. Peter would put the winch in gear and raise the palette up onto the dock. Another poor, tired, hungry fool would horse the bales onto the truck bed, and another worker (or two) would stack them, building them as high as they could behind the cab, then filling the load forward until the truck was full.

Meantime, the people on the barge would load another palette. On and on. That stuff weighed one hundred to one hundred twenty pounds per bale. We were handling maybe twenty tons of hay. The last step was to lash the hay, cover it with plastic as well as possible, then climb in the truck, put 'er into gear, and creak home. I finally crawled in the door at about 9:00 p.m., having eaten my last meal about fifteen hours before. Whew, you talk about wore out. Gimme something to eat, a beer, and let me kick back.

Needless to say, the next day I was feeling a bit tired. Too bad. This was the day that we were unloading the hay from the trucks, and stashing it in Dick's and Karl's barns. I didn't really feel like looking at that stuff again, much less handling it and unloading it yet one more time. But, there you are. Toss the bales off the truck, horse them into the barn, and stack them, first in the loft, then in the main barn. Man, we have handled these same bales so many times in the past thirty-six hours we practically knew their names.

The job was finally completed. Karl, who has never been particularly pleasant to me, came over and said, "Well, you made the grade." Swell.

Sometimes I wonder how many times in this life I'm going to have to listen to someone say, 'Well, you made the grade." I know it's meant to be a compliment, but, whew, this process of making it can be very fatiguing.

31

Casey

A shout, "Buckwheat, your uncle Charlie's in town," brought me out onto the porch of the shack Justine and I were living in down by Long Bay. We were working for Nancy Varney at the time, about a quarter mile up a steep trail from her farm. I asked Justine what she was talking about.

She said, "Nancy got a call from the store that your uncle Charlie is on the island. You do have an Uncle Charlie, don't you?"

I said, "I used to have, but he died about twenty years ago." I decided to trudge down to the farm and see what was up.

When I got to the house Nancy explained the call. It seems that whoever Uncle Charlie was he had called from the store. He said that he was going to start walking down to the island. I just shrugged. She said, "Well, you'd better take the truck and find out what's going on." Sometimes things are a little boring in the bush, and you want to be the first to get any fresh news. I got in the Ranger and drove out the pot-holed driveway and up the pot-holed road toward False Bay, about five miles away.

I got almost to the teapot house when I saw a good-looking, middle-aged man, with a pack and a face pink from exertion. He had evidently walked about a half-mile from the store. He was definitely not in island shape. You got into shape very quickly on the rock. We looked at each other and he said, "You're not Bob W."

I said, "No, but I may know him." I asked Charlie where he got my name.

He said, "When I asked at the store they didn't know any Bob W, and said that it was probably Buckwheat Bob, who was down at Nancy's. She gave me the phone number." It was a tad disquieting that they knew that much about me but, oh well.

The situation caused a dilemma for me. I was one of maybe three people on the island who knew Bob W's last name. Now it must be understood that a lot of people in our situation used false names, one real name but no last name or a nickname. There were many reasons for this; often because their real name might ring a bell with someone in authority. In the current case Bob (or K, as he was known here) was, like me, illegally in the country. He was living with T, who was also illegal. I knew this, because until recently they had been living in my old squatter's shack at Sandy Beach.

The situation was complicated by the fact that K and T had been discovered by the RCMP, and theoretically deported. They had bid everyone adieu and sailed off on a friend's boat, later circling, disembarked on the other side of the island, and were hiding out several hundred yards from where they had lived before. They were living in a plastic shelter behind Bruce's shack, across the bay from my old squatter's shack. I was one of the few who were aware that they were back on the island. We knew that there were snitches around, and they would be pretty quick to smell out something like that.

Outlaws are very reticent people when communicating with strangers. I was wondering how to deal with this situation. Who was this guy I was dealing with? He said he was an uncle, but how did I know this? What should I do?

After thinking it over I said, "Do you have some identification?" He pulled out a card that identified him as a pilot for Southwest Airways. From all mannerisms Charlie was not a Canadian, naturally born at least. He reeked of

American. I also figured that if the RCMP had American agents masquerading as airline pilots, the game was probably pretty much up for all of us.

I told him to get in the car, threw his pack in the back, and started down the road. I described the situation to him during the trip, and he didn't respond too much, which was a good sign. I drove down Millicheap Road to the bottom and parked the truck and said, "We'll have to go on foot from here."

The "trail," which I had built years ago, was not marked because we didn't want people to be able to follow it to the shack. Charlie must have thought he had gotten involved in some Central American-type insurgency or something. When we got to my old shack, I told him to stay there until I checked things out, and crashed into the woods.

I went around to Bruce's cabin to confer. When I got there I found that Bruce's parents had arrived for a visit. We knew each other. I asked if Bruce was around and they said no, that he would be back in a while. I asked if K and T were around, and Bruce's dad said, "Oh no, they don't live here anymore. They left the Island."

I thought, *Oh shit, Bruce hasn't told them that they are living about a hundred yards back in the bush. Now what am I going to do?*

Bruce showed up a little while later and I beckoned to him so we could talk privately. When I told him what was going on he said, "Yeah, I didn't tell my folks K and T were back, but it's cool. I'll have K go over and make contact."

I went back across the bay and told Charlie that everything was cool and he would be contacted shortly, shook hands, and walked back to the truck.

32

Piano

Here's another example of life in the boonies. K and T were living in my old shack on Sandy Beach. They moved into their tree house, built inside a cluster of four to five Douglas fir trees facing southeast, the direction of winter storms. Even though I visited them in their hutch, I was no expert at the ins and outs of tree-house living. Nor, for that matter, did I have any desire to become one. They decided to make the old place I had built, that they had been living in, into their rec room. It was a ten by ten-foot dirt floor pole shack (made of discarded stuff from the area), which by the way was still standing, sort of, in the year 2011. T was a concert pianist, who had lived without a piano for some years. K and T were destitute on the physical level, as many of us had been for some time. T would go to the community center, several miles walk, to play the piano when she couldn't stand it anymore; but she yearned for her own instrument.

She managed to get ownership of a used upright piano that lived in Victoria, B.C., about ninety miles to the south. Finding the piano and acquiring ownership was the easy part. We had to plan the operation for getting it home as if we were planning the Normandy Invasion, because the logistics were so staggering. Someone with a pickup volunteered to haul it from Victoria to

French Creek, where the ferry docked. The hauler had to be at the ferry dock by the time the boat arrived in French Creek. Hopefully there would be a work crew on the ferry, to help load the piano. Everything went OK to this point. There had to be a truck at the ferry dock on the island, waiting to unload the piano and get it onto the truck somehow.

Now, if you are thinking that all we have to do is drive up there to Sandy Beach, no such luck. There was no road. The shack was on the low bluffs next to the bay. The plan was for the Lindseys' Boston Whaler to sail from Marshall's Beach, where they lived, around the point to Tucker Bay, a shallow crescent about two miles wide with Sandy Beach, Conn Bay, and then a small inlet called Tucker Bay within the crescent. We drove the piano down to Tucker Bay, the only public access to the beach that we could drive to. When the whaler arrived, we loaded the piano on the boat. We then hurried over to Sandy Beach, to be there when the whaler arrived. We had to beat the bush about a quarter of a mile to get there. One of the scheduling considerations was that it had to be delivered sometime near high tide, so we wouldn't have to carry it too far over beach logs. We timed the tide pretty well. There are two things you always know when you live near the sea; they are: (1) wind conditions and directions and (2) the tides.

We had to horse the piano over a couple of beach logs then up a little trail about one hundred and fifty feet. The whole operation worked like a charm.

33

Walking

Walking wouldn't seem to be a subject you could write a whole story about. I mean, how difficult can it be? Just put one foot in front of the other, be moderately careful not to trip, step up for curbs, and, depending on your inclination, you might want to avoid cracks.

I was raised in the foothills of the northern California Sierra Mountains. My father grew up in the Sacramento Valley, and later lived in the Sierras around Quincy. He spent the time he had left over from logging and, I assume, general carousing by hunting and fishing. He loved the outdoors. Naturally my brother and I inherited this tradition.

Let me tell you, there is some rugged country in the Sierras. The country is geologically quite young, composed of lava and granite, with much of the terrain formed by glaciers during the ice age.

The various tributaries of the Feather River had stretches with names like Stag Point; Bald Rock Canyon, which was my favorite mud hole, and the roughest country I have ever seen; Rich Bar, which produced a lot of gold in the day; and Caribou. Some had local colloquial names, such as Joe's Upper and Lower Holes, named for Joe Felipe, a coach at my high school, who really loved fishing the Middle Fork.

I remember once when I was in my teens, I went fishing with my father. We went down into Bald Rock Canyon, the lower end, which isn't too tough, but it was a thousand feet of switchbacks, both down and then back up. I was oblivious to the hardship. I remember on another trip, us fourteen-year-olds had been racing up the hill while the old farts, like the outdoorsmen in their thirties and forties, were huffing and cussing at us and saying, "What's the goddamn hurry!"

On this particular trip we went down into Bald Rock Canyon and caught some fish. From the bottom of the trail you can only move up and down the river about two hundred yards, then, if you can find a way up the wall of the canyon you can climb hand over hand up maybe two hundred feet until you find a bit of trail or crevasse and move along this until you find a way back down to the river. There are many spots on that riverbed that have never been trod upon. We climbed, explored, fished, and had a great time. Then we climbed out of that hellhole, drove the jeep to the Brush Creek Tavern and Store, better known as Manuel's. It was named after Manuel Souza, as fine a gentleman as you'll ever find, short and slightly stout with black hair and mustache and a twinkle in his eye.

We had just climbed about a thousand feet up a granite canyon, in near hundred-degree, summer northern California heat. We were tired, sore, dirty, and thirsty. We entered the old log tavern and store, sat down at one of the bar stools, and looked at the beer, panting.

Manuel (pronounced Man-u-al, not Man-well) asked what it'd be.

My father said, "Two beers."

Manuel looked at me—skinny sixteen or seventeen years old—pointed his thumb and asked, "Is he old enough?"

My dad nodded and said, "He's old enough."

Manuel nodded, and popped the beers. I had cold shivers running up and down my spine. "He's old enough," he'd said. I know I failed to live up to many of his expectations, but on that day, and a few more thereafter, I had been "old enough."

My brother and I used to hike into Bald Rock Falls, down and across a shear granite face of the great bald rock dome that stood two thousand feet above the river. This stretch of water had never been traversed at river level. The canyon was a mystical experience for me as a teenager. I almost lost my life several times on these trips, terrifying. The frightening power of the natural world. This is just a canyon, not a moving menace like hurricanes or earthquakes. It's just . . . there.

When I would climb down and finally get to camp, the only possible spot big enough to lie down was a flat rock shelf. Not fun wrapped up in an army blanket and trying to sleep on this rock. It made me feel very inadequate. I guess you learn that nature is not malevolent; it's just indifferent.

That place was magnificent. There were stories from the Indians concerning U-I-NO, who was a monster and lived in the canyon, and killed anyone who went down there. I think the Indians were trying to scare out white men from one of their best fishing spots. Walking, and footing in general, was very important, of course. I learned a lot of walking skills navigating those canyons. I became a canyon insider, and learned from old-timers about different trails.

A few adults went fishing down there. It was a terrible trip for fishing, because it was so rugged, and because if you caught something you would most likely have to carry it out. A twenty-five- or thirty-pound salmon gets heavy after a while. I remember one time we walked out with three salmon and thirty-five trout, wrapped in a wet army blanket. Although they would never admit it, I think the older folks were having mystical experiences too.

I found the feelings of insignificance at the bottom of the canyon exhilarating. I could feel the power of its inertia. I strongly remember a healthy fir tree growing out of a solid granite crevasse. How it rooted and got its nutrition I don't know. It was a wonderful reminder of the tenacious vigor of life. I don't know what my parents thought of these teenage boys going down there by themselves. They knew how treacherous the country was, and my mother never showed any fear. Knowing her she must have experienced much concern over the years. But that all happened much later.

During the war, my father—a coach and schoolteacher during the winter—ran a blister-rust control camp for the Forest Service. My summers were spent living in tent-houses with no electricity and often no running water. They would often run the generator at night, but not during the day. Most of the time I was alone, unless you count my brother, who was two to six years old during that time. He did not offer a lot of companionship to a brother who was four years older. The camps were in heavenly places like Granite Basin, Camp Almanor, Canyon Dam, and Gansner Bar.

A child being allowed to spend the whole summer in country like this was the ultimate fantasy for me. I had grown up reading and listening to tales of the old west. It was a family tradition. The only place I had to play was a camp full of high school football players or skid-row bums within an entire National Forest, with no other people around. How's that for a kid's dream?

The blister-rust camps were over three thousand feet above sea level. The National Forests were closed, and really bare of people during WWII. I had pretty much the whole Plumas National Forest to myself. I mean, this was hyperspace.

There were a number of bears in our area. One summer we had a big garbage pit behind the camp. Every night just about dusk, two or three bears would come running out of the forest and jump into the pit. There were lots of old tin cans in the pit, and of course they would rattle like hell when those bears would land. The cans rattling would scare them, or at least they pretended to be scared, and they would hightail it back into the forest. About two minutes later here they would come back, running out of the woods to jump into the pit where the cans would rattle. It seemed they would repeat this game until they got tired. Of course, everyone would go out each night and watch the spectacle. This was in the early 1940s before TV, and movies were a long way away.

One time a bear broke into the cookhouse and stole all the bacon. His (or a relative's) fate was sealed by that unspeakable outrage. We ate him a few days later.

One day I found an old rusted-out bear trap. Wow. I roped it to a tree and set it. I remember thinking, "I'm gonna catch a bear." Now, boys my age back then used to play games like they were going to trap bears. Because of Roy Rogers and Gene Autry cowboys, the frontier was really in vogue, but I was *living* in real bear country, with a real bear trap. I'm sure that the trap was broken; hell, it had probably been rusting away for twenty to thirty years, but that is a very small challenge for the imagination of a nine- or ten-year-old boy. I had a real bear trap, and I was going to trap a bear. I mean, there is such a thing as being too real. Luckily I never caught one.

I built a hidden fort, a hideout inside a hollow log. I even had a real gold mine. There was an abandoned hard-rock quartz mine about a half-mile from the camp, over the hill and down on the north fork of the Feather River. Whew, did my mother get mad when she found out that the camp cook had taken me down to the river. I came back with a sack full of quartz rock.

Get rich. I must have pulverized about ten pounds of rocks and extracted about a hundredth of an ounce of gold before that fantasy faded out, only to be replaced by another. Who knows what, maybe trapping a bear.

One of my father's jobs was to stake out, with string, the areas that were to be worked by the crews in order to grub (eradicate) gooseberry plants, which carry the pine blister rust disease. He would walk section lines, with string and a compass. Sometimes I would go with him. This was a laugh. About the only groundcover up there was Manzanita, a very pretty hard wood scrub, and buck brush, which has straight shoots going in all directions and half-inch-thick stickers attached to the shoots. My dad was about six foot three and he would wear thick pants, because you couldn't go around brush when staking out a straight line. I would love to go with him, and crash through this stuff all day. I don't know what I must have been thinking, struggling through all that brush. You can see that I started walking in the woods at a reasonably young age. I later walked the trails in these granite-lava canyons for a number of years, through the slash of second-growth forests. God, what a horror they are.

If I had stayed close to civilization, and wandered the woods as a means of recreation, I would never have thought too much about how to walk in the bush.

But later in life, when I moved to the woods to live, I had to confront my style, so to speak. When walking in the woods, it is necessary to be able to see ahead at all times when you are traveling cross-country or following trails. After all, we are as much prey as any other creature in the forest. You can't be looking where you are stepping, even if you are traveling through rock, fallen trees, brush, etc. How do you do that? I don't know. All I know is that when I got to the woods in later years, I just walked that way, weight on the balls of my feet, knees slightly bent, good balance, and a lowered center of gravity. This was especially import-ant when I was carrying a lot of weight on my back. High weight raises your center of gravity, and makes you wobbly. I guess when I walk I lift my knees high, and kind of feel with my feet. I'm sure that I take peek breaks from time to time, but even though I try to watch myself walking, I don't notice looking directly in front of my path.

After learning to do this, try following an animal trail that is unfamiliar. All trails in the woods were originally animal trails. Animal trails go everywhere. The challenge is to get from wherever I am to wherever I want to go using trails. Therefore, I have to have a place I want to go, and know the approximate direction I have to go to get there.

Now comes the fun part. I always have to know where I am in relation to where I am going. Therefore, I have to know that if I am going due north, and that bearing is impossible to follow, maybe because of cliffs, then I have to keep looking for branches in the trail that seem to lead back in the direction I want to go.

In order to follow the contour of the trail, I have to constantly gaze as far ahead as possible. Most trails die out in many places, especially in rocks and water, so I have to guess or anticipate where it is likely to be found again. I gaze ahead, keeping in mind what the line of the trail is like behind me, and look for the easiest way to my destination. Animals are not stupid. I don't mean that they can solve quadratic equations in their heads, but they don't like brush or dead-end cliffs much more than you or me. Oh, I admit that they can sort of screw you up sometimes. Deer, for example. In the first place most of them are shorter than us, and they can definitely get through lower spots than are comfortable for white men. But more importantly, they can jump a hell of a lot higher and farther than I can, so when they get in a little trouble they just jump out. Also, in case you don't know it, they are quite agile, and seem to like to scramble up and down the sides of granite canyons; although, I have seen a carcass of an unlucky young deer every once in a while at the bottom of a cliff. Ordinarily these mountainsides are negotiable by someone like me, but sometimes I wish I hadn't tried.

Sheep, on the other hand are just natural trailblazers. They like to flock, don't like brush any more than I do, and can't jump. I'm not talking about mountain sheep; the only ones I know are feral, once domestic sheep. You can bet they know the best way from A to B through heavy brush. Conversely, if I end up stuck in a place where there is no reasonably fresh sheep shit anywhere near, then pard, I am probably in the wrong place.

Getting back to following trails. I get a sense of where a trail is going, by looking as far ahead as I can, and projecting its overall direction. Even if I lose it right ahead, I may be able to pick it up farther on.

After practicing for a while it becomes a sense, and I don't even think about it. So I learn how to walk without looking down, always looking ahead and around, always ready to go limp if I stumble, so I won't sprain or break anything. As an agile teenager running along four-inch-wide trails four hundred feet above rocks was normal. I guess all teenagers think they are bulletproof. I'm young. I'm agile. No problem.

Even before I moved to the woods I learned a couple of sad lessons. I got off cheap, but after that I tried to be mighty careful. One time I was hiking the John Muir Trail with some friends. We happened upon some wondrous elixir that is often smoked, and got feeling very good. I was carrying a fifty-pound pack and not paying attention. I tripped over a rock and came down on the back of my neck. Fortunately, the pack frame hit the ground, which took most of the blow. I ended up with only a slightly strained neck.

Another time, I was alone and coming down off Sugarloaf Mountain, up above Big Bear Lake, east of LA. I was alone. Taking these gigantic leaps, I built up this great momentum, then came down on a rock, twisted my ankle, and did a shoulder roll. The next thing I knew I was on my feet still running down the mountain. I had just done a complete flip. Again, I hit on the pack frame; that saved me some embarrassment. I could have been very much messed up. Again, I got lucky, and this time I was alone. I almost always hike alone, and usually cross-country, so it could have been a long time, like months, before anyone found me.

After that I began to think that maybe I wasn't bulletproof after all. In essence this revelation meant that I had to develop a whole new set of walking habits. I would have to learn to concentrate on every step. Not look, but think before I stepped.

Some of the things I learned about hiking and scaling are how to do the quick step and how to relax if you slip or stumble to keep from spraining an ankle. The quick step is like a limp. If I'm walking on a cliff or mountainside and see a spot that doesn't look too firm, maybe I stop and try it a little just to get the feel and visualize my next two steps. Then I take the two steps starting with my inside foot, quickly kick off the spot with the bad footing with the outside foot, letting my momentum carry me, so that I don't put my full weight on it, then quickly step onto the firm footing with my inside foot. That way if the questionable footing gives way, I will still probably make it to the next step. Also, I can't lose my balance. At any time there is trouble on the side of a mountain, I try to lower my center of gravity.

One of my favorite things is walking in the forest at night. Anywhere while it's pitch black works, with the caveat that you have to be fairly familiar with the trail. My how I concentrate on the universe around me. All of my senses are as alert as they will ever be. Well, I might concentrate a bit if I were in a war zone and there were snipers around, I guess.

Navigating in the dark is a total mind-body thing. I must have a mental map of where I am going. I've found out that I have to be able to know directions at night. I think what I do is to visualize the whole path in my mind, from where I started to where I'm going. It is important to remember where I have already been. It is quite possible that I might have to backtrack to a familiar spot. How familiar? Who knows? For some reason I seem to know where I am. There have to be various landmarks along the way, so hopefully you know which landmarks you have passed, and therefore should be able to get back to the last one and regroup if necessary. One of the most unnerving things I have found is arriving at a landmark that I thought I had already passed. Then say, "Where the heck am I?"

The actual walking is the easiest part. I walk with the weight on the balls of my feet, knees high, and always in balance, so that if I stumble, or walk off a cliff, I won't fall down. And I walk s-l-o-w-l-y when I'm not sure of the way. Using this technique I find that I am feeling the way with the bottoms of my feet, even if I am wearing gumboots. I can feel what kind of terrain I'm on, whether it's mineral, soil, grass, or brush. It is usually easy to tell if I'm off a path. I start running into things. Some forest paths have low overhang, so just getting whapped in the eyes doesn't necessarily mean that I'm off the path. But if I feel sticks and rocks under my feet, and I know the trail is not supposed to have sticks and rocks in it, that's a pretty good indication that I'm off the trail. I just have to remember to stop if I'm not sure where I am, and try to remember how to get back to the last landmark. As the Indians used to say, there is a big difference between being lost and just not knowing exactly where you are.

There are tricks to it. One very important one is that even when it is pitch black, the sky is just slightly brighter than surrounding forests and mountains. By watching the tips of the trees, I can barely discern the sky in the clearing above a road or path.

There are also senses that we are not ordinarily aware of. I can actually feel if the trail is clear ahead. I can sense bushes and trees before I touch them. It is really uncanny to be tooling down the path at night, not really noticing that I can't see anything, and just knowing precisely where the path is. Another trick is, if I get into brush I try to back out. I don't want to get turned around. That could cause trouble. Sometimes I'm better off just closing my eyes.

Another trick is, when watching ahead look slightly away from the direction I am going, and use my peripheral vision. We seem to perceive slight outlines better that way. It's really sort of ominous when I'm walking through this totally dark forest, and see or feel an even darker dark, and an oppressive presence. You stop and there is a big rock, or a tree or a building.

I remember one frustrating time I was walking back home with a friend, after a rather riotous evening at the Canadian Legion. My buddy and I were pretty well sloshed, walking home, pitch black, and came to this blacker-than-black I'm talking about. I knew exactly where we were. I was pretty sure. We were almost home . . . oh, say a hundred and fifty yards, and we had just encountered this huge cedar tree. Right here you lose the path for about twenty feet, because it sort of goes under the lower boughs and around the very edge of the tree. I knew where I was, and I knew exactly how the trail bent right there, and I couldn't find it. After a while I began to wonder if I was really where I thought I was.

If I just can't find the trail I must backtrack to the last known spot, relax, stop shaking, and start again. You must remember where you have been. There have been times when, if I had gotten off a path and lost my bearings, I would have had to walk as much as two miles in horrible bush; two miles if I could manage to walk and crawl through tons of salmonberry bushes and swamps and cliffs and old logging slash, and then do this in a straight line so that I didn't circle around. Not a pleasant thought. This time I had to backtrack about five times before I was able to find the trail again.

It can even get very scary in the daytime. I've been lost, er, I mean haven't known exactly where I was, many times during the daytime. The trail to our squatter's shack from the other direction was about a hundred and twenty yards of pure desperation. Since our family was in Canada illegally, we tried to keep our residence as secret as possible. For that reason I built the cabins so that they would be difficult to see from either the cove or the ocean. To get in by this trail

I would walk down Main Road, the primary north–south artery on the Island, take a dirt road about two hundred and fifty yards down to almost where it dead-ends at the ocean, then jig left a bit up a dirt path, and dive under a cedar tree. There was a cliff face between the shack and the dirt road, so we would either have to go away from our destination and up the hill behind the shack in order to hit the high trail, or work out along the cliff. A hint of a lower trail along the bluff seemed to have been picked out by sheep that must have gotten lost long ago. No fresh sheep shit.

This was a very dangerous trail, especially at night. I dug it out in a few places by some heavy work with a mattock and sledgehammer and crow bar, so it only went about twenty yards along the side of the cliff, but that was enough. One older friend of ours, with a fifty-pound pack on his back, fell about fifteen feet into the rocks. He chipped some vertebrae in his back, and was laid up for quite awhile.

We left all the logs and stuff in the trail so it wouldn't look like a trail if Sergeant Preston and his wonder dog, King, ever got inquisitive. This was OK, unless you were trying to get home at night without a light. As I remember, the trail went something like this:

You had to duck under a low cedar tree to get started. It was very easy to miss in the pitch black. There was about ten feet of real trail at the start, so at least you would know that you had once been on the trail. Next you had to climb over several branches and small logs. At this point it didn't feel like you were on the trail. Then it threaded through the trees, took a dip to the right between two trees that were very close together, then alongside a large decaying log. Next you had to step over a medium-sized log. Now you cut to the right past a small fir tree and, hopefully, started feeling rocks under your feet. If you can feel rock that means you have almost made it to the cliff, the scary place. You start easing ahead, because you are almost to the edge of the bluff. The only problem is you can't see it, and haven't the slightest idea how far ahead it is, and you're already going slightly downhill. There is a pretty good-sized Douglas fir tree hanging precariously over the cliff, right where the trail turns to the left and along the cliff. This is where my friend fell, and he fell in the daytime. Hopefully you run, but not literally, into that fir. Then you know where you are.

When you start going side-hill, it becomes necessary to lean sideways toward the cliff face, and hold yourself away from it with your arm. You can't stand up straight in that situation because it's hard to maintain balance. So you're kinda inching along, and then about twenty yards along the trail branches slightly uphill. Take this branch and you are finally back in the woods on a brushed trail and home.

There was an abandoned mailbox on the road down to the bay, which usually contained a candle lantern, some candles, and matches. One time three of us—Mara, her ten-year-old daughter, and I—were coming home from a party. The two of us were pretty blitzed and it was pitch black. We looked in the mailbox: no lantern or candles.

Mara had not gotten into the "walking in the dark stuff" as much as I had at that time, and I think she started to get a little frightened, for which I can't really blame her. However, there we were. It's a little difficult trying to focus your consciousness to become one with the trail while someone is nagging you.

"Why didn't you leave a candle lantern in the old mailbox?"

"I saw it last week. I guess someone took it."

"Well why the Christ didn't you leave two?"

Stuff like that. Finally she said, "I'm not going one step farther. You go to the cabin and get a candle lantern and we'll stay right here." At that point I considered leaving her there for a while to try to get a bit of an attitude adjustment, but of course I didn't. After all, her daughter was with her. Also I was too chicken. I mean, you leave them out on the cliff for a while, and they can really go off on you when they finally make it back. I know this all sounds sort of strange, but it's not really a game. It is a way of measuring your environment, really coming to know it as a complete tactile entity.

We have really lost our ability to function with nature, can't directly perceive the power and energy in the natural environment. When you can walk on a trail in the dark, you begin to understand how trees grow and how a wild animal mingles with his environment.

I remember more than once while hiking the John Muir Trail—gliding over the terrain up steep, seemingly insurmountable cliffs with ease; in all directions peaks and crags between eleven thousand and fourteen thousand feet as far as I could see—thinking how far from civilization I really was, and realizing that if the tiny trail I was following, so faint that sometimes I would lose it, were to suddenly disappear, I would be much, much closer to being up the proverbial shit creek. Without maps and marked trails, we perceive the wilderness in wildly different terms.

34

Insect Repeller

When I returned to the island after my music period ended, I moved in with Justine. We were caretakers of Edith's old house on Lennie Road. The year after Justine and I had left the island I boarded the ferry for what was to become my annual tourist trip to Lasqueti, the place I always feel is home. I still knew some of the people who were on the ferry, and I ran into my friend Kevin. After greetings Kevin asked me, "Do you remember the insect repeller you gave me shortly before you left the island?"

I replied, "Yes, did it work?"

He said, "No, but I have a funny story to tell you."

My mind went back to the incident. All my life I have been a techie. I was intrigued with electronics, and I was fourteen years old when I got my first amateur radio license.

My generation was born during the depression, but was raised during WWII and the reinvention of civilization after the war ended. I guess we were more prone to idealism in those days, and wanted to believe that technology would save the world, and make everyone happy.

I first started to question that premise after the introduction of computers to industry. I believed that with automated accounting by banks, for example, automation would give them more time and energy to assist customers. What I found out was just the opposite. Once the parameters for cost-effective accounting were set, the industry just dropped all people who didn't fit the profile. Who needs trash anyway? As I saw it the technology was making all the management decisions, and I didn't like it.

Eventually I got out of the tech business, and completely changed my lifestyle to exclude technology as much as possible. While on Lasqueti Island someone gave me a battery-powered radio, so the first paw was in the door. That was the extent of the technological "creep" until the school acquired an Apple II computer. I was the only one on the island with any computer experience, so I developed a couple of applications and programs for the school. I was taking a small amount of money under the table by assisting a special needs student and used the computer as a teaching aid. I had finally come to the conclusion, while sitting in a cabin in Canada, that technology had taken over the world while I had been enjoying the pristine lifestyle. The only way I could cope with the future was to try to re-enter the real world somehow. It was also a chance to go the next level with my music, try to actually make some money.

Radio Shack to the rescue. I bought a ten dollar Radio Shack four-channel mike mixer and a fifteen dollar "junk" portable condenser tape recorder mike, but it had surprisingly good fidelity. I bought a Bill Lawrence snap-in guitar pickup, and viola! I was in business, if I could locate a P.A. amplifier to play my stuff through. I dealt with the problem in several ways. Some of the halls I played in had some sort of sound system, so I was at least partially teched up. I also rented gear on occasion.

I had a very enjoyable summer until my house burned down, along with all my electronic stuff. Fortunately it didn't have a value of more than a hundred dollars total. I moved back to the States, and started the next phase of my life: Playing music in Oregon the next winter.

I managed to replace the stuff that burned up, plus I acquired a Fender Vibralux guitar amplifier, and I was in the music business, more or less. Over the next year or so I made some refinements. I bought Craig Anderton's book *Electronic Projects for Musicians,* and was instantly transported. Most of my electronic experience had been pre-solid state, old tube stuff, but I got into the modern world pretty fast. I built a compressor and this really improved my instrument sound, which needed all the help it could get.

I finally crashed and burned while playing music on Vancouver Island. I could not continue with the music. I returned to the Lasqueti Island bloody (figuratively speaking) but unbowed. Mostly. After I was back on the island a while I began again tinkering a bit with electronics.

I had a collection of circuit boards and components, and constructed several devices. One problem was that I didn't have electricity to power my soldering iron, a twenty-watt Radio Shack pencil iron, and was forced to heat it on my propane stove, an interesting irony in the hi-tech '80s. I connected with Rob, who lived on the island, and he graciously allowed me to use his tools and equipment, which made assembly much more fun.

While reading through a *Popular Electronics Magazine* one day I ran across an article that contained diagrams for construction of an ultrasonic insect repeller. Although the general impression was that these things didn't work, I decided to build one. I wired up the circuit board and installed it in a Top tobacco can. I cut a round hole in the top for the transducer.

When it was ready, I turned the switch on, the LED lit up but I couldn't hear anything. Of course not, it was ultrasonic. As I was wondering how to test the device, the cat climbed through the cat door and sat down on the kitchen floor. I turned the repeller on and pointed it toward the cat. His ears perked and he went straight up in the air then crashed back out through the door. Far out. It works. At least it would repel cats, though I couldn't prove that it would inhibit insects. The device did elicit some local interest.

Kevin and Nancy lived at the south end of the Island. Kevin came to visit one day and asked me about the repeller. I gave him a demo, not terrifically impressive, since you couldn't hear anything and the cat was nowhere to be found.

He told me that Nancy was allergic to wasp stings and was very much afraid of them. He asked me if I thought the device might work to keep insects away from her. I told him that we were leaving the island soon, and I had no use for the device; he could have it, if he wanted it. He accepted the gift and I left the island.

I have to interject here and say that since there were many insects in this climate there were also a great many bats; and since most roofs and walls were made with shakes, they became home for the bats. Most houses had bat populations and they were generally welcomed, since they kept the insects down.

Kevin told his story. "One day I accidentally left the repeller turned on while it was on the kitchen table, and I went outside to work. When Nancy came out of the bedroom, she saw about a dozen bats staggering around the room totally disoriented. She ran out of the house screaming, and accused me of trying to kill her."

After we finally managed to stop laughing all I could do was apologize for developing such an infernal device. See, I told you that you can't trust technology.

Although you can still buy ultrasonic insect repellers, the electronics engineers still say they don't work, but you and I know different, don't we?

35

The Move

Things had gotten to the point that Justine and I were considering leaving Canada. It was hard to contemplate, because we were caretaking for one of the older houses, which had rather humble beginnings. It was an idyllic spot. It was originally a storage shed, kind of a halfway house for feed and supplies that were later moved down the trail to the Livingston homestead. Sometime later a floor, a sort of foundation, and several rooms had been added. The foundation was logs propped up with rocks, shakes, and in some cases skyhooks, because there really was nothing holding them up. Magic. It did have one distinction; it had a brick chimney, which was extremely desirable in wood-burning environs, though rare. It wasn't really much of a house, but it was home, and it was free.

The house was above Lennie Road (one-lane dirt), on the beginnings of the steep slope up to Johnson's Bluff and several hundred yards from Jodi's corner. I originally knew it as Arnie's Corner, when Arnie lived there. Ed Darwin, one of the old-timers on the island, told me that he first knew it as Welsh's Corner, when Ab Welsh moved there in 1915. Place names mean something in the bush. Across the road there was a large funky shake shed, which contained the left-over materials from the sixteen-foot dory boat that Heather had built by hand.

In a rural setting like this your space extends to where you bump up against someone else's space. At times the result of this bumping up can cause conflicts. The settlers had tried many ways to enrich their diet. As experiments, they planted a lot of different types of fruit trees, to see which would survive in this hostile environment. The survivors included some varieties that almost defy imagination. We had 'Banana apples', 'Northern Spies', 'Kings', 'Transparents' (the source of many gallons of wine each year on the Island), and many, many varieties that were unidentifiable after all these years. Included in our yard were various varieties of plums. There were 'Damsons', 'Prune', 'Peach Plum', and, believe it or not, 'Apricot Plum', which looked and tasted a lot like apricots. I don't know where the hell these came from or how they were developed, but we were very popular with our friends during plum season.

One of the factors for both Justine and I considering leaving the area was that we were illegally in Canada. This caused more than a few problems. At one point Justine made the observation that after five years she was sick and tired of being nice to everyone, even the few assholes who lived up there. Lasqueti was, rightly or wrongly, notorious in Canada for harboring malcontents, dope smokers, and illegal Americans. Probably some citizens fell into all three categories. Most of the old-timers were of a live and let live persuasion. There were, of course, several vindictive people who were not above snitching anything and everything to the RCMP. Fortunately for all, most of them were really unreliable sources of information, so the cops didn't pay too much attention to them.

As in any family or community there were feuds and frictions. These put great pressures on us, since some of the people involved were good friends. We had to be very careful not to become too involved. One event that comes to mind is the feud between Bruce and the Whittles over a marauding dog that mysteriously disappeared. But that is stuff for another story someday, maybe.

For me, this was my second stint on the island, and I had been there for a total of nine years. I had always thought that I would find some way to become landed, so I could live there legally. The easiest way would have been to marry a

Canadian lady. The problem was that it seemed that the women I got together with were illegal Americans like me. I had offers from good sisters to do a "marriage of convenience," but it would have been a major and difficult commitment for them, primarily because I was older than most of the immigrant Americans, and did not fit the profile of a desirable new citizen. This is somewhat ironic, since most of the Americans the government thought they wanted were draft dodgers and politicals who had no real affinity for Canada, nor appreciation for that wonderful country. I on the other hand loved it and would readily have defended it with arms if necessary. I think that's why I had so many Canadian friends.

Another way to get into the system would have been to create a false identity, with credentials that would be acceptable to the powers that be. I actually started to do this the first summer I spent in Hope, B.C. At that time I tried to get a false Social Insurance card. I probably should have pursued this, as it turned out later, but I chickened out. Anyway, I was into being a fugitive mountain man and false identity wasn't part of the persona I was establishing. I was trying to be invisible. Another way to get in would have been to go to the city and try to get a real job that Canada needed to have filled, even if by an American. However, by this time I was so bushed that the very thought of being in the city or trying to con a governmental functionary into believing I was legit brought out a cold sweat.

I was getting worn down, having no social net whatsoever, and having been very lucky not to be in the wrong place at the wrong time. A serious illness or accident could be enough to endanger the viability of our residence in the country. Also, I would appreciate not having to dive into the brush every time I saw a Mountie. I could tell you some stories about fugitive paranoia.

Justine had been living on the island for about five years. She arrived barely able to walk after recovering from being smashed almost to death by a killer wave. Her medical history, if written down on paper, would probably have devastated a small forest. She was suffering from post-polio syndrome, and her inability to adjust to temperature fluctuations finally done her in up in the North Country.

Another factor in the decision was that ways of making a living seemed to be drying up. The job with the special needs student ended. This, plus other odd jobs and Justine's crafts, had enabled us to slip by. It was tough, however. I was very nervous about going out in the real world after all of these years, but gradually we realized that our trip was closing down. This came to a head when the Canadian government announced that there was going to be a restricted amnesty for illegal aliens who had been in the country continuously for more than five years. Armed with letters from nearly everyone on the island attesting to my wonderful character and community spirit, I visited a lawyer in Vancouver. He read my letters and said, "That's all fine, and will probably help after you prove you have been in the country all this time. Can you prove it?"

Oh shit. No, I couldn't prove it. My trip had been to not show up on any records, to not draw anything from the social institutions, to be invisible. It was explained to me that the intent of the law was to legitimize those who had been living in the cities, working, using false papers, and ripping off the establishment. I had done so well in not costing the government anything that I didn't qualify. Well, so much for good clean living; perhaps not always totally clean, I guess.

So in the late fall we decided to take the plunge. The first thing on the list was to get rid of the solid trash we had accumulated over five years. We borrowed the Varney's small pickup and rounded up the trash. To my astonishment we were able to get rid of it in two small pickup loads. I am probably more proud of that than anything else I achieved during that time.

We didn't have a vehicle or a place to go after we left the island, so we had a logistical problem just getting out of there. After cleaning the homestead up, the next thing was to get rid of the usable stuff we had accumulated. Finally after giving and selling what we could we ended up with maybe twelve boxes of possessions. We stored about five boxes in Jodi's loft, and kept the last seven or eight. Justine was in her element, weeding stuff out and writing endless lists. The trip would require several luggage transfers, but we would make it if we were lucky.

We were in luck on one level at least, because at that time there was a taxi in operation on the island. We could use that to get our stuff and us to the ferry landing. There had been several taxi services on the island over the prior fifteen years, but none of them had lasted very long. There were three different problems with what could have been a lucrative business in other surrounds. The first was that because of the roads, the average life span of a new vehicle was probably twelve thousand miles more or less, depending on your driving habits and the weight of the vehicle. Smaller Jap trucks lasted pretty well, heavy American pickups you could hear rattling for a mile off after about the first six thousand miles.

The second problem was that gasoline was very expensive on the island. The owner of the inn/restaurant/gas pump could pretty much charge what he wanted. Of course, you could use boat gas, which was cheaper and wasn't taxed, but they put purple dye in boat gas, and you could see it if you took the air cleaner off and inspected the carburetor. The Mounties actually did that when they would raid this small island. And as noted before, there was no regular auto repair facility on the island.

But as I say, we were lucky. Bill Lynch, author and stage director, hiding out from civilization on Lasqueti, was using his Dodge van as a taxi. The first part of the trip was reasonably painless. Bill drove up to our house and we loaded the boxes and suitcases we were taking with us. He dropped us at False Bay. We lugged our gear down the gangway and stowed it on the ferry. Phase one completed.

It must be understood that timing was very important in this operation. We had to get to Victoria, about a hundred and fifty kilometers down Vancouver Island, by about 11:30 in order to meet our next rendezvous with the *Black Ball* ferry to Anacortes, Washington.

Gerry and Fienny were waiting at French Creek in their Dodge van. We carried our boxes off the ferry, down the dock, and out to the van. Phase two successful.

We raced down the hundred miles of island highway to Victoria, and got to the dock just as the Anacortes ferry was pulling in. Phase three completed.

When the cars finally began leaving the ferry, our friend Kiefer pulled his old Dodge Dart in next to Gerry's van, and we transferred our loot. We hugged Gerry and Fienny goodbye and drove back onto the ferry as it turned around to go back to the U.S. Phase four completed.

Now, for the first time, we were able to begin realizing that we were on our way to a frightening new experience. First, however, we had to explain our existence to the American Customs and Immigration agent.

This unfortunate functionary was traveling on the ferry, and strode up to us to ask who we were and why we were there. It had always been my policy to tell the truth, even if it proved to be complicated, unless the truth could cause serious trouble. It couldn't hurt us at this time. We had no warrants out on us, and we were undeniably Americans, and we had not broken any U.S. laws by living in Canada.

As I told our story, I could see the discouragement mounting in his eyes. "Why do I have to deal with this today?" I'm sure that although he was in a business that heard many stories, there was nothing in the manual to cover the story he was hearing now. The only fear that I had was that he would make us unload that stuff one more time today, so that he could paw through it and find out what we were really up to. He decided not to do this, but he really looked through our pockets, packs, and Justine's purse before admitting defeat and leaving us more or less in peace.

The next step was to drive Kiefer to his home near Seattle, and he would loan us his car for a week or so. We arrived in Anacortes, Washington, and debarked on the exciting new adventure. As we pulled off the ferry, with all the traffic zooming around us, Justine announced, "Now let's find a First Interstate Bank and deposit our money and get some ATM cards."

Say what??? It was at that point that I began to realize what the future looked like. Oh no!

Epilogue

Justine and I bounced around California for a year or so, living on seasonal and temp work. We finally split up, and at age forty-nine I moved in with my parents. I managed to get some retraining money from the government, and spent one semester boning up on computers and accounting. I realized that I would have to use whatever tech expertise I had in my next phase of life.

Although most tech stuff was happening in the Bay Area, I realized that I might be able to handle a city the size of Sacramento, but any place larger was out of the question. So, destitute I applied to the state personnel board, and the upshot is that within a month I was a programmer/analyst, making (for me) undreamed amounts of money. Don't tell me God doesn't have a sense of humor. All I had to do was earn it.

I was hired by an old programming buddy, Bill, who had prospered during the time I was having fun. He had a somewhat sadistic sense of humor, and dropped me into the most pressure-packed unit in the agency, the Information Center. For a while I was pretty worthless, and everyone was asking who I was and why I was there. We were a part of the Legislative Counsel Bureau, and were tasked with providing all the information services for the Legislature, the

Legislative Counsel, and the Legislative Analyst office. When I left civilization in 1970, personal computers were not even dreamed of. It was hard to realize that these little devices had more computing power than the mainframes of my day. And . . . I had been living without even electricity all that time.

My warrior training held me in good stead. I simplified my life as much as possible. All this money was going into my bank account, and I was going to get out of there as quick as possible. Or so I told myself. I knew I was probably going to be around for the long haul, and let's be honest: for all that time I'd been away I hadn't worked at one job more than three months, and I really liked it that way. So I said, "Ok, they've got me but they only have a piece of me. Just as much as they pay for."

One advantage, possibly the thing that allowed me to work in this environment, was that I was by nature a techie. That is, or used to be, a respected station in life. When you make stuff or fix stuff it isn't hard to evaluate how good you are at it, and if you are good they leave you alone. I had no desire for management at all.

After I'd been on the job about three months, and was becoming somewhat productive, my old buddy Bill and I were talking at a party. He told me that he had nothing but good reports about me. That made me feel good. I told him, "Well Bill, this is only the third hardest thing I have ever had to do in my life. The hardest was that first winter on Lasqueti Island. The second was learning to live on nothing." So I was prepared. I had to pick up fifteen years of technology in a very short time.

I made up my mind to make sure I didn't develop any attachments to Sacramento. When I finally managed to extricate from this job, I'd be on my way far from work computers and cities. I developed and managed a state-of-the-art (sort of) graphics, video, multimedia shop, and provided expertise with these media services to the legislature, as well as other users of the Legislative Data Center. I pretty much did it all: hardware, software, and network. During this period I did very little music. I did write or start many of the stories in this book.

As soon as my retirement papers went through, I was out of Sacramento and back to Oroville, to care for my aging father, my mother having passed away shortly before my retirement. I seem to have come in a complete circle. I took care of my dad for several years until he passed away. During that time I had started getting heavily involved in the local folk music scene. Music would be a big part of this current phase of the movie. I have been letting the world come to me for many years. Don Juan is supposed to have advised to choose the path with heart. I have tried.

I remember a passage from a book I read many years ago. According to the protagonist a junkie remarked, "Life doesn't give a rats ass who lives it." That always stuck in my memory. Certainly life on the planet has become at least as grotesque as I envisioned it so many years ago. I am really heart sick at the lack of respect and contempt Western civilization has bestowed upon our mother. Having said that, I feel indebted to life for the gift and strive to use the time I have left to justify my use of it. This book is a part of that process.

Acknowledgments

I Originally wanted to publish the stories and vignettes I had written with little personal involvement in it. Loretta Rector generously volunteered to do an edit. After she had finished it and had mostly liked the stories, she asked me why I wasn't in the book. I told her that I wanted to be like Jack Kerouac, chronicling the movement, not about himself. No conceit in my family. She would not accept that and said it must be about me, expand my personality.

That was not what I was looking for at the time. I just wanted to get rid of the god damned thing. However, I started writing a story over the stories I had already written. I don't know how to thank her for the hundreds hours I spent re-writing the manuscript to be sort of an autobiography. This was not my idea, but now that it's done I am pretty happy with the result. Loretta was right.

I'd also like to thank Bob Lupoli, who took over as my agent to try to find a publisher. Neither of us knew anything about publishing. He worked very diligently and between us we managed to get rejected by at least two hundred different publishers. What a team. Good work Bob.

Kaye and Dan Wilson gave valuable assistance on the cover design.

Alex Karamanis, Author of *Alex's Bedtime Stories* on Amazon, for editing and book review.

Finally, thanks to all the fabulous characters inhabiting these stories and the many who were not included, who so enriched my life.

I inadvertently left out a very important person/institution on Lasqueti Island. I have fortunately reached the age at which I can blame everything on incipient dementia and diminished responsibility. Laurence Fisher was a young man who owned the Lasqueti Land Company Ltd, a large piece of land originally organized for logging and real-estate sales. Laurence used much of the land to form a land sharing co-op which provided young people on the island a cost-effective way of gaining property and a home. He also founded Wildwood Works, a small manufacturer of wood products made from tree branches, many of Yew, using Native art designs. The endeavor also provided some local employment. The Coop has recently donated land and supported a successful effort to build a health clinic and eventually retirement habitation for elderly islanders. This project is called 'The Last Resort Society' and was named in honor of Laurence's mother.

CPSIA information can be obtained
at www.ICGtesting.com
Printed in the USA
FSOW02n1756180916
25162FS